THE BEST OF WESTERN EUROPEAN COOKING

THE BEST OF WESTERN EUROPEAN COOKING

Kay Shaw Nelson

The John Day Company
New York

Designed by Ingrid Beckman

Manufactured in the United States of America

Library of Congress Cataloging in Publication Data

Nelson, Kay Shaw.
  The best of Western European cooking.

  Includes index.
  1. Cookery, European. I. Title.
TX723.5.A1N43   641.5'94   75-33345
ISBN 0-381-98286-6
10 9 8 7 6 5 4 3 2 1

TO
Rae and Wayne
My
Convivial Dining
And
Traveling Companions

Contents

Introduction:
Western Europe and Its Cuisines

FROM SCANDINAVIA to the Iberian Peninsula, from the British
Isles to Austria, the pleasures of the table are ever present and
ever rewarding. The art of cookery flourishes no less creatively
in provincial hideaways than in glamorous capitals, to the delight alike of knowledgeable native and enterprising visitor.

It is not surprising that Americans find the cuisines of Western Europe fascinating to explore. For in these nations we find
the origins of our own culinary heritage, as we have since the
days only a few generations back, when the Continental grand
tour was a mark of the well-to-do. The leisurely grand tour may
have given way to the modern tourist trip, but Continental delicacies and culinary variety still abound.

Norway, Sweden, Finland, and Denmark; Ireland, Scotland,
Wales, and England; Belgium, the Netherlands, and Luxembourg; West Germany, Austria, and Switzerland; Italy, Spain,
and Portugal; and, above all, France—each of these nations has
developed over the centuries a distinctive and individual cuisine.
In a few cases, regional similarities may exist, but never same-
ness. None of these countries is vast in territory, but each has
made maximum use of the products of field, forest, sea, and

stream. Born of national pride or necessity, culinary treasures have been created in royal palace, peasant hut, or seaside shack and evolved against the checkered background of European history.

From the Romans, who for centuries ruled a great part of the area we now call Western Europe, the peoples of these lands learned the fundamentals of agriculture, viniculture, animal husbandry, cooking, and dining. Unfortunately, with the invasions of nomadic vandals from the north and northeast and the collapse of the Empire, this precious legacy was destroyed. The fruits of Roman culture temporarily sank into oblivion.

During the Dark Ages, when rulers from the north took over the formerly civilized lands, Europeans returned to their previous barbaric ways of living. Fields weren't tended, and the wild forests grew back. Humans foraged for whatever they could find. During these troubled times of constant warfare the great cities fell into ruin.

Gradually, however, permanent settlements began to rise again through the banding together of isolated groups ruled by lords who dominated the peasant workers. With the feudal system, the manors became self-supporting units, growing and preparing their own foodstuffs and other daily needs. Very often in times of drought, famine, or warfare, or even in more peaceful days, those in charge of the large estates surfeited themselves with great haunches of meat, wild game, and poultry, while the less fortunate struggled to find ingredients to mix a batch of bread, which became the staff of life. One item that became most important was salt, necessary to preserve the meat of animals, which were slaughtered in great quantity; also crucial were spices for flavorings and preservatives.

It was in the monasteries, the only places of tranquillity in those turbulent times, that the arts bequeathed by the Romans were preserved. The monks cultivated herb and vegetable gardens, as well as orchards and vineyards, and had special rooms for baking, brewing, and preserving. From their grapes and fruits were made their highly prized wines and liqueurs. These religious sanctuaries became the only "inns" of the time, and travelers welcomed by the monks were not only thankful but impressed with the hospitality and fine fare.

One such wayfarer was Charlemagne, an impressive figure who loved the delights of the table. When crowned Holy Roman

Emperor in A.D. 800, he became the first European ruler to advocate the improvement of man's daily living. As the first great unifying force for the scattered peoples, he inspired the feudal barons to revitalize agriculture, domesticate animals, and raise the standard of living. He also attempted to improve dining customs.

Thus at his court Charlemagne encouraged such niceties as using the point of a dagger, instead of the fingers, to pick up food. And, with some sensitivity to decor, he had his bare dining room carpeted with flowers, the walls covered with ivy, and the tables blanketed with fresh roses. The Emperor even permitted women to dine at his feasts—on condition that they not use "noxious perfumes."

Quantity of food was far more important than quality throughout medieval times. Wooden tables were so heavily laden with enormous platters of viands that they became known as "groaning boards." Gradually, more variety in food was provided, in part as the result of the seasonal fairs, or markets, which were set up at strategic crossroad cities. As workers and their masters gathered, often from considerable distances, merchants displayed and sold their wares, minstrels entertained, and everyone made merry with feasting and drinking. These profitable and convivial events developed over the years into the fabulous fairs still celebrated with great gusto throughout Europe. They were also the beginnings of what is now the flourishing Common Market.

From earliest times the Europeans, as other primitive folk, had been guided by the forces of nature for their daily living, seasonal celebrations, and family beliefs. Planting, harvesting, and feast days acquired certain meaningful rites and practices. As Christianity spread throughout Western Europe, and the power of the Church increased, many of the pagan customs and celebrations were adopted by the new religion for holidays that are still observed in Europe and in America.

The Church was also responsible for the popularity of what became a very important European food: fish. Instructed to eat only "fysshe" on Fridays, fast days, and during Lent, which amounted to quite a large number of days, Christians eagerly sought out the fruits of the Atlantic, northern seas, and inland waters. Even moats surrounding the castles were stocked with ample supplies of fish so as to be readily available.

Although a very sad phase of European history, the religious wars of the Middle Ages between the Christian nations of the West and the Muslims contributed to the improvement of the daily fare. For survivors among the vast numbers of zealots who flocked to Constantinople and beyond returned to their homelands with a number of "new" foods, particularly fruits, nuts, and spices, and methods of cooking that furthered gastronomic fashions and progress.

The greatest influence on the development of Europe's culture, including the cuisine, however, came from Italy during the Renaissance. During the 1500s and 1600s the arts of the flourishing Italians spread to France and other European countries, bringing a period of new and great enlightenment to the previously darkened Continent. Also contributing considerably to the advancement of gastronomic matters and the exchange of culinary ideas were the intermarriages among the leading royal houses of Europe, particularly those of Britain, France, Spain, and Italy.

In fact, the foundation of the Great French cuisine may be attributed to one of these politically arranged marriages. In 1533, an Italian princess, Catherine de'Medici, only fourteen years old but heiress of the richest and most noble family of her country, arrived in France to marry a young prince, Francis, who was later to rule as King Henry II. With Catherine came an impressive entourage of aides and cooks, all well versed in the elegant manners and culinary customs of the aristocratic families of Florence.

During her reign, Queen Catherine, a prodigious diner, altered French court habits considerably. She placed great emphasis on tasteful table settings, starring imported Venetian glassware, handsome silver and gold ornaments, ruffled embroidered linen cloths, and elegant chinaware. She also brought women back to the dining room and, at her fabulous banquets, introduced and popularized such delicacies as artichoke hearts, veal dishes, truffles, delicate cakes, and beautifully garnished confections.

It is not certain, however, whether the Queen attempted to persuade the members of the court to utilize another Italian import, the fork. We do know that the two-pronged implement, brought originally to Venice by a Byzantine princess, was not readily accepted in Europe, except in Italy. Frenchmen, devoted to the use of dagger tips or fingers for choice morsels, contended that the fork "spoiled the taste of the food." The English took great pleasure in deriding the innovation as a foreign affectation designed for "sissies." Even the clergy felt compelled to speak out against the fork. One aroused cleric declared it to be "impious because it assumes that God's own good gifts are unfit to be touched by human hands."

It was quite another matter, however, with the foods that reached Europe, via the Near East, from the Orient. For the all-important spices were becoming increasingly difficult to procure. By the latter half of the fifteenth century, the extension of Turkish and Arabic power was making it almost impossible for spices to reach the Continent, either by caravan through central Europe or through the port of Venice. The need for and pursuit of spices opened up new and golden eras for the European nations, which embarked on adventurous explorations and the establishment of colonial empires around the world.

As we all know, among the leaders of these explorations were the Spaniards, who were enjoying their golden age in the fifteenth century. Previously, the Moors had established a thriving and refined civilization on the Iberian Peninsula and, through them, the tables of Europe had been enriched with more plentiful supplies of fruits, vegetables, and rich desserts, as well as by the use of such foods as rice, saffron, and cinnamon. From the New World discoveries of the Spanish adventurers came a fabulous wealth of other precious fare, which was intermingled with the European cuisines to make them the most lavish and interesting of the world. The conquistadors brought back to Spain the tomato, turkey, sweet and hot peppers, maize or corn, pineapples, avocados, cacao beans for chocolate, beans, squashes, vanilla, and white and sweet potatoes.

The styles of the day, in culinary as well as other fields, were established by the powerful royal courts, which had great influence on the development of the national kitchens.

Across the Channel in England, for example, progress in the refinement of dining took longer to develop than on the Continent. These were the days of rousing feasts, with eating and drinking to excess. The powerful Tudor monarch, Henry VIII, was a gargantuan diner who devoured at will enormous quantities of richly seasoned dishes, barons of beef, highly spiced stews, enormous pies, and wines. We are indebted to him for the development of the great Christmas feast of 12 joyful days, which became a happy and democratic celebration for all the population to observe, with garlanded boars' heads, peacocks, bowls of wassail, rectangular mince pies, plum puddings, fruitcakes, and a long list of other favorite fare.

His daughter, Queen Elizabeth I, who ruled during the peak of the New World explorations, was a hearty diner too, beginning the day with sizable portions of meats and tankards of ale. Since then, the English have always favored substantial breakfasts including, however, more varied dishes. The Queen was also extremely fond of sweets, which she devoured in considerable quantities throughout the day. During her reign, the whole nation developed one great sweet tooth. Cooks devised rich puddings, cakes, marmalades, custards, sweetmeats, marchpanes, and sweetened drinks, served by the hundreds at some parties. This liking persists today, and the British are still extremely fond of their great number of sweets, particularly desserts, two of which, cherry and apple pie, became virtually national dishes in America.

During the Elizabethan period, there began a great emphasis on the home production and preparation of foods, drinks, and "remedies." Members of the nobility and the middle class strove to outdo each other in improving the products of their gardens, orchards, breweries, bakeries, smokehouses, and kitchens. A great deal of time and effort was spent on these pursuits, and the English cuisine developed to theretofore unknown heights. In particular, vegetables and salads, utilizing such exotic ingredients as flower petals and buds, as well as rich condiments and sauces, became fashionable. Americans adopted many of the sauces, notably ketchup.

Very important to the improvement and increasing interest in gastronomy in England and on the Continent were the growing number of cookbooks being published. From ancient times man had been fascinated with recording favorite recipes and giving culinary advice, and books with gastronomic subjects were among the first written. The earliest that still survives is credited to a Roman, Apicius, who wined, dined, and wrote during the first century.

The oldest known English cookbook, *The Form of Cury* (old word for cooking), included favorite recipes of Richard the Lion-Hearted, a devotee of fine food. It was a French writer, La

Varenne, who wrote the first tome establishing culinary rules and principles, as well as introducing refinements in cookery and dining. His *Le Cuisinier français* appeared in 1651.

This book, often called the culinary bible of the day, was of utmost importance, particularly because it was printed during the reign of Louis XIV, *Le Roi Soleil*, who, although an enormous eater, was dedicated to the improvement of the art of cookery and the pleasure of dining. His great chef, Béchamel, created the world's most famous sauce which bears his name. The Sun King constructed at Versailles a glorious palace to display to all of Europe the power and grandeur of his court. Not only were the entertaining rooms of matchless magnificence, but the gardens, orchards, bakeries, wine cellars, and kitchens were the largest ever built. Countless numbers of servants toiled for the great banquets where dining was an impressive spectacle served in courses according to protocol. One such feast comprised "168 garnished dishes or plates, not counting the various foodstuffs served as dessert."

Although great attention was paid to the order and service of these lengthy repasts, formality was occasionally tempered by royal whim. One contemporary account chattily states that "it sometimes happened that the King, who was very dexterous, amused himself by throwing little balls of bread at the ladies and allowed all of them to throw them at him." On one occasion, this bread-tossing led to the throwing of whole rolls, oranges, and apples. And a lady-in-waiting to the king's daughter, "who was hurt when the King threw a roll at her, threw a salad at him, fully seasoned."

During Louis's reign, coffee, tea, and chocolate became fashionable beverages; dining rooms became an important part of Continental homes; table appointments were improved; and it became very social to entertain with intimate suppers, *petits soupers*. In Paris, cafés were flourishing at which the most popular attractions were the ices and ice creams introduced by a Sicilian. Also opening in larger numbers were restaurants (meaning restoratives), which gradually increased their fare from only soups to long lists of elegant creations.

The Sun King must have been delighted to know that the fame of the French court spread quickly across northern and central Europe and that customs established at Versailles and Paris became the model for other royal families. The preeminence of the French table had been established. French culinary creations were copied on palace, restaurant, and hotel menus *en français* and served throughout the Continent. Every emperor and empress, king and queen, as well as lesser royalty, had to have chefs who were French or French trained.

These great chefs brought the French cuisine to its full achievement during the eighteenth century. One of the most talented, Marie-Antoine Carême, "cook of kings and king of cooks," served the French royal court, the English prince regent, and Czar Alexander, among other notables. He was particularly famous for his elaborate pastries and lengthy cookery texts embellished with lavish illustrations.

The era produced many great and famous cookbooks. One was written by an eccentric gourmet, Anthelme Brillat-Savarin, who left a glorious monument to the art of good eating in his *Physiology of Taste*. In another, *Le Grand Dictionnaire de cuisine*, a lifetime effort of Alexandre Dumas, the noted author and amateur cook, described foods and cookery with personal appeal. And a later cookbook of the nineteenth century, *A Guide to Modern Cookery*, by the greatest chef of *la belle époque*, Auguste Escoffier, remains a classic.

Despite the strong French culinary influence on the Continent, particularly the royal courts, which still persists, the national cuisines of the various European countries developed quite independently from those of the aristocracy. These reflected the characteristics of the people, the climates, and the influences from neighboring lands. Interestingly, each emerged to be unique, although some countries do share gastronomic preferences. As one example, consider the British Isles. Although the English, Scots, Welsh, and Irish dine on some of the same fare, each has definite culinary traditions that are proudly maintained.

From earliest times, the peoples of these very important islands retained a stubborn preference for their own favorite fare, trying to shun as much as possible influences from the Continent. They have always been very fond of dishes made with their favorite grains. With barley, oats, rye, and wheat their cooks created an impressive number of superb dishes, such as nourishing porridges, hearty soups, puddings, dumplings, breads, doughnuts, pancakes, scones, buns, crumpets, fascinating cakes, and cookies, to say nothing of the quick snack inspired by the Earl of Sandwich.

British baked goods in great variety are particularly relished for the national custom of afternoon tea, or the later light high tea, at which other dishes are also served.

The British are justifiably proud of their meats, particularly the joints or roasts of beef and saddles or crowns of lamb or mutton. Lesser cuts are made into interesting soups, stews, pies, puddings, and pastries quite different from those of other cuisines. Beef has long been the most popular meat, and indeed the English became known as Beefeaters, the name given to the handsomely costumed warders at the Tower of London. The strong men who protected the Tower were supposedly given this name because a visitor from Italy in 1669 commenting on the reason for their strength, remarked that they were "great eaters of beef, of which a very large ration is given them daily and they might be called beef-eaters." Presumably the well-known English gin named for them is equally strong.

Greatly prized by sportsmen and gourmets are the British wild game and noble birds, particularly the pheasant, partridge, and grouse. Also superb fare are the numerous fish and shellfish dishes prepared with fresh varieties from the nearby waters. Long masters at the art of cheese-making, the British enjoy their Stilton, the king of blue cheese, or Cheddar, for snacks or at the end of a meal. But they also utilize a number of their excellent cheeses to make such inviting creations as rarebits and pies, some served as savories at the end of a meal, a custom peculiar to the English.

Visiting Britain today, it is possible to enjoy numerous gastronomic experiences. Such large cities as London and Edinburgh have noble restaurants featuring the finest of native specialties. Two particular treats are afternoon tea and the hearty breakfast, which features a number of superb dishes. While touring the charming countryside, there are many homes and inns that welcome tourists for "bed and breakfast," which is to say a comfortable night's lodging and a generous morning repast.

And one must not forget the great and ancient British institution, the pub. Scotland is famous for its whiskey and England for its gin, but every man's drink is the flavorful beer, which flows from taps in great quantity at pubs of every description, bearing every conceivable name, and seemingly around every corner. These inviting gathering places are generally cozy and informal, their ale and beer superb, and their fare inexpensive and interesting. Pubs cater to the taste of everyone.

Across the sea in Ireland there are also pubs, and the Irish love to visit them. There is a saying, "It's hard to sing with an empty glass." They might prefer to have it filled with their famous native whiskey, but most likely it will be the favorite beer, of which the black foamy stout is an interesting and distinctive brew.

The Irish have another saying: "Laughter is gayest when the hunger is best." And indeed they love to sit and enjoy their snacks, called "snap-ups," hearty soups, meat pies, rib-sticking stews, clever potato creations, country hams, flavorful seafood, and a great variety of baked goods with inventive names. What is sometimes lacking in variety is made up in the deliciousness of the fresh and excellent fare. For the tourists who love to visit the small Emerald Isle, there are handsome modernized hotel-restaurant castles, country inns, and a chain of great southern hotels featuring good local dishes.

Like the other northern lands of Europe, those of Scandinavia have culinary customs dating back to ancient times. In the days of the Vikings necessity made the rugged and isolated people rely on catches from the icy seas and animals of the forests for most of their food. From the land came, during the short summer, tasty fruits, particularly berries, and vegetables. The Vikings developed a traditional hospitality that still exists. Parties in the olden days were lengthy infrequent get-togethers for which guests trekked or rowed long distances to the walled castles for merry days of feasting and drinking. Then began the custom of setting up a cold board with a vast assortment of foods as a gesture of welcome and hospitality for travel-weary guests. Very often each person arrived bearing contributions such as regional specialties of cheese, game, smoked fish, or fruits.

Later a number of inviting warm dishes were added to the cold, and by the eighteenth century the Swedes had developed the great array of interesting fare the rest of the world would know as *smörgåsbord*. The wealth of these culinary gifts alone does honor to the cooks of Scandinavia. But there are also great soups, fish and meat puddings, seafood specialties, flavorful vegetable combinations, and a rich repertoire of baked goods—breads, cakes, cookies, and pastries—many of which have become standard ingredients in American Christmas celebrations.

For the traveler in Finland, Sweden, and Norway, the culinary treats are many. To savor the great salmon, flavorful crayfish, smoked fish, reindeer, venison, cloudberries, crisp flat crackers, and interesting cheeses, with beer and *snaps* (also called akvavit in Scandinavia), is ever a great experience.

On the Continent, the Danes also relied heavily on fish and shellfish, but their country has become world famous for its dairy products. Butter, cheese, eggs, and pork are sought-after delicacies. From the moment of arrival in Denmark, one is aware of the unusual importance of food. The Danes are boastfully a nation of trenchermen, dining well and with pleasure several times daily. Dinner is taken at six in the evening, it is said, so there will be time for another meal, or at least a substantial snack, before bedtime. One soon finds that cookery has a special place in the Danish culture and, like the charming towns, lovely landscape, and idyllic islands, that it reflects the happiness and creativity of the people.

Perhaps the most famous element of the cuisine is the *Smørrebrød*, or open-face sandwich, which is universally offered in infinite variety. The "spread breads" please the eye, as well as the palate, and making them is truly an art. The Danes also have excellent seafood dishes, good "country dishes," such as famous meatballs, pork combinations, thick soups, highly esteemed poultry preparations, the famous Danish pastries, and a number of rich desserts.

While traveling in Denmark one is constantly lured to the table by culinary temptations. The most captivating city in this respect is Copenhagen, where it doesn't take long to discover that the Danes are anything but melancholy. The air of gaiety is everywhere, and everyone seems bent on enjoying the varied delights. The restaurants and cafés of the city are of great appeal, but a particular magnet for all gourmets and fun-lovers is the unforgettable Tivoli Gardens, a city oasis alive with every conceivable enticing entertainment, entrancing to both young and old. Here, after a repast to be remembered, it is easy to understand an alliterative advertisement for Denmark that proclaims the country to be "Famous for Food, Fun and Fairy Tales." No idle boast that food ranks first.

Another country also famous for its dairy products is the Netherlands, popularly known as Holland. The Dutch are hearty eaters, and their fare reflects their tastes. In this small country one finds thick soups and stews; pork, sausage, potato, and cabbage dishes; robust breads; substantial desserts; and internationally known cheeses. Thanks to the adventurous Dutch seamen and colonists, the cuisine is also spiced with the exotic foods of other lands, particularly the East Indies. Clippers of their early great fleets returned home laden with fascinating cargoes from faraway places. A New World gift, chocolate, was readily adopted and creatively used for the great Dutch candies. Coffee from the Indonesian island of Java (which was nicknamed for it) is drunk in great quantities. Indonesian dishes, such as *nasi goreng, sates,* and the remarkable rice table (*rijstafel*), found a second home in Holland. Curries and spices are liberally used. From the Dutch the world also acquired many culinary gifts, including the incomparable hollandaise sauce.

One of the most opulent of the European cuisines is that of Holland's next-door neighbor, Belgium. Its fare, however, reflects the cultural and linguistic division of the country between the Flemish and the Walloons. While the food of the north is similar to that of Holland, the southern specialties of the Walloons are akin to those of France. Throughout the nation, gastronomy is taken seriously and the pleasures of the culinary arts are constantly indulged. Street vendors tempt passers-by with superb mussels, snails, eels, and the national favorite, *pommes frites.* Sweet waffles, pastries, and other confections can be purchased at open shop windows. Everywhere in evidence are sausages, seafood, Ardennes ham, game, and poultry. Vegetables, such as Brussels sprouts, tender white asparagus, crisp endive, and hop sprouts, as well as fresh fruits in season, are truly delights. Beer is the national drink and is also used creatively in the cookery.

Dining in the restaurants of Belgium is never disappointing. In Liège, Namur, delightful Bruges, northern coastal towns, the ancient port of Antwerp, or beautiful Brussels, there can be found some of the Continent's best restaurants, each with superbly prepared local specialties.

Far more basic and much better known to Americans is the fare of Germany. Hearty and substantial, the food is quite fitting for the cold climate and daily hard work. The national cuisine was developed by the peasants or workers, whose viands differed considerably from those of the nobility. The regional specialties are diverse, adding to the appeal of dining in Germany.

Generally speaking, the Germans are particularly devoted to pork products. They love their sausages and have created great varieties of them. Americans acquired some of their finest, including the hot dog or frankfurter, named for the German banking center; the familiar hamburger is named for the busy German seaport. When it comes to starch, the Germans are no weight watchers. The potato is the national vegetable, cooked and served in great quantity. Many meals feature the beloved dumplings. And noodles are favorite southern dishes. Between meals, wholesome breads with butter are common snacks. And if one has a yen for sweets, the shelves of bakers, *Konditoreien* (pastry shops), and department stores bulge with attractive displays of any number of them.

The Germans love to eat at home with family and friends, but they are also devoted to the pursuit of dining out in their numerous public eating houses. For snacks, there are indoor and outdoor cafés, as well as vendors plying the streets. Even at the markets or in the stores it is always possible to find some aromatic hot sausages or sandwiches, and an assortment of cold foods, including smoked fish, particularly herring and eel. Also, at any time during the day or evening it is customary to pause at a *Keller* for a beer or two, or a *Weinstube* to sample the incomparable wines. Restaurant menus are lengthy with nourishing soups, cabbage and root vegetable dishes, richly sauced meats, hearty casseroles, and game of particular deliciousness.

A love of good living has long been important to the southern neighbors of the Germans, the Austrians, who well understand the appreciation of good music, fine wines, and gastronomic delights. They cook as they sing, with happiness, enthusiasm, and imagination. Each dish reflects a light and artistic touch.

Over the centuries, the Austrian cuisine has been greatly influenced by its neighbors, particularly in central Europe, the Balkans, and, to a lesser degree, the Mediterranean and Western

Europe. From Hungary the Austrians acquired a fondness for paprika and goulashes. Italians introduced pasta. From the Balkans came valuable spices, rice dishes, and baklava pastry for the spectacular strudels. Dumplings and sauerkraut were German contributions. Russia and Poland offered sour cream and pickled foods.

The Austrians drew on the culinary traditions and foods of others but also added their own imaginative touches.

Austrian gastronomy reached its pinnacle in the kitchens of Vienna, long an important crossroads of central Europe and the cultural center and capital of the great Austro-Hungarian Empire. The culinary extravagance and luxury of meals served in the handsome palaces of the beautiful and gay city became legendary.

Today, as in yesteryear, it is delightful to dine anywhere in Austria, but especially in Vienna. Particularly inviting are the colorful and friendly restaurants with local specialties, such as the rich soups, fish from the lakes and rivers, veal, pork and game dishes, boiled beef, goulashes, chicken preparations, noodles and dumplings, and the great sweet desserts.

The Viennese love their ubiquitous coffeehouses where one can sit and read or relax with a cup or two of delicious coffee, which is served in appealing variety. Also enjoyable are the little suburban taverns or houses called *Heuriger*, where the atmosphere is friendly and gay, and the purpose of gathering together is to sample the new local wines (*heurigen Weine*) with convivial companions.

In another small European nation, Switzerland, a beautiful and inviting land, the cuisine, as the culture, has been influenced extensively by its three neighbors, France, Italy, and Germany. Thus, in areas of Switzerland bordering these countries the menus may feature dishes borrowed from, or similar to, other cuisines.

There are also, however, great Swiss specialties, and the cooks have long been noted for an ardent concern for fine fare. Fortunately they are blessed with the best and freshest of food, readily available from productive farmlands and well-tended animals and poultry. Outstanding among the renowned Swiss dairy products are the cheeses, eaten as snacks, or for supper with bread and milk, and which are used in making delicious dishes such as the internationally known fondue or the less famous *raclette*.

In Switzerland one also finds excellent meats, particularly pork and veal, inviting vegetable creations, delicious tarts and breads, fascinating cakes, pastries, and candies. Each November the Swiss enjoy a spree in celebration of one of their favorite foods, the onion. At the colorful Onion Market of Berne, Switzerland's picturesque capital and one of Europe's best-preserved medieval cities, celebrants buy onions, sample onion dishes, and drink the excellent wines, available also at other times in good quantity and variety.

Switzerland's southern neighbor, Italy, has an ancient and complex cuisine, both European and Mediterranean. Throughout the country one is able to dine superbly in restaurants, ranging from the chic and expensive to the unpretentious and inexpensive. Furthermore, eating in Italy is a good deal of fun, for the people welcome the pleasures of the table at any time of the day or evening. Nothing interferes with eating and drinking.

When contemplating the Italian cuisine, Americans are apt to think only of the specialties of the southern region, since many cooks from this area emigrated to the United States and opened restaurants. In Italy it is indeed pleasurable to sample these more familiar dishes, such as antipasti, pasta creations, veal specialties, and tomato and eggplant combinations. The restaurants of Naples and Rome offer the best of them.

But while wandering about central and northern Italy and dining in such lovely, historic cities as Florence, Genoa, Bologna, Venice, and Milan, the versatility of the Italian cuisine can be fully appreciated. For the cookery ranges through a profusion of superb soups, seafood specialties, imaginative meat preparations, rice and cornmeal delicacies, imaginative cakes and ice creams, and superb cheeses. As to wines, the repertoire is one of the world's best of diverse selections, including many not as well known as chianti, but all well worth sampling.

To the west, Spain, like Italy, is a part of Europe but is also a Mediterranean area. Its cuisine is of lesser variety and renown but is of unusual interest. Uniquely, it is the only one on the Continent with oriental overtones, brought by the African Moors, who during their 500 years of rule introduced eastern rice dishes, spices, citrus fruits, nuts, peaches, dates, and other fruits, as well as rich, very sweet desserts.

Earlier, seamen had already brought from the Near East two very important and staple crops, olives and grapes. From the New World came tomatoes, red and green peppers, both mild and hot, and aromatic allspice, which the Spaniards readily adopted as treasured fare.

It was after the inclusion of these American contributions that the Spanish cuisine became fully developed, reaching its peak during the sixteenth century when the Spanish court was the most illustrious in Europe. The French cuisine did not influence the royal houses of the Spaniards as greatly as it did the other royal houses in the north. The Spanish cuisine is marked most definitely by internal regional differences.

Spain is a large country of contrasting climate and geography, and even the national dishes, such as the great and hearty soups and stews of many meats, especially pork products and legumes, are prepared differently in various locales. The cuisines of the south, dependent on olive oil, rice, fresh vegetables, seafood, and lighter fare in general, really belong to the Mediterranean. The food prepared in the north is more hearty, relying on meats, game, Atlantic seafood, and spicy seasonings.

The Spaniards are most independent about their eating, and the proud Basques, if given an opportunity, will gladly debate with the equally prideful Catalonians the goodness of their national dishes. This is one of the reasons that it is a great pleasure to travel through Spain, observing and enjoying the differences. The Spaniards love to dine out-of-doors whenever weather permits, and in the southern regions that is possible most of the year. To visitors it seems that this pastime of eating and drinking goes on most of the day and evening, for food is ever available at outdoor cafés, bars, and restaurants, whether chic or of humble aspect. One thing is common to all of Spain, however, and that is the late, late hour of serving dinner, normally about ten o'clock.

The cuisine of Spain's neighbor, Portugal, the small westernmost nation of the Continent, developed with traditions of individualism and isolation. For, although these two countries constitute the Iberian Peninsula, they are separated by rugged mountains and their culture and cookery bear few resemblances.

The Portuguese have always had to rely on their basic re-

sources for their daily fare. And, befitting a small country with
a 350-mile coastline, often described as a terrace overlooking the
Atlantic, the waters of this ocean have been important for many
aspects of daily living. Seafaring traditions date back to the
Phoenicians. During Portugal's golden age in the fifteenth century, however, its daring explorers became heroes of the day
for reaching all corners of a newly discovered world.

Portuguese who settled in America in such locales as Massa-
chusetts and California, both coastal regions, brought their traditional methods of cookery with them. The Portuguese influence is even stronger in some of the Caribbean islands and South
American countries. Little wonder that their coffee is one of
Europe's best, for their ties with Brazil have long been close.

The basic diet of the Portuguese relies heavily on seafood,
available in staggering quantity and variety. The national favorite is salt codfish taken from faraway Atlantic waters for
centuries. It is made, so the legend goes, into 365 preparations.
The Portuguese are also great lovers of soups, dried beans and
green beans, rice dishes, pork, great salads, magnificent fruits,
and unique, very sweet desserts. Their preferred flavoring is
fresh coriander.

Although gay people who love music, dancing, flowers, good
red wine, and sunshine, the Portuguese have long been known for
their inner sadness. Thus, tourists to Portugal seek out the colorful fairs (romarias) and folk festivals, which seem to be held
all the time, to enjoy the singing, beautiful costumes, local vinho,
and very often, grilled fresh sardines. But special attractions
for visitors are also the fado houses, where the music of the sadness of the people, called fado (fate), is the main attraction.

Whenever one dines in Portugal—in humble restaurants or in
the grand hotel dining rooms of Lisbon and the renowned coastal
resorts—there will be interesting and distinctive food and a variety of excellent local wines, including the two most famous,
Port from the north and Madeira from the islands of the same
name.

The glories of the French cuisine have already been mentioned, but it may be remarked that French cookery, both classic
and country, is still considered to be the best in the world. While
in France, it is most difficult not to be constantly drawn to the
temptations of the table. The provincial fare is much too com-

plex to discuss individually, but generally speaking, one of the best ways to enjoy it is to order the *spécialités de la maison* at the inns and restaurants. Of course, the glorious creations of the renowned dining places of Paris, Lyons, and Bordeaux, to name only a trio of the gastronomic cities, are incomparable.

According to a French saying, a meal without wine is tantamount to a day without sun. The French produce more wine than any other country, and they also appreciate it more. *Vins ordinaires*, served generally in open carafes, may be as appealing to sample as the more expensive bottled vintages. It all depends on where you are, what you're eating, and the limitations of your pocketbook.

Suffice it to say that dining in France is one of the great pleasures of a lifetime.

Lesser known than the cuisines of the larger countries of Europe are those of the smaller nations of Luxembourg, Andorra, Lichtenstein, and Monaco, each individual and inviting. While enjoying a culinary Continental tour, they should not be forgotten, and some notable specialties of their kitchens are included herein.

This collection of recipes is selective rather than comprehensive and is intended to present distinctive and delectable examples of the various Continental cuisines. It is hoped that pleasant memories will be evoked for those who have resided or traveled in Western Europe. Others may find an opportunity to savor and appreciate the intriguing variety of the best from the Continental kitchens.

THE BEST
OF WESTERN
EUROPEAN
COOKING

1

Appetizers

IN WESTERN EUROPE the rich repertoire of marvelous morsels served prior to a luncheon or dinner is most important to the repast that follows. For, as an introduction to the main part of the meal, appetizers set the scene and have the gastronomic role of whetting the appetite.

The peoples of these countries do not normally partake of pre-prandial libations without something to eat. Thus, whether a few or several, humble or luxurious, simple or complex, appetizers are carefully prepared and slowly savored.

Customarily, the food served with drinks, or as a first course at the table, is light and delicate, planned to marry well with the menu that will follow. This, however, is not always the case. In these cuisines there are a number of appealing appetizer presentations that are a sort of a meal-before-the-meal.

The custom of serving and enjoying an elaborate galaxy of stimulating dishes with drinks before dining probably began in Europe, in Scandinavia. The Vikings partook of hearty fare from a cold board while imbibing their strong spirits. The Danes still are fond of their *kolde bord*. By the eighteenth century the Swedes had devised an inviting "akvavit buffet" as an introduction to the festive meal. Guests stood near a separate table in the corner of a dining room or adjoining area, and sampled fish, cheese, and bread and butter, while drinking akvavit.

As more dishes were added, the spread became known as the herring buffet, because of the predominance of several preparations made with that favorite fish. By the nineteenth century, with the addition of warm dishes and an expanded repertoire, the delightful institution known as *smörgåsbord* was enjoyed throughout the country.

The idea evidently appealed to the Russians, who borrowed it from the Swedes and, while drinking copious quantities of vodka, partook of a formidable display of native specialties which they called *zakuski* ("bite down"). They, like the Scandinavians, were fond of salt fish dishes but added their own variations, such as caviar, pancakes, and filled doughs.

From Russia this inviting custom spread to other parts of Europe, particularly France where it was renamed *hors d'oeuvre à la russe*, meaning "outside the chef's work, Russian-style." Formerly appetizers had been called *petites entrées*. For the French there was less emphasis on the fish specialties preferred in the northern countries, and more on vegetable creations, attractive egg dishes, garnished canapés, filled pastries, rich salads, sausages, *pâtés, terrines*, and *galantines*. Today the French enjoy their assortment of hors d'oeuvre as a prelude to luncheon. In restaurants the hors d'oeuvre often is a handsome display, with the delicacies served in individual glass dishes, called *raviers*, and wheeled in a cart to the guests for each to make his own choice. In private homes, the fare may be a simple combination of olives, sausages, and a few raw vegetables, but it will be relished with an *apéritif* or wine as much as a grander presentation.

In Italy the well-known *antipasti* ("before the meal") is a colorful and attractive combination of seafood, raw and cooked vegetables, sausages, olives, and highly seasoned prepared dishes, generally rich with oil, designed to abate the effects of any drinks or wine served with them. The Spaniards love their *tapas* and *entremeses*—which may include almonds, olives, skewered tidbits, deep-fried fritters, and seafood, with sherry or other wines—particularly while watching the evening *paseo*, or population parade, a national pastime.

Both the Austrians and the Germans call their impressive appetizer arrays *Vorspeisen* ("before foods"). Enjoyed with *Schnaps*, wine, or beer will be a few selections or a copious spread of smoked fish, herring in marinades and sauces, pickles, several sausages, composite salads, filled pastries, canapés, cheeses, *pâtés*, and raw or pickled vegetables.

Although the other European countries do not have traditional appetizer spreads, they do enjoy their favorite before-the-meal delights. The English are partial to their oysters, preferably those from Colchester or Whitstable served only with fresh lemon juice and buttered thin brown bread. Other favorites are smoked trout, potted shrimps, whitebait, and quail or gulls' eggs. The Scots are understandably fond of their smoked salmon, mackerel, and iced melon, the latter served traditionally with sugar and ginger. In Ireland, the Galway oysters, which are eaten with stout and brown bread, and the Dublin Bay prawns and native salmon are sought-after delicacies.

The Belgians enjoy some of the French specialties as hors d'oeuvre but are also fond of their oysters from Zeeland, snails, thin Ardennes ham, and a particular favorite, baby green eels, as before-the-meal fare with their national drink, beer. In Holland, eating goes on all day so it is sometimes difficult to distinguish appetizers from snacks, but certainly smoked fish, herring, Zeeland oysters, plovers' eggs, and cheese preparations, served with *genever* gin or beer, rate highly with the Dutch. In both Switzerland and Portugal the local cured meat, beef in the former, and ham in the latter, are notable specialties taken with the excellent local wines.

While traveling in Western Europe, it is of course most pleasurable to sample the local appetizer delicacies, very often available only in season. Certainly the fresh and smoked seafood, rich *pâtés*, well-seasoned sausages, caviar, and exquisite pastry specialties, such as one served at the Pyramide restaurant in Vienne, France, *brioche de foie gras*, are memorable treats.

But it should be remembered also that such is the fondness for a before-the-meal treat that very often a more humble food will be relished. I have observed the pleasure of a gentleman in Germany slowly sipping a glass of beer while carefully eating a single hard-boiled egg. To the French, one of the great hors d'oeuvre delights is one or more long red radishes, with the green leaves left on, served with butter and salt. For the Italians a slice or two of salami or some sardines, with crusty bread, are a welcome treat.

Some of the best and most popular Western European appetizers belong more properly in the category of salads, and recipes for them are included in Chapter 8.

This selection is representative of the various Continental cuisines, and from it a choice of taste tempters may be made that should prove a worthy and intriguing overture to any meal.

ENGLISH POTTED SHRIMP

An excellent appetizer to keep ready in the refrigerator for unexpected guests or to enjoy for a special occasion. It is simple to prepare and a delight to savor. The English claim that their most flavorful shrimp come from the waters of the North Sea off the Yorkshire coast. Those used for this dish are the tiny or minuscule varieties sold generally in our stores in jars or cans. Potted shrimp spread on hot toast are a great English favorite for high tea but they also make a good appetizer or first course.

½ pound butter
½ teaspoon mace or nutmeg
¼ teaspoon cayenne pepper
Salt, pepper to taste

2 cups cleaned, drained canned
  or bottled tiny shrimp OR
1 pound shelled, cooked fresh
  tiny shrimp

Combine ¼ pound of butter, the mace (or nutmeg), cayenne, salt, and pepper in a saucepan and heat until the butter is melted and foamy. Add the shrimp and heat about 1 minute. Spoon into small containers—custard cups, pots, small dishes—dividing evenly between them. Add the remaining butter to the saucepan and, when melted, pour over the shrimp. Cool. Cover or tie waxed paper over the tops and refrigerate at least overnight. The shrimp will keep several days. Serve with hot toast. Makes 6 servings.

DUTCH BITTERBALLEN

These appealing little snacks are called meatballs but are more similar to croquettes.

¼ cup butter
¼ cup flour
1 cup beef or veal broth
1 teaspoon Worcestershire
  sauce
Freshly grated nutmeg, to
  taste
Salt, freshly ground pepper to
  taste

3 tablespoons finely chopped
  onion
2 tablespoons chopped fresh
  parsley
1½ cups finely chopped cooked
  beef or veal
Bread crumbs
1 to 2 eggs, beaten
Fat for deep frying

Melt the butter in a saucepan. Mix in the flour. Add the broth, a little at a time, and cook, stirring, until smooth and thick. Add the Worcestershire, nutmeg, salt, pepper, onion, parsley, and meat. Cook over low heat for 15 minutes, stirring occasionally. Remove from the heat and spoon into a buttered pie plate. Spread evenly. Chill about 2 hours. Shape into small bite-size balls. Roll in bread crumbs, then beaten egg, and again in bread crumbs. Refrigerate at least 1 hour, preferably 2. Fry in hot deep fat (390°F. on frying thermometer) until golden brown. Drain on absorbent paper. Serve very hot with sharp mustard. Makes about 35 pieces.

SWEDISH DILL SALMON

Salmon, one of the most highly prized fish of Scandinavia, is prepared in many ways. A simple but cherished salmon dish is one of uncooked pickled or cured dill-flavored salmon served with a sweet-sour mustard-dill sauce. This dish, called *gravlax* in Swedish, is a specialty of the *smörgåsbord*.

4 pounds fresh salmon,
  center cut
3 tablespoons coarse salt
3 tablespoons sugar

1 tablespoon white
  peppercorns, crushed
1 large bunch fresh dill

Remove the backbone and other bones from the salmon and cut in half lengthwise. Combine the salt, sugar, and pepper and rub over the insides of the fish. Place one piece, skin side down, in a large bowl or serving dish. Place the dill over the salmon. Top with the other piece of fish, skin side up. Place a heavy platter of some other dish over the salmon to weight it down. Refrigerate, covered, for 24 hours. Turn the fish once or twice during this period. When finished, remove the salmon from the dish and scrape off the seasonings and dill. Cut off the skin and slice the salmon diagonally into thin slices. Serve the slices of salmon garnished with fresh dill and the skin slices, and with the sauce, *gravlaxsas* (see page 207). Makes 8 to 10 servings.

HAM CORNETS FROM VIENNA

Attractive and easy-to-prepare appetizers are ham cornets filled with combinations of favorite foods of the Viennese.

1 package (8 ounces) cream
  cheese
1 cup sour cream
1 tablespoon freshly grated or
  prepared horseradish

¼ cup minced chives
Paprika, salt, pepper to taste
12 4-inch squares thinly sliced
  boiled ham

Combine the cheese, sour cream, horseradish, chives, paprika, salt, and pepper. Spread over the ham slices and roll into cornets or cone shapes. Fasten with toothpicks and chill. Sprinkle the tops with paprika. Makes 12 servings.

FILLING VARIATIONS:

1. Spread the ham slices with pork or liver *pâté* and roll up. Decorate the open ends with slices of hard-cooked egg and sprinklings of parsley.

2. Sauté chopped mushrooms in butter. Flavor with lemon juice and nutmeg. Mix with sour cream. Garnish the tops with chopped fresh dill.

DANISH SMØRREBRØD

A marvelous Danish creation is the artistic open-faced sandwich, *Smørrebrød* or buttered bread, which is universally available in infinite variety at snack bars, in homes, at cafés, or in opulent restaurants. It is everybody's favorite for luncheon. In Denmark each public eating place has a *Smørrebrød Kart*, or menu, sometimes in several languages and sometimes literally a yard long, with incredible variations listed, often according to ingredients. At Copenhagen's Hôtel d'Angleterre the 137 selections include categories of fresh, smoked, or salted fish and meats, sausages, eggs, salads, vegetables, and 15 choices of cheese. Some *Smørrebrød* have been given curious names. On a motel-restaurant *Kart* in northern Jutland, among the specialties were Neptune Maiden, Silvertop, Hawaii Touts, Rally Fantasi, Love Maiden, and Rush Hour.

Every Dane seems to be an expert on the preparation of *Smørrebrød*, an expertise that has passed from one generation to the next. Actually the sandwiches are buttered bread with "something" on top, generally two or more ingredients. Yet the final product, eaten with a knife and fork, is more than a mere sandwich. The choice and preparation of the proper foods make the sandwiches works of art. Very important, for example, is the selection of bread, which must be of firm texture and thinly sliced. Crusty white, dark rye, pumpernickel, or sour rye may be used, but the Danes prefer the thin, square slices of dark rye (*Rugbrød*). Whichever kind is used, it should complement the flavor of the topping, for example, spicy foods on white, and heavy combinations on firmer bread. Also important is a generous layer of excellent butter covering the entire slice. This keeps the bread from getting soggy and provides an anchor for the toppings.

The choice of toppings, called *Paalaeg* ("something laid on") is limited only by one's imagination. They may be simple or complex. Flavors, however, must harmonize and firm foods should be placed over salads and vice versa. Color contrasts should also be considered. The first layer, placed over the butter, may be slices of cold meat, cooked fish, salami, tomato or cucumber slices, liver paste, smoked salmon, seafood salads, cheeses, or hard-cooked eggs. Over this will be arranged the garnishes: chopped aspic, cold fried onions, raw egg yolks, grated horseradish, tomato or radish slices, vegetable strips, raw onion rings, dill or parsley sprigs, slices of cold scrambled eggs, pickles, lemon twists, mayonnaise, asparagus tips, pickled beets, anchovy fillets, or slivers of herring.

When eaten for meals, the Danes have several *Smørrebrød*. In fact, courses of them can be served. First one of fish, then of meat, a salad, and finally one of cheese. Americans very often serve these sandwiches as appetizers or first courses. They should be made as close to serving time as possible so they will be fresh. Some suggestions are given below:

1. Danish liverpaste, bacon, and sliced mushrooms.
2. Sliced pork loin with cold pickled beets or red cabbage.
3. Tuna fish with sliced cucumber garnish.
4. Roast beef with fried egg and onions.
5. Fried fish fillets with tartar sauce.
6. Egg and tomato slices with mayonnaise and chopped chives.
7. Ham, cheese, and chopped parsley.
8. Shrimp, crab, or lobster salad on lettuce with slice of pimiento.
9. Camembert with a radish flower on lettuce.
10. Smoked salmon on lettuce with horseradish-flavored whipped cream.

BELGIAN OEUFS MEULEMEESTER

This delicious egg and shrimp appetizer has long been favorite fare in historic Bruges, the "Venice of the north," once among the richest cities of Europe, and still enchanting to visit to view its art treasures, architecture, and canals. It is an unforgettable experience to dine on inviting Belgian specialties at a terrace restaurant in this lovely city of Flanders, in full view of the old church belfry and one of the languid canals.

6 hard-cooked eggs
½ pound (about 10) cleaned, shelled, cooked shrimp
¾ cup light cream or milk
2 tablespoons chopped fresh parsley

1 teaspoon minced chervil
2 tablespoons sharp mustard
½ cup grated Parmesan cheese
Salt, freshly ground pepper to taste
1 tablespoon butter

Shell the eggs and cut them into shreds. Cut the shrimp into bite-size pieces. Combine the eggs and shrimp with the cream, parsley, chervil, mustard, and ⅓ cup of cheese. Season with salt and pepper. Spoon into 4 individual baking dishes or one large shallow dish. Sprinkle with the remaining cheese and dot with butter. Bake in a preheated hot oven (400°F.) for about 10 minutes, long enough to heat through and for the top to become golden. Makes 4 servings.

FRENCH PORK RILLETTES

A very popular French hors d'oeuvre, sold commercially in great quantity, *rillettes* are actually shredded meat, generally pork, packed into small pots. They are not difficult to prepare and may be kept in the refrigerator for several days to be used as needed.

2 pounds breast of pork
1 to 2 garlic cloves
½ teaspoon dried marjoram

¼ teaspoon dried thyme
Pinch mace (optional)
Salt, pepper to taste

Remove the rind from the pork and cut the pork into pieces. Put in a large saucepan with the remaining ingredients and ½ cup of water. Cook slowly, covered, for 1½ hours. stirring now then. When cooked, drain and cool the meat. Remove any skin and bones. Separate the meat from the fat, reserving the fat. With two forks, tear the meat into shreds and put into small earthenware, china, or other pots or small dishes. Heat the fat to melt it and pour over the meat. Chill in the refrigerator. Serve with crusty French bread and butter. Makes 6 to 8 servings.

BEEFSTEAK TARTARE

A most popular Western European appetizer, served as a first course or sometimes as an entrée, is raw ground beef combined with raw egg yolks and seasonings. Most often the mound of beef, with the egg and other ingredients, is served on individual plates to be combined by each person. For cocktail parties or buffets, all the ingredients may be mixed beforehand and then served on a wooden board, tray, or platter, surrounded by bread and butter. The name is believed to have derived from the Tartar practice of scraping and eating raw meat. In fact, purists maintain that the best meat for this dish is that achieved by scraping lean beef. Normally, however, ground beef is used. It should be freshly ground and put through the grinder at least twice.

Of the many times that I have enjoyed this appetizer, I recall it most vividly from a dinner at the restaurant Bold Hotel in the lovely picturesque town of Oberammergau, famous for its breathtaking Alpine beauty, decorated Bavarian houses, meticulous wood carvings, and the Passion play that is presented by local actors every decade. Facing a delightful mural of the charming town, we dined on remarkable fare. My beefsteak tartare had been previously mixed and was presented on a slice of pumpernickel, covered with raw onion rings, and surrounded by tomato, pickle, and cucumber slices.

Europeans partake of this dish sometimes also in the late morning, and many insist it is one of the best restoratives after an evening of celebrating.

½ pound lean round or sirloin   2 raw egg yolks
steak

Garnishes:

finely chopped onion, capers, caraway seeds, chopped anchovy fillets, chopped gherkins, grated fresh horseradish, chopped fresh parsley, minced chives

Accompaniments:
pepper mill, Worcestershire sauce, mustard, lemon juice

Ask the butcher to grind the meat twice and plan to buy it shortly before serving. The meat should be as fresh as possible.

Divide the meat into 2 portions. Shape into 2 mounds on individual serving plates. With the back of a spoon make a depression in the center of each mound of meat, for the egg yolks. Serve surrounded by separate dishes of any desired number of the garnishes, or place spoonfuls of them on the plate around the meat. Place the accompaniments on the table for each person to use as desired. Makes 2 servings.

SPANISH HAM FRITTERS

For *entremeses*, or appetizers, the Spaniards enjoy small fritters that can be picked up with toothpicks. The *buñuelitos* are made with cheese, fish, chicken, hard-cooked eggs, or this popular food, ham. A good accompaniment is dry sherry.

1 cup all-purpose flour
½ teaspoon salt
2 large eggs, separated
½ cup water
¾ cup diced cooked ham

1 tablespoon finely chopped
    onion
½ teaspoon paprika
Pepper to taste

In a bowl, combine the flour and salt. Mix together the egg yolks and water, and stir into the flour. Beat 1 minute. Beat the egg whites until stiff. Fold them and the ham, onion, paprika, and pepper into the batter. Drop a tablespoon at a time into hot deep fat (375°F. on a frying thermometer) and cook, turning once, until golden on all sides. Remove with a slotted spoon and drain. Serve hot or lukewarm. Makes about 20 fritters.

DUBLIN BAY PRAWN COCKTAIL

A great deal of confusion exists about prawns and shrimp. Actually a prawn is a crustacean that somewhat resembles the shrimp but is not of the same family. Prawns vary in size and are sometimes sold as shrimp. A delicacy that comes from Dublin Bay, and is highly prized by the Irish and other Europeans as well, has been named a prawn but is yet another crustacean. It is described by some persons as a small variety of lobster and by others as a baby cray-fish. Anyone who is fortunate enough to have the oppor-tunity of savoring the large and tender shellfish needn't worry about the error in the name. This cocktail may be made with shrimp or prawns as as a substitute.

¼ cup whipped heavy cream
¼ cup tomato catsup
Juice of 2 large lemons
1 teaspoon Worcestershire
  sauce
½ to 1 teaspoon freshly grated

or prepared horseradish
Salt, pepper to taste
½ cup shredded lettuce
½ cup chopped celery
24 large cleaned, shelled,
  cooked prawns or shrimps

Combine the cream, catsup, lemon juice, Worcestershire, horseradish, salt, and pepper. Chill. When ready to serve, place the lettuce and celery, dividing evenly, in 4 stemmed glasses. Ar-range 6 prawns in each glass. Cover with the sauce. Makes 4 servings.

NORWEGIAN SNITTER

Like all Scandinavians, the Norwegians are very fond of open-faced sandwiches made with a wide variety of foods. Those eaten for supper are smaller and less elaborate than *Smørrebrød* and are called *snitter*. They should be of a size that can be eaten with the fingers. Serve on a large plate accompanied by light beer and akvavit or *snaps*. These are but four possible suggestions.

1. Arrange slices of hard-cooked eggs, overlapping, on well-buttered white bread. Arrange anchovy fillets over them. Sprin-kle with chopped parsley.
2. Combine diced cooked meat, beef or veal, with mayonnaise, chopped pickle, a little mustard, salt, and pepper. Place a let-

tuce leaf on buttered dark bread. Top with some of the meat mixture. Garnish with a tomato slice.

3. Arrange tiny shelled and cooked shrimp, smoked salmon, herring, or any other kind of seafood on buttered pumpernickel. Sprinkle with lemon juice. Garnish with a thin slice of cucumber and chopped fresh dill.

4. Spread Norwegian *gjetost,* brown goat's cheese (or another Norwegian cheese), or buttered white bread and garnish with a radish slice.

DUTCH CHEESE TRUFFLES

This simple appetizer combines three favorite Dutch foods: cheese, butter, and pumpernickel. Either the round, crimson-coated Edam or the yellow Gouda may be used. Both are mild, firm, and similar in flavor.

½ pound butter, softened
¼ pound grated Gouda or
  Edam cheese
¼ teaspoon paprika

Salt, freshly ground pepper,
  grated nutmeg to taste
3 to 4 slices pumpernickel

Combine the butter, cheese, paprika, salt, pepper, and nutmeg and mix well. Chill for 20 minutes. Shape into small balls. Chill 30 minutes. Toast the pumpernickel twice and whirl in a blender or crush with a rolling pin to make crumbs. Roll each cheese ball in the crumbs. Makes about 20 truffles.

ITALIAN STUFFED MUSHROOMS

1 pound large fresh
  mushrooms
1 garlic clove, crushed
1 cup minced cooked ham
2 tablespoons chopped parsley

2 tablespoons grated
  Parmesan cheese
2 tablespoons fine dry bread
  crumbs
Salt, pepper to taste
Olive oil

Wash and dry the mushrooms. Pull off the stems and use for some other dish. Combine the remaining ingredients, except the olive oil. Spoon into the mushroom caps and sprinkle with olive oil. Arrange in an oiled shallow baking dish. Bake in a preheated moderate oven (350°F.) for about 20 minutes. While cooking, sprinkle with more oil so the mixture will not be too dry. Serve hot. Makes 4 servings as a first course.

KLEINE VORSPEISEN OF GERMANY

For their parties, both intimate and large, the Germans (and Austrians) prepare attractive displays of their *Vorspeisen*. Generally some of the foods will be purchased in their well stocked delicatessens. Others are prepared at home. Among the purchased fare may be smoked fish (herring or eel), other herring dishes such as roll mops, a variety of sausages and cheeses, thin slices of cold meats, types of *pâté*, pickles, and pickled vegetables. With these may also be served hot or cold salads of seafood, chicken, or meat, stuffed tomatoes, mushrooms, filled puff pastries, handsome stuffed eggs, and elaborately garnished canapes.

For a small selection of appetizers from Germany an attractive platter can be made with the following:

1. Roll ham slices around canned white asparagus. Garnish the top of each roll with one stalk of asparagus and a strip of pimiento.

2. Fill small tomatoes with ham, cheese, or liver *pâté*, and dot the caps with bits of mayonnaise. Replace caps over the fillings.

3. Arrange thin slices of salami, cold meats, and cheese, overlapping each other, and garnish with pickles.

4. Cut any kind of smoked or canned fish into bite-size pieces and garnish with chopped dill and lemon wedges.

Serve with the platter two or more kinds of white and dark bread, pats of butter, and mustard.

ENGLISH SAUSAGE ROLLS

The English are very fond of combining meat and flaky pastry into a number of interesting dishes. This is one of the simplest but is always an inviting appetizer.

24 link pork sausages   ½ cup lard or shortening
1½ cups flour   4 tablespoons cold water
¾ teaspoon salt   1 small egg, beaten

Partially cook the sausages by frying to release most of the grease. Drain on paper toweling and cool.

Sift the flour and salt into a bowl. Cut in the lard and add the water. When combined, roll out on a floured board. The pastry should be quite thin. Cut into strips, 2½ by 3 inches each. Place 1 sausage link in the center of each strip. Roll up, leaving the ends of the sausage out, and seal with cold water. Make a couple of small slashes across the top of each. Brush the tops with beaten egg. Arrange on a greased cookie sheet. Bake in a preheated hot oven (425°F.) for about 20 minutes, until the crust is crisp and golden. Serve hot. Makes about 24; the exact number will depend on the thickness of the pastry.

NORTHERN EUROPEAN SMOKED FISH

Northern Europeans are very partial to a variety of kinds of smoked fish, which they consider to be the best of appetizers. Although each country has its favorites, all of the fish are generally highly regarded. The British consider smoked salmon to be the aristocrat, and certainly smoked salmon from Scotland is superlative. In Britain there are also superb smoked herring, which are fare staples. Some kinds are more familiar to Americans than others. Kippers, the great breakfast dish but also an appetizer, is a herring that is split open before being smoked. Herring prepared in this manner have a stronger flavor from the smoking. The finest are those cured in the villages of Scotland's eastern coast. Two types of herring that have been left whole before smoking are called bloaters, which are smoked only a short time and are a great specialty of Yarmouth, and bucklings, which are smoked longer.

One of the best known of the British split smoked fish is Findon haddock (called finnan haddie by the Scots), named for the fishing village in Scotland where the particular method of curing originated. The British are also fond of cod's roe, eels, trout, and mackerel, which, as with the salmon and herring, they eat with only fresh lemon juice and bread and butter.

The Germans are devotees of their highly respected Baltic herring specialties, some similar to those of the British; but their preference is smoked eel, served with buttered rye bread. In Scandinavia, smoked salmon, mackerel, herring, and eel are great favorites, featured particularly in the *Smørrebrød* and *smörgåsbord*.

Although the main purpose of smoking fish is to preserve it, the process also imparts a characteristic and appealing flavor to the fish. Thus, as appetizers they are best served *au naturel* with only attractive garnishes and lemon juice, if desired. While you are traveling in northern European countries these specialties are well worth seeking. Fortunately, they may be enjoyed at home since they are widely exported and are available in American stores.

GERMAN MUSHROOMS ON TOAST

Mushrooms are favorite German fare and are served in a number of inviting dishes for *Vorspeisen*. This variation of *Champignon-Schnitte* is a good appetizer or first course.

1 pound fresh mushrooms	Salt, freshly ground pepper,
½ cup butter	grated nutmeg to taste
Juice of 1 large lemon	8 toasted firm white bread
¼ cup flour	slices, crusts removed
1½ cups rich brown gravy	Chopped fresh parsley
½ cup white wine	

Wash the mushrooms quickly or wipe with wet paper toweling to remove any dirt. Cut off any tough stem ends. Cut crosswise into thin slices. Heat the butter and lemon juice in a large skillet. Add the sliced mushrooms and sauté over medium heat for 2 minutes. Stir in the flour and then half the gravy. Cook, stirring, 1 minute. Add the remaining gravy, white wine, salt, pepper, and nutmeg and cook, stirring, 1 or 2 minutes, until the mixture is thickened. Cut the toast into triangles and spoon the hot mushroom mixture over them. Sprinkle the top with parsley. Makes 4 to 6 servings.

HORS D'OEUVRE JARDINIÈRE

A very attractive first course that can be served also as a luncheon entrée.

6 medium tomatoes
1¼ cups diced cooked ham
1 cup cooked peas
1 cup diced cooked potatoes
¾ cup mayonnaise
2 teaspoons prepared sharp
    mustard
Salt, pepper to taste
3 large eggs, hard-cooked

1 tablespoon fine dry bread
    crumbs
1 tablespoon grated Parmesan
    cheese
1 tablespoon wine vinegar
2 tablespoons chopped fresh
    parsley
Lettuce leaves

Cut a slice from the stem end of each tomato. Carefully scoop out the pulp, seeds, and liquid. Invert the tomatoes to drain. Combine the ham, peas, and potatoes. Carefully mix with the mayonnaise and mustard. Season with salt and pepper. Spoon into the tomato shells.

Peel the hard-cooked eggs and cut into halves crosswise. Take out the yolks and mash them. Combine the yolks with the bread crumbs, cheese, and vinegar. Spoon into the egg shells. Place the eggs, yolk sides down, over the tomatoes. Sprinkle the top of the eggs with parsley. Arrange the stuffed tomatoes on lettuce leaves. Chill. Makes 6 servings.

AUSTRIAN LIPTAUER

From the Hungarians, the Austrians borrowed one of their favorite appetizers which is commonly called Liptauer. The name derives from a Hungarian soft white cheese which originated in a province called Liptauer or

Liptoi. The dish is served in two ways. The first and traditional is the one I enjoyed at Vienna's Weisser Rauchfangkehrer ("white chimneysweep") restaurant. This was a large piece of white cheese in the center of a plate surrounded with tiny mounds of chopped chives, mustard, chopped onions, freshly ground pepper, chopped anchovies, and paprika. The idea of the dish is that since the cheese has little flavor, each bite, mixed with one of the seasonings, will be different. The second version is to combine the cheese with the seasonings and serve it as a spread in the form of a mound or another desirable shape. Additional seasonings that can be also used include caraway seeds, chopped gherkins, and capers. Cream or pot cheese is a good substitute for the Liptauer. This is but one of the many preparations.

2 packages (3 ounces each) cream cheese
¼ cup butter
2 tablespoons chopped drained capers
1 tablespoon chopped chives
2 tablespoons chopped onions
2 flat anchovy fillets, minced
2 teaspoons sharp mustard
2 tablespoons paprika
Pepper to taste

Cream the cheese and butter together. Add the remaining ingredients and mix well. Shape into a mound on a plate. Chill. Serve surrounded with thin pumpernickel slices or other dark bread. Makes about 4 to 6 servings.

PESCADO EN ESCABECHE

A popular appetizer in Spain and Portugal is pickled fish made spicy with seasonings.

2 pounds white-fleshed fillets
Flour
Salt, pepper to taste
About 1⅓ cups olive oil
2 large onions, sliced
1 cup wine vinegar
2 bay leaves
2 garlic cloves
¼ teaspoon crushed red peppers

Cut the fillets into 1-inch pieces and remove any skin. Dust with flour and season with salt and pepper. Heat ⅓ cup olive oil in a skillet and fry the fish in it until golden on both sides. Remove from the heat. Drain and cool. Add the onions to the drippings, adding more oil if necessary, and fry until soft. Mix in 1 cup of oil and the remaining ingredients and bring to a boil. Remove from the stove.

Arrange half the fillets in a deep bowl or glass dish. Cover with half the marinade. Repeat the layers. Leave, covered, in the refrigerator for 24 hours. Makes 6 to 8 servings.

Herring Appetizers

The most important to mankind of all the species of fish has been the humble salt herring, caught in large quantities in the North and Baltic seas, as well as in the Atlantic. By the twelfth century it had become staple fare in all of northern Europe, treasured for its high protein and low cost. Its value further increased when processes for curing and salting were improved. Over the centuries, when food was scarce, herring prevented starvation. Armies were fed on it. And governments fought over the fish. One struggle between the French and English became known as the Battle of the Herrings. The overthrow of Charles I of England was partially due to his interference in the free herring fishing rights of his own subjects. The Dutch became the envy and enemy of all their neighbors for their domination of the herring interests; because of this their vast foreign fleet was built. Northern towns were created because of the fish. In fact, one adage has it that "the foundations of Amsterdam were laid on herring bones."

The herring is still so popular and important in Holland that the spring arrival of the first catch of the *groene haring*, ("green herring"), is a widely celebrated and colorful national event. A barrel of the culinary prizes is formally presented to the queen. In the northern coastal villages it is great fun to watch the expertise of the Dutch in handling a snack of raw herring. Held by the tail, the fish is dipped in raw onion and then nibbled, leaving only the framework of bones.

Americans, who really do not appreciate the versatility of herring as a food, are ever amazed to discover the number of interesting dishes made with it when visiting these northern countries. Simple raw or pickled fillets will be handsomely served. I recall a restaurant in Bonn where, on a terrace overlooking the Rhine, my herring, garnished only with raw onion rings, was brought to the table on ice carved in the shape of a fish. There are numerous marinades for herring appetizers, and the fish is artfully combined with other foods to make interesting appetizer salads. Herring is very important to the preparation of *Smørrebrød* and is the gastronomic star of *smörgåsbord*, served in in a number of interesting creations. Included here are three herring recipes. Others will be given in following chapters.

SWEDISH PICKLED HERRING

This dish, *inlagd sill*, is very popular for the herring buffet of *smörgåsbord*.

2 large salt herring	4 whole allspice, crushed
1 cup white vinegar	1 bay leaf
½ cup sugar	1 large onion, chopped or
4 peppercorns, crushed	sliced

Soak the herring in water to cover for 24 hours. Change the water several times. Clean, bone, and skin the herring. Cut diagonally into bite-size pieces. Arrange in a bowl. In a saucepan combine the vinegar, sugar, peppercorns, allspice, and bay leaf. Bring to a boil and pour over the herring. Refrigerate, covered, overnight. Drain and serve garnished with chopped or sliced onion. This may be served with hot or cold boiled potatoes if desired. Makes about 12 *smörgåsbord* servings.

HERRING SALAD FROM SWEDEN

Another favorite herring dish for *smörgåsbord*.

1 large salt herring	1 cup diced cooked meat, veal
2 medium tart apples, pared	or beef
and sliced	1/3 cup wine vinegar
3 cold boiled medium potatoes,	2 tablespoons sugar
diced	Pepper to taste
3 medium cooked beets, diced	1 hard-cooked egg
1 gherkin, chopped	1/2 cup heavy cream

Soak the herring in water to cover overnight, changing the water several times. Clean, bone, and skin the herring. Dice. Mix with the remaining ingredients, except the egg and cream. Pack into a mold or bowl. Refrigerate. When ready to serve, turn out on a platter and garnish with the white and yolk of the egg, chopped separately. Serve with thick cream lightly whipped. Makes 6 to 8 servings for *smörgåsbord*.

GERMAN ROLL MOPS

This is one of the most popular German appetizers and is commonly sold in stores but may be prepared at home.

12 salt herring fillets	1 cup water
Hot prepared mustard	2 teaspoons sugar
2 tablespoons capers, drained	6 peppercorns
2 large onions, thinly sliced	6 juniper berries
3 large dill pickles, cut into 12	2 small bay leaves
pieces	2 teaspoons sugar
1½ cups cider vinegar	

Soak the herring in cold water to cover for 24 hours, changing the water 3 or 4 times. Drain. Remove any bones from the herring; wash and wipe dry. Lay a fillet, skin side down, on a flat surface. Spread with mustard. At one end, place ½ teaspoon capers, some onion slices, and 1 piece of pickle; roll up. Secure with toothpicks. Repeat with each fillet. Place in layers in a large, nonmetallic bowl or dish.

Combine the remaining ingredients in a saucepan and bring to a boil. Reduce the heat and cook slowly, uncovered, for 5 minutes. Cool and pour over the herring. Add any remaining onion rings. Cover with foil and refrigerate 4 to 6 days before serving. Drain. Some on individual plates if desired. Makes 6 servings offering 2 to each person.

SWISS ONION CHEESE TART

A superb Swiss dish similar to the famous French *quiche*.

1 pie crust for 9-inch pie	2 cups milk
3 tablespoons butter	4 eggs, beaten
3 large onions, thinly sliced	2 cups grated Swiss cheese
1 tablespoon flour	Salt, pepper to taste

Prepare the pie crust and fit into a pie plate. Melt the butter in a saucepan or skillet. Add the onions and sauté until tender. Mix in the flour and 1 cup milk. Cook, stirring, for 1 minute. Combine with the remaining ingredients and turn into the pie crust. Bake in a preheated moderate oven (350°F.) for about 40 minutes, until a knife inserted into the pie comes out clean. Cut into wedges. Serve hot. Makes 6 servings.

SCOTCH EGGS

An innovative appetizer that can be prepared beforehand.

1 pound sausage meat	6 hard-cooked eggs, shelled
2 tablespoons chopped fresh parsley	Flour
2 tablespoons minced onion	1 egg, beaten
1/8 teaspoon cayenne	Fine dry bread crumbs
Salt, pepper to taste	Deep fat for frying

Combine the sausage, parsley, onion, cayenne, salt, and pepper and mix well. Roll out evenly on a piece of waxed paper. Dust each egg lightly with flour. Coat each egg with sausage mixture to cover completely. Roll each egg in beaten egg and then in bread crumbs. Fry in hot deep fat (375°F. on a frying thermometer) for about 5 minutes. To serve, cut into halves. Makes 6 servings.

GERMAN EGG AND TOMATO "MUSHROOMS"

In Germany, and Austria as well, the beloved mushrooms are symbols of good luck. Wooden, china, glass, and ceramic replicas of white-stemmed mushrooms with white and red speckled caps are commonly sold as ornaments for Christmas trees, as table decorations, as salt and pepper shakers, and for other uses. Some cook devised an edible replica of this symbol. The "mushroom" is a favorite garnish, or can be eaten as an appetizer. It is simple to prepare and attractive to serve.

Cut a slice from the end of a hard-cooked egg so it will stand upright. Spoon out ½ of a medium tomato to remove the pulp, seeds, and liquid. Fit over the egg to form a "cap." Decorate the tomato top with tiny specks of mayonnaise.

Scandinavian Smörgåsbord

Outside Sweden, the best known of the Swedish culinary attractions is the gastronomic delight called *smörgåsbord*, a groaning board of many fascinating and inventive creations. Unfortunately, duplications of this glorious spread, served around the world, do not very often do justice to the original buffet meal as it was evolved by the Swedes. Therefore, it is interesting to note both the gastronomic past and present of this festive fare.

It probably could be said that the first *smörgåsbord* was created by the ancient Vikings, who welcomed travelers and guests to a cold board. But the Swedes point out that more recent origins are traced to the "akvavit buffet," an eighteenth-century array of appetizers, served with akvavit, while standing and awaiting a more formal seated meal. Traditional fare was butter and bread, cheese and herring, termed *Smor, ost och sill,* which over the years became shortened to SOS and was a symbol used frequently on restaurant menus. This abbreviation still exists on some of them.

Swedes, always partial to herring, added more dishes made with this fish and the event became known as a "herring buffet." A particular centerpiece was a large barrel-like container with six faucets dispensing six kinds of akvavit. Gradually, warm creations were added to the cold dishes and by the eighteenth century the appetizer display was a glorious one featured for all special events in the Swedish homes.

Sad to say, while the *smörgåsbord* gained popularity in other lands, it lost favor in its homeland and the custom of serving it almost disappeared. Fortunately, in recent years, some interested cooks promoted its revival and the *smörgåsbord* served in Sweden today, particularly Stockholm, is more glorious than ever. The most opulent restaurant spread in that city, and probably the world, is served at the Operakallaren, a restaurant owned and directed by Sweden's foremost gastronome, Tore Wretman. It is a glorious repast of over 60 dishes surrounding a beautiful akvavit dispenser served from a gigantic buffet table in the center of a lovely dining room. Another *smörgåsbord* that I particularly enjoyed was not as varied or spectacular to behold but was still a memorable experience. This one was featured at the Stallmastaregarden ("stablemaster's lodge"), a lovely restaurant or inn outside Stockholm that once belonged to a stablemaster, and is the city's oldest restaurant, dating from 1754. The dining room is small and comfortable, and, in the summer, the garden is inviting for an after-meal coffee.

The ceremony is important to full appreciation of the *smörgåsbord.* For, although all the foods are placed on a large table, they are served in courses of three or four, with clean plates and silver for each. Each diner may help himself to as much food as he wishes, but generally it is wise to begin with small helpings as there are just too many temptations to sample in one meal.

As in yesteryear, the meal begins with what is called the herring buffet, an assortment of cold dishes starring herring, some other fish, both mild and strong cheeses, and bread and butter. Particularly noteworthy are pickled fillets with sour cream and chives, marinated pickled herring (*inlagd sill*), a creation called glass blower's (*glasmastarsill*), and spiced herring with vegetables. There might be also caviar, cod's roe, Swedish anchovies, and an intriguing display called Bird's Nest—raw egg yolks surrounded by anchovies, pickled beets, onions, and capers, all on a bed of lettuce.

For the next course, the array of cold fare continues with more fish dishes such as smoked eel and salmon; jellied salmon's fins and dill-cured salmon; cold meat cuts, including reindeer; attractive egg dishes; sausages; *pâtés*; ham and pork preparations; relishes, pickles; and an array of colorful salads made with vegetables, meats, poultry, and seafood.

The hot buffet, *smavarmt*, is the third presentation and generally features meatballs, herring dishes, soufflés, casseroles, hashes, veal stuffed onion rolls, and Jansson's Temptation (baked potatoes and anchovies, p. 109).

If anyone is interested or can manage it, dessert will be either fresh fruit or a piece of cake, followed by good strong coffee.

BAGNA CAUDA OF PIEDMONT

A beloved specialty of Northern Italy's region of Piedmont is a hot dip for a variety of raw vegetables. The name is taken from the Italian "hot bath" and the dish may be served as an appetizer. In Italy it is also often a snack or, as on Christmas Eve, a whole meal. Generally the ingredients include a fair amount of olive oil, butter, garlic, and anchovy fillets. Delectable but rare white truffles are also commonly added. Some variations include heavy cream. For the vegetables, the Italians like to include the cardoon, a relative of the artichoke. The sauce, in a chafing dish or small earthenware casserole, is kept warm over a spirit lamp or candle warmer. An electric hot tray could also be used.

½ cup butter	1 cup heavy cream
½ cup olive oil	Assortment of raw vegetables:
8 anchovy fillets, drained and minced	carrot sticks, green onions, strips of green peppers,
2 to 4 cloves garlic, chopped	cucumber slices, slices of
1 canned white truffle, finely chopped (optional)	zucchini, cauliflowerets, small whole mushrooms

Melt the butter over low heat and heat the oil in a saucepan. Add the anchovies, garlic, and truffles, and slowly add the cream, stirring constantly. Be careful not to boil. When heated, pour into a chafing dish or small casserole and put over a spirit lamp or candle warmer to keep warm. Dip the prepared raw vegetables into the warm sauce. Makes about 6 servings.

2

Soups

FROM THE KITCHENS of Western Europe has emerged a wealth
of imaginative and diverse savory soups that can be relished
with great delight on any occasion. Whether a *consommé*,
crème, potage, sopa, purée, velouté or a hearty regional specialty,
each is rewarding to prepare and proffer. We Americans are
indeed fortunate in that some in this galaxy have been inter-
woven into our cuisine and thus are familiar fare. Many others
may be a pleasant discovery.

The art of soup-making has long been an essential and laud-
able achievement. In fact, soups were among man's first culinary creations. The first of them were doubtless prepared by
putting meat, bones, liquid, and perhaps some seasonings, in
empty animal-skin bags. Also added were hot stones to cook
them. Later, as clay containers were created, the ingredients
became more varied and were cooked slowly over direct heat.
Thus was devised the first *pot au feu* ("pot on the fire").

In Europe the early wealthy Romans enjoyed a variety of intricate soups at their lengthy banquets, while lesser folk subsisted on more basic and hearty creations. From the cookbook by
Apicius, believed to have been written in the first century A.D.,

we can determine that there was an excellent array of earthenware and bronze pots and kettles for preparing soup. Contemporary visitors to the ruins of Pompeii can view a fascinating collection of them, as well as other kitchen equipment recovered from various excavations.

As have other peoples, the Romans made their soup with a variety of staples such as legumes, vegetables, seafood, meat, and poultry, but they made them distinguishable by the addition of incredible combinations of strong flavorings. In fact, they actually disguised rather than enhanced the natural appeal of the foods. They also added sweet-and-sour mixtures to their thick pottages, a taste preference that spread to other European cuisines.

During the Dark Ages, after the fall of the Roman Empire, there were no resources for fancy experimentation with soups or any other fare. It was a time of foraging for anything to keep alive, and soups became the mainstay of the daily diet. Basic creations filled with grains and other accessible foods, they provided warmth and nourishment. The first soup kitchens, which would be revived over and over again in times of need, were established in the monasteries. Countless numbers of hungry unfortunates were thus able to survive.

The first written treatise dealing with soups is found in the oldest French cookbook in existence, *Le Viandier*, written about 1375 by a chef known as Taillevent. From this work one can assume that a most popular ingredient in several well-flavored soups was bread. Supposedly it was the custom of the time to dip great chunks of whole-grained bread into communal pots of rich broth.

The word for soup evolved from *sop*, the name for a piece of bread dipped in meat broth during the Middle Ages. About the twelfth century the broth was called *sop* or *soupe*, and other ingredients were added to the liquid. In the cuisines of Western Europe there are still many similar words. In Austria, Denmark, Germany, and Norway, for example, the dish is *Suppe*. In Spain and Portugal it is *sopa*; in Holland *soep* and Sweden *soppa*. The Italians use the word *zuppa* for some of their repertoire and the French likewise designate one category as *soupe*, a more hearty variation than a *potage*. A notable exception to this similarity of appellations is the Finnish *keitto*.

Basic bowls of liquid mixtures were also known as pottages,

gruels, and brews. But as refinements in gastronomy improved, so did the preparation of soups. During and after the sixteenth century, talented French cooks led the way by evolving the art of making numerous varieties of soups to heights theretofore unknown. For they no longer prepared them by merely combining foods together, but devised stocks, sauces, and seasonings that enhanced their flavors and gave them new refinement and distinction. These would become classical creations which have become standard items at royal and other distinguished repasts throughout the Continent.

It was Louis XIV, however, who introduced at his court the innovative protocol of serving various dishes as separate courses. Previously all the fare had been put on the table together. Although the Sun King himself began a dinner with a variety of soups, it became the custom at Continental banquets to commence with two of them, one clear and one thick. The great chef, Escoffier, probably best described this role of soups when he said they should perform like "an overture in a light opera (divulging) what is to be the dominant phrase of the melody throughout."

As we all know, these soups, served as first courses at dinners, are light ones, designed to stimulate the appetite, and should marry well with the remainder of the menu. Each of the European cuisines has developed a number of particular favorites that, in addition to those French classical ones, are served at restaurants, hotels, and in homes.

One of the best and most regal is the English turtle soup, which, because of its intricate preparation and expense, is not made in the home. An ancient recipe begins "Take a turtle weighing about 50 pounds." But the soups made in London today require three 140-pound turtles, imported from the West Indies, to make some 50 gallons of soup such as are required for a large gathering like the Lord Mayor's traditional banquet for a thousand or more guests. Also needed are vast amounts of rich stock, a considerable quantity of sherry, and sweet white wine. In England there is no soup to compare with this one, and it was Lewis Carroll who so aptly serenaded it as "Beautiful Soup, so rich and green,/Waiting in a hot tureen!"

Soups serve other functions as well, and many of the hearty varieties for centuries have traditionally constituted meals by themselves in European homes. Some soups are also eaten as

snacks or in the wee hours of the morning as a restorative or
effective remedy after a night of celebrating.

Suffice it to say that soups are very important throughout
Western Europe. Recipes and descriptive data in this chapter
will reveal national favorites and differences, but the marvelous
collection will also attest to some other words of Escoffier.
"Soup," he wrote, "puts the heart at ease, calms down the vi-
olence of hunger, eliminates the tensions of the day, and awak-
ens and refines the appetite."

SPARGELSUPPE FROM GERMANY

Germans are partial to asparagus soup that is made traditionally with white asparagus (see p. 189). One of the
best restaurants in which to sample the asparagus soups is
at Nuremberg's atmospheric Goldenes Posthorn, just below
the imposing castle-fortress (*Burg*), where in 1958 the
handsome green and white *Spargel Karte* (menu) with 57
inviting white asparagus specialties included the following
soups: consommé with *Spargel*; fresh *Spargel* cream soup;
terrine of *Spargel* soup with chicken; turtle soup with *Spargel*; and fresh lobster soup with *Spargel*. This *Spargel-
suppe* may be made with white or green asparagus.

1 pound fresh white or green   2 tablespoons flour
  asparagus   2 egg yolks, lightly beaten
Water   Freshly ground pepper and
2 teaspoons sugar   grated nutmeg to taste
Salt to taste   3 tablespoons chopped fresh
1 cup light cream   parsley
2 tablespoons soft butter

If white asparagus is used, it must be peeled from just below
the tip to the base. For green asparagus, trim off the scales and
any tough stalk ends. Wash well and cut into 1-inch pieces, reserving the tips. Put 5 cups of water in a kettle and bring to a
boil. Add the asparagus pieces and sugar and season lightly
with salt. Lower the heat and cook slowly, covered, about 12
minutes, or until the asparagus is tender. Cook the tips sep-

arately in salted boiling water to cover until tender. Drain the
tips and set aside. Put the cooked asparagus pieces and liquid
through a sieve or whirl in a blender until smooth. Heat in a
saucepan. Add the cream. Combine the butter and flour until
smooth and form into tiny balls. Drop into the soup and cook
slowly, stirring, until thickened. Mix 2 or 3 tablespoons of the
hot soup with the egg yolks and return mixture to the kettle.
Add the asparagus tips, pepper, and nutmeg. Season with salt.
Leave on the stove only a few minutes, stirring. Serve garnished
with the parsley. Serves 6.

DUTCH VEGETABLE SOUP WITH MEATBALLS

The Dutch are great devotees of meatballs, *balletjes*,
which they serve in a number of inviting dishes. This is one
of their great favorites. It can be served as a one-dish
meal for dinner or supper.

1 pound ground veal
1 egg
2 teaspoons curry powder
Salt, pepper to taste
2 slices white bread, without
  crusts
¼ cup milk
1 large onion, chopped
1 large carrot, scraped and
  chopped

1 large leek, white part only,
  cleaned and thinly sliced
1 large celery stalk, cleaned
  and chopped
2 tablespoons butter or
  margarine
1 tablespoon vegetable oil
1½ quarts beef bouillon
¼ teaspoon dried marjoram
1½ cups broken vermicelli
¼ cup chopped fresh parsley

Combine the veal, egg, curry powder, salt, and pepper in a
large bowl and work together with the hands or a spoon until
well mixed. Soak the bread in milk to cover. Squeeze dry and
break into tiny pieces. Add to the veal mixture and mix again
to combine thoroughly all the ingredients. Shape into 1½-inch
balls and set aside. Sauté the onion, carrot, leek, and celery
in the butter and oil in a large kettle over low heat for 10 minutes. Add the bouillon and marjoram and season with salt and
and pepper. Bring to a boil. Lower the heat and cook slowly,
covered, for 30 minutes. Add the meatballs and cook about an-

other 20 minutes, or until they are done. Meanwhile, cook the vermicelli in boiling water until just tender; drain. When the meatballs are cooked, add the vermicelli. Remove from the heat and serve garnished with the parsley. Serves 8.

SCOTCH BROTH

The most traditional of all the Scottish soups is one called barley broth or Scotch broth, a beloved family one-dish meal which has given nourishment to Scots for centuries. Made with mutton or lamb, barley, and vegetables, it is indeed a worthy combination. While dining in Scotland one can generally sample the soup in any restaurant or inn as it is a standard menu item, superb on any occasion.

2 pounds neck or breast of
  lamb, cut up
2 quarts water
Salt to taste
4 peppercorns, bruised
½ cup of pearl barley

1 cup diced carrots
1 cup sliced onions
1 medium turnip, peeled and
  diced
3 tablespoons chopped fresh
  parsley

Put the lamb in a large kettle. Add the water and season with salt. Bring to a boil and remove any scum from the top. Add the peppercorns and barley and lower the heat. Cook slowly, covered, for 2 hours. Take off the stove and remove the meat. Cool. Cut the meat from the bones and trim any fat from it. Put the meat back in the kettle and discard the bones. Add the carrots, onions, and turnip and return to the stove. Bring to a boil. Lower the heat and cook slowly, covered, for 30 minutes. Correct the seasoning. Remove and discard the peppercorns. Stir in the parsley. Serves 6 to 8.

SOUPE À L'OIGNON AU GRATIN

Among all the noble dishes made with the humble and versatile onion, none is better than a rich soup topped with toasted French bread and grated cheese. It is a marvelous dish any time of the day or night but is particularly relished in France as a restorative in the wee hours of the morning after a night of celebrating. In Paris it was long traditional to finish a fun evening with one or more bowls of onion soup at Les Halles at about 4 A.M. This was before the colorful market was moved outside the city. The custom has persisted in other places, however, and there are any number of bistros, restaurants, or cafés where one can dine on this great soup. I recall the thrill of being initiated into this custom just before the sun came up at a popular Paris supper club, La Calavados, where nonstop service continues all night amid a gay atmosphere enlivened with vivacious personalities. Since then I've been a consistent devotee of this great *soupe* served anywhere at any time.

1½ pounds (about 5 cups sliced) onions, peeled and thinly sliced
3 tablespoons butter
3 tablespoons vegetable oil
1 teaspoon sugar
Salt, pepper to taste

6 cups beef bouillon
½ cup dry white wine
1 or more slices of toasted French bread
About 1¼ cups Grated Gruyère or Swiss cheese
Melted butter

Sauté the onions in the butter and oil in a large heavy saucepan over moderate heat until limp. Add the sugar and mix well. Season with salt and pepper. Pour in the bouillon and bring to a boil. Lower the heat and simmer, covered, for 20 minutes. Add the wine and continue to cook slowly for 10 minutes. Ladle into earthenware or other ovenproof bowls. Top with one or more slices of toasted French bread. Sprinkle generously with cheese. Sprinkle the top with melted butter. Put in a preheated moderate oven (375°F.) for 20 minutes or until the cheese is melted. Then put under the broiler for a few minutes, until golden and crusty on top. Serve in the dishes. Serves 6.

PORTUGUESE CALDO VERDE

The most popular soup in Portugal's northwestern region of Minho is *caldo verde*, green soup, made with potatoes and a deep green kale unlike that grown elsewhere. The soup is basic and humble but flavorful with olive oil and garlic and topped with sausages. The Portuguese eat their native type of corn bread (*broa*) with it.

1 pound fresh kale	Salt, pepper to taste
4 medium potatoes, pared	¼ pound smoked garlic
8 cups cold water	sausage, cooked, and sliced
¼ cup olive oil	into ¼-inch rounds

Wash the kale and cut off the stems. Slice into shreds as thin as possible. Put the potatoes, water, oil, salt, and pepper in a saucepan and bring to a boil. Lower the heat and cook slowly, covered, for about 5 minutes, or until the potatoes are tender. Remove from the stove and put the mixture through a sieve or purée it. Return to the saucepan and add the strips of kale. Continue to cook about 15 minutes longer, or until the kale is tender. Serve with the sausage on top of the soup. Serves 6.

NORWEGIAN FISKESUPPE

Bergen, Norway's second largest city and capital of the West Land (*Vestlandet*), is an atmospheric port where it is a particular delight to wander along the quay of the old town. Another fascination is to watch the fishing boats leaving and returning with some of the world's best fruits of the sea. Because of this bountiful and excellent supply, Norwegians are devotees of a great many seafood dishes, including flavorful fish soups. One of their favorite fish for making them is *pale* or young coalfish of the cod family. Its distinctive and appealing flavor is outstanding. To make this soup, use any firm white-fleshed fish such as pollock, haddock, or cod as a substitute.

2 pounds raw fish trimmings,	Salt to taste
(bones, heads, skin, tails)	4 quarts water
1 medium onion stuck with 3	3 tablespoons butter or
cloves	margarine
1 bay leaf	1 cup sliced leeks
6 peppercorns, bruised	

1 small celeriac (celery root),
pared and cubed
1 cup sliced carrots
4 medium potatoes, diced
1½ pounds boneless
white-fleshed fish, cleaned

2 egg yolks
⅓ to ½ cup sour cream, at
room temperature
⅓ cup chopped fresh parsley

Put the fish trimmings, onion with the cloves, bay leaf, peppercorns, salt, and water in a large kettle. Bring to a boil. Lower the heat and simmer, covered, for 30 minutes. Strain the broth. Melt the butter in a large kettle and add the leeks, celeriac, carrots, and potatoes and sauté for 5 minutes. Add the fish and cook about 10 minutes longer, until the fish is tender. Remove the fish to a platter and keep warm. In a small bowl, beat the egg yolks and add some of the hot broth. Pour back into the soup. Add the sour cream and leave on low heat a few minutes, stirring. Break up the fish into bite-size pieces and add to the soup. Remove from the heat. Serve garnished with the parsley. Serves 6 to 8.

DUTCH ERWTENSOEP

The national soup of Holland, *erwtensoep*, made with green split peas, pork, and vegetables, is a hearty one-dish meal. Properly prepared, it should be so thick that a spoon can stand upright in the rich purée. Since it is better if cooked the day beforehand, left overnight, and then reheated, many housewives do this purposely. A traditional accompaniment is pumpernickel.

2 cups (1 pound) split green
peas, washed and drained
3 quarts water
Salt to taste
2 large pigs' feet, cleaned and
split
1 pound smoked bacon or pork
in one piece
4 medium leeks, white parts

and 2 inches of the green,
cleaned and sliced thickly
4 medium potatoes, pared and
diced
1 medium celeriac (celery
root), peeled and diced
Pepper to taste
½ pound frankfurters, sliced
into ½-inch rounds

Put the split peas, water, and salt in a large kettle and bring to a boil. Reduce the heat and simmer, covered, for 1 hour. Add the pigs' feet and bacon and continue to cook for another hour. Then add the leeks, potatoes, celeriac, and pepper and continue to cook for another 30 minutes. Remove from the heat and take out the pigs' feet and bacon. Cut any meat from the feet, discarding the bones and skin. Cut the bacon into slices. Return the meat and bacon to the kettle and add the frankfurter slices. Check the seasoning. Reheat over a low fire or leave overnight and reheat the next day. Serves 8.

DANISH COLD BUTTERMILK SOUP

Scandinavians are devotees of sour milk products, which have long been important to them as foods. One of the most interesting dishes made with buttermilk is a Danish summer soup, served with spoonfuls of whipped cream floating on the top, with the unpronounceable name of *Kaernemaelkskoldskaal.*

3 eggs	1 teaspoon vanilla extract
¼ to ½ cup sugar	1½ quarts cold buttermilk
Juice of 1 medium lemon	Whipped heavy cream
1 tablespoon grated lemon	(optional)
rind	

Beat the eggs in a large bowl with an electric beater or whisk. Slowly add the sugar, the exact amount according to the desired taste. Add the lemon juice, lemon rind, vanilla, and the buttermilk, two cups at a time. Continue to beat until well mixed and smooth. Chill. Serve with spoonfuls of whipped cream floating on top. Serves 6 to 8.

SWISS MUSHROOM BOUILLON

One of the most popular foods in Western Europe is the mushroom; both wild and cultivated varieties are used extensively in the various cuisines. Some of the most superb creations are mushroom soups. One of the simplest, yet most refreshing and excellent as a first course, is this one from Switzerland.

¾ pound fresh mushrooms	Freshly grated pepper to taste
8 cups beef bouillon	⅓ cup minced green onions or
1 cup dry sherry	chives

Rinse the mushrooms quickly or wipe them with damp paper toweling to remove any dirt. Cut off any tough stem ends. Slice thickly lengthwise through the caps. Put with the bouillon in a large saucepan and bring to a boil. Lower the heat and cook slowly, covered, for 10 minutes. Add the sherry and pepper and remove from the heat. Serve garnished with the onions or chives. Serves 8.

LE WATERZOOI DE VOLAILLE FROM BELGIUM

One of the most characteristic of the northern Belgian or Flemish dishes is a flavorful creation called *waterzooi*, a soup-stew which is made either with fish or chicken. (See recipe on p. 110.) One of the delightful places to enjoy it is in the ancient art city of Ghent, famous for its museums and flowers. While dining at the Cordial restaurant and thinking of bygone days, it is not difficult to realize that this inviting town was among Europe's greatest and richest cities during the fifteenth century.

2 medium onions, chopped	6 cups chicken broth or bouillon
2 medium leeks, white parts only, cleaned and thinly sliced	1 bay leaf
	4 whole cloves
	½ teaspoon dried thyme
3 medium stalks celery, chopped	3 parsley sprigs
	6 peppercorns
2 medium carrots, scraped and chopped	Salt to taste
	¼ cup all-purpose flour
11 tablespoons (approximately) butter or margarine	2 egg yolks
	Juice of 1 large lemon
	1 large lemon, sliced
4½ to 5 pounds broiler-fryer chickens, cut in pieces, washed and dried	¼ cup chopped fresh parsley

Sauté the onions, leeks, celery, and carrots in ¼ cup of butter in a large kettle over low heat for 5 minutes. Remove with a slotted spoon to a plate. Melt ¼ cup of butter in the kettle and sauté the chicken pieces on both sides in it. It will not be possible to do all of them at the same time. Add more butter if needed. When the sautéeing is finished, return the sautéed vegetables and all the chicken pieces to the kettle. Add also the chicken broth, bay leaf, cloves, thyme, parsley sprigs, peppercorns, and salt. Bring to a boil. Lower the heat and cook slowly, covered, about 30 minutes, or until the chicken is tender. Remove from the stove and, with tongs, take out the chicken pieces. Keep them warm. Strain the broth into another kettle and leave over low heat.

Melt 3 tablespoons of butter in a saucepan. Stir in the flour and mix well. Pour in 2 cups of the hot broth and cook slowly, stirring, until the mixture thickens. Mix into the broth that is in the kettle, stirring over low heat. Beat the egg yolks slightly with the lemon juice and add a little of the hot broth, then return to the kettle. Mix well and remove at once from the heat. Correct the seasoning. To serve, pour the broth over the warm chicken pieces. Garnish with the lemon slices and chopped parsley. Serves 8.

If you wish to prepare the soup beforehand, do not add the egg yolks and lemon slices until just before serving.

VENETIAN RISI E BISI

A characteristic dish of Venice, rice and peas, or *risi e bisi,* is served both as a soup and a vegetable, depending on the amount of liquid. Each is preferably made with sweet tender fresh peas; those of Venice are particularly flavorful. This dish was a featured specialty of the official banquets once given in the spectacular dining rooms of the Palace of the Doges. I recall it, however, from a lovely evening meal at the Taverna la Fenice, one of the city's best restaurants, which has a fascinating menu and outdoor terrace.

⅓ cup chopped bacon or ham   3 tablespoons butter or olive
1 medium onion, minced   oil

½ cup uncooked rice
6 cups rich chicken broth or
  bouillon
Salt, pepper to taste

2 cups fresh or frozen green
  peas
Grated Parmesan cheese,
  preferably freshly grated

Combine the bacon, onion, and butter in a large saucepan and
sauté until the onion is tender. Add the rice and sauté until the
grains are well coated and translucent, about 5 minutes. Add
the chicken broth and bring to a boil. Season with salt and
pepper. Lower the heat and cook slowly, covered, for 20 minutes, or until the rice grains are just tender. Add the peas, allowing about 10 minutes if fresh, and about 5 minutes if frozen.
When tender, remove from the heat. Serve sprinkled with the
grated Parmesan. Serves 6 to 8.

SPANISH QUARTER-OF-AN-HOUR SOUP

A very popular and excellent soup served in Spanish restaurants is called *sopa al cuarto de hora*, although it is not
prepared in fifteen minutes. The time, however, is well
worth the effort as it is a flavorful medley of inviting ingredients typical of the Spanish colorful and flavorful *sopas*.

⅓ cup diced bacon or ham
1 or 2 tablespoons olive oil
1 medium onion, chopped
2 medium garlic cloves,
  crushed or minced
1 large tomato, peeled and
  chopped
1 teaspoon paprika
6 cups chicken broth
2 cans (7½ ounces each)
  minced clams, undrained

½ cup uncooked rice
Salt, pepper to taste
1 cup fresh or frozen green
  peas
1 cup cleaned small or medium
  canned shrimp
2 hard-cooked eggs, shelled
  and chopped
1 canned pimiento, cut into
  strips

Combine the bacon, oil (use 2 tablespoons if ham rather than
bacon is used), onion, and garlic in a kettle. Heat the ingredients and sauté for 5 minutes. Add the tomato and paprika and
sauté about 3 minutes longer, until mushy. Pour in the broth

and clams, with their liquid, and bring to a boil. Stir in the rice. Season with salt and pepper. Lower the heat and cook over a medium fire, uncovered, for 15 minutes. Add the peas and shrimp and cook 10 minutes longer, if the peas are fresh, or 5 minutes, if they are frozen. Serve garnished with the eggs and pimiento. Serves 8 to 10.

Fresh, rather than canned, shrimp may be used. If so, sauté them with the onions until pink and remove. Return to the soup shortly before serving.

POTAGE PARMENTIER

This flavorful leek and potato soup is named for Antoine-Auguste Parmentier, a French horticulturist, who during the late eighteenth century worked tirelessly to have the despised potato accepted as a valuable and economical food. He not only cultivated the white tubers and served them at dinner parties but presented a bouquet of their pretty blossoms to Louis XIV. They gained further popularity when Marie-Antoinette wore the blossoms in her hair, and eventually potato dishes became not only acceptable but sought-after fare. Any dish named Parmentier means that it includes potatoes.

4 medium leeks, white parts and 1 inch of the green, washed and sliced	6 cups chicken broth or water Salt, pepper to taste
4 tablespoons butter	1 cup light cream or milk
4 medium potatoes, pared and diced (about 4 cups)	2 tablespoons chopped chives or fresh parsley

Sauté the leeks in 2 tablespoons of butter in a large saucepan or kettle over low heat until tender. Add the potatoes, broth, salt, and pepper and bring to a boil. Lower the heat and cook slowly, covered, until tender, about 20 minutes. Put through a food mill or sieve, or whirl in a blender until smooth. Return to the saucepan. Add the cream and the remaining 2 tablespoons of butter. Correct the seasoning. Serve garnished with the chives or parsley. Serves 4 to 6.

CACCIUCCO ALLA LIVORNESE

One of the great Mediterranean seafood soups is a thick and flavorful one that takes its name from the Tuscan port of Livorno or Leghorn. It is eaten generally as a main course and any visitor to this colorful coastal region will relish the memory of a luncheon of *cacciucco* at an outdoor restaurant. Like all seafood specialties of this area, the dish is not easy to duplicate elsewhere, as the local fruits of the sea are simply not available. Strange and spiny creatures such as octopus and shellfish provide a marvelous flavor.

3 pounds mixed seafood (Suggestions include lobster, shrimp, cod, haddock, mackerel, snapper, sea bass, or rockfish.)
1 large onion, chopped
2 to 3 garlic cloves, minced
1/3 to 1/2 cup olive oil
1/2 teaspoon crumbled dried sage
2 medium bay leaves
Salt, black and red pepper to taste
1/4 cup tomato paste
1/2 cup dry white wine
Garlic toast

Cut the fish into good-sized serving pieces. If lobster is used, clean and separate the body from the claws. Cut into similar-sized pieces. Sauté the onion and garlic in the oil, the amount according to taste, in a large kettle until tender. Add the sage, bay leaves, salt and peppers, and mix well. Cook 1 minute. Stir in the tomato paste and add the wine. Bring to a boil. Add the seafood and lower the heat. Cook very slowly, covered, about 15 minutes, until the seafood is tender. (If the seafood varies considerably in texture, add the firmer pieces first and then the softer pieces.) Meanwhile, prepare the garlic toast. Spread 6 or 12 pieces (one or two per serving) of crusty Italian bread with a mixture of crushed garlic and olive oil. Bake in a preheated moderate oven 350°F., for about 12 minutes, or until crisp. To serve, arrange the toast in large soup bowls. Put the pieces of seafood over the bread and spoon the broth over it. Or serve the broth separately. Serves 6.

SWISS MEHLSUPPE

A popular soup in Switzerland throughout the year is a simple flour one called *Mehlsuppe*. It is particularly associated, however, with the gay *Fasnacht*, or carnival celebration, and most Swiss agree that the soup is best in Basel. There the whole population turns out for a spirited lantern parade beginning at 4 A.M., and restaurants serve great quantities of the soup and onion pie to the gay celebrants until dawn. Thus fortified, they can report for a morning's work and then commence merrymaking all over again in the afternoon.

5 tablespoons butter
5 tablespoons flour
6 cups hot beef bouillon or
  water
1 medium onion stuck with 4
  cloves

1 bay leaf
Salt to taste
1½ cups stale bread croutons
½ cup grated Gruyère or
  Swiss cheese

Melt the butter in a heavy saucepan. Stir in the flour and cook over medium heat, stirring, until the mixture is smooth and deep brown. Be careful not to burn the mixture. Remove from the stove and add the hot bouillon, stirring until smooth. Add the onion with the cloves, the bay leaf, and salt. Return to the stove and cook over very low heat for 1 hour. Stir occasionally while cooking. Remove and discard the onion and bay leaf. Serve with the croutons floating on the surface and sprinkled with the cheese. Serves 6.

GULYAS SUPPE FROM AUSTRIA

In both Austria and Germany a favorite home and restaurant soup is the Hungarian goulash *Suppe*, richly flavored with paprika. It can be and often is a meal by itself or a midmorning snack, particularly relished in cold weather. I recall it as a most satisfying quick luncheon while stopping at German *Autobahn* restaurants or while sightseeing in Austria. The seasoning of the Austrian soup differs from the traditional Hungarian in that it includes caraway seeds, marjoram, and lemon peel.

4 medium onions, chopped
2 to 3 garlic cloves, crushed
6 tablespoons lard or bacon
  drippings
3 to 4 tablespoons paprika,
  preferably Hungarian
3 pounds beef chuck or round,
  cut into 1-inch cubes

2 large tomatoes, peeled and
  chopped
2 tablespoons caraway seeds
2 teaspoons dried marjoram
1 teaspoon minced lemon peel
2 quarts water
Salt, pepper to taste
4 medium potatoes, pared and
  cut into small cubes

Sauté the onions and garlic in the lard in a large kettle over low heat until tender. Stir in the paprika and cook for 1 minute. Add the beef cubes, several at a time, and brown on all sides. Add the tomatoes, caraway seeds, marjoram, lemon peel, water, salt, and pepper and bring to a boil. Lower the heat and simmer, covered, for 1 hour. Add the potatoes and continue to cook slowly for about 30 minutes longer, or until tender. Serves 12.

SCOTCH COCK-A-LEEKIE

Although of Scottish origin, this flavorful chicken-and-leek soup is popular throughout the British Isles. Its name was acquired most probably because at one time it was made with a cockerel. Some versions include the addition of pitted prunes, an innovation that is denounced as a French heresy by Scots, who scorn a sweet flavor in the soup.

1 stewing chicken, about 5
  pounds, washed
5 quarts water

12 leeks, white parts and 2
  inches of green stems, washed
  and cut into ½-inch slices

4 parsley sprigs
1 bay leaf
½ teaspoon dried thyme
Salt, pepper to taste

½ cup pearl barley
2 tablespoons chopped fresh
  parsley

Put the chicken in a large kettle and add the water. Bring to a boil and, with a skimmer or spoon, remove any scum that has risen to the surface. Add the remaining ingredients, except the chopped parsley, and lower the heat. Cook slowly, partially covered, until the chicken is tender, about 2½ hours. Remove the chicken to a large plate or platter and when slightly cooled, remove and discard the skin. Take the meat from the bones and cut into bite-size pieces. Discard the bones. Remove and discard the parsley sprigs and bay leaf from the liquid. Take off any scum from the surface of the liquid and return the chicken pieces to the kettle. Put back on the stove long enough to heat through. Serve garnished with the chopped parsley. Serves 10 to 12.

FINNISH KESÄKEITTO

In Finland a marvelous summer vegetable soup called *kesäkeitto* is eaten as a main dish accompanied by open-faced sandwiches of cold sliced meat. It is prepared there when the garden-fresh vegetables are at their peak of tenderness. It can be made, however, with a combination of fresh and frozen vegetables, although the flavor will not be exactly as good. It is a superb, delectable, and attractive soup that can be enjoyed any time during the year.

2 cups thinly sliced leeks or
  onions
2 cups cut-up cauliflower
2 cups cut-up green beans
1 cup shelled fresh or frozen
  green peas
1 cup thinly sliced carrots
2 cups diced potatoes

5 cups boiling water
1 tablespoon sugar
6 tablespoons flour
Salt, pepper to taste
6 cups hot milk
2 tablespoons butter
⅓ cup chopped fresh parsley

Put the vegetables and boiling water in a large kettle. Add the sugar, salt, and pepper and bring to a boil. Lower the heat and cook slowly, covered, until the vegetables are just tender, about 20 minutes. Meanwhile, combine the flour and milk and mix until smooth. Pour into the kettle and mix well. Cook slowly, stirring, a few minutes. Remove from the heat and add the butter and parsley. Serves 8 to 10.

AUSTRIAN RINDSUPPE

Of all the great Austrian soups, the star of the repertoire is beef soup, *Rindsuppe*. It serves many culinary roles, however. The meat and vegetables cooked in it can be taken out and served as a meal. The bouillon or stock is then strained and clarified and used to enrich other dishes or is served by itself as a clear bouillon. As the latter it generally has the addition of any of a number of garnishes such as noodles, semolina, rice, a diverse selection of dumplings, strips of unsweetened cooked pancakes, a raw egg yolk or egg, julienne-cut vegetables, or an Austrian specialty, deep-fried dough "peas" called *Backerbsen*. The clear broth plus the added garnish acquire the name of the latter. Thus one with liver dumplings is called *Leberknödelsuppe*. Austrian cooks have devised many ways of preparing this soup, and no two recipes are the same. Each is made with the finest of ingredients. This recipe is one variation and can be eaten as a regular soup or, as in Austria, with the meat and vegetables removed, the bouillon clarified, and served with a favorite garnish.

2 to 2½ pounds beef bones, cracked
3 pounds soup beef, chuck, or other beef
3 tablespoons butter or vegetable oil
3 quarts water
Salt, pepper to taste
1 large onion, thinly sliced
2 medium leeks, white parts only, cleaned and thinly sliced
2 medium carrots, scraped and thinly sliced
1 celeriac, celery root, pared and cubed
3 small turnips, pared and cubed
2 cups cut-up cauliflower
4 sprigs parsley
2 medium bay leaves
½ teaspoon dried thyme

Scald the bones and rinse in cold water. Wipe dry the meat. Heat the butter in a large kettle and brown the meat in it on all sides. Add the bones, water, salt, and pepper. Slowly bring to a full simmer and remove any scum from the top. Cook over very low heat, partially covered, for 1½ hours. Again remove any scum from the top. Add the remaining ingredients and continue to cook until the vegetables and meat are tender, about 1 hour longer. Remove and discard the parsley sprigs and bay leaves. Take out the meat and cut into bite-size pieces, discarding any bones and gristle. Return the meat to the soup. Serves 8 to 10.

GERMAN LENTIL SAUSAGE EINTOPF

Very characteristic and basic to German cookery is a hearty and nourishing *Eintopf*, or one-pot dish that can be a thick soup or stew. *Eintopf* creations are enjoyed at family tables or amid the convivial *gemütlich* atmosphere of an inn, tavern, or restaurant. This one is made with two very popular German foods, lentils and sausages. It is reminiscent of an *Eintopf* I enjoyed at the Schneefernerhaus, the highest hotel in Germany, atop the Zugspitze, reached through a long tunnel after ascending the steep mountain by rail. It is a lovely restaurant overlooking a broad skiing area and with a spectacular view of the German and Austrian country side.

6 slices bacon, diced
2 medium onions, sliced
2 leeks, white parts only, cleaned and sliced
2 medium carrots, scraped and diced
1 cup diced ham
2 cups lentils, washed and drained
5 cups water
1 medium celery stalk, with leaves, diced

½ teaspoon dried thyme
Salt, pepper to taste
1 can (1 pound) tomatoes, undrained
4 cups tomato juice
10 frankfurters, thickly sliced
2 cups broken pasta (spaghetti, macaroni, or noodles), cooked and drained
3 tablespoons cider vinegar
⅓ cup chopped fresh parsley

Fry the bacon in a large heavy kettle or casserole and add the onions, leeks, carrots, and ham. Sauté for 5 minutes. Add the lentils, water, celery, thyme, salt, and pepper, and bring to a boil. Lower the heat and cook slowly, covered, about 30 minutes, or until most of the liquid is absorbed and the lentils are soft. Add the tomatoes, tomato juice, frankfurter slices, and pasta. Cook another 10 minutes. Stir in the vinegar and remove from the stove. Serve sprinkled with the parsley. Serves 8 to 10.

For a thinner soup, add more tomato juice.

POTAGE AUX HERBES FROM BELGIUM

Some of the world's oldest and best soups have been those made with herbs. But those prepared today in Belgium and France are made with what are called *herbes potagères*, pot herbs or vegetables. These are a combination of vegetable greens such as lettuce, sorrel, spinach, sea kale, and purslane. This soup variation is refreshing and innovative and is made with greens and herbs.

2 tablespoons butter
1/3 cup chopped chives or green
 onions
1 cup shredded lettuce
1/2 cup shredded sorrel or
 spinach
1/2 cup chopped watercress
1/4 cup chopped fresh parsley
6 cups beef bouillon
1 teaspoon sugar
Salt, pepper to taste
1 cup light cream

Melt the butter in a heavy saucepan and sauté the chives in it until tender. Add the lettuce, sorrel or spinach, watercress, and parsley. Simmer, covered, for 10 minutes. Add the beef bouillon, sugar, salt, and pepper and simmer, covered, 30 minutes longer. Stir occasionally. Add the cream and leave on the stove long enough to heat through. Serves 6 to 8.

PETITE MARMITE

The classic one-dish meal of France, *petite marmite* or small pot, rich with beef, chicken, and vegetables, derives its name from the pot in which it is traditionally cooked

and served. It is a great restaurant dish well worth seeking
out in any part of France. The broth is very often served
over toasted French bread in bowls, with the meat and vegetables being offered separately on a platter.

2 medium onions, sliced
2 tablespoons butter or
 vegetable oil
2 pounds chuck or other beef
 in one piece
1 pound beef soup bones
2 pounds chicken wings
3 quarts beef bouillon or water
2 medium bay leaves
4 whole cloves
4 parsley sprigs
½ teaspoon dried thyme
6 peppercorns, bruised

Salt, to taste
3 medium leeks, white parts
 only, cleaned and sliced
 thickly
4 medium carrots, scraped and
 cut into 1-inch pieces
4 medium white turnips,
 peeled and quartered
1 loaf French bread, sliced
 thickly and toasted
Grated Parmesan cheese,
 preferably freshly grated

Sauté the onions in the butter in a large kettle over low heat
until tender. Add the beef, beef bones, chicken wings, bouillon,
bay leaves, cloves, parsley sprigs, thyme, peppercorns, and salt,
and bring slowly to a full simmer. Remove any scum. Cook
very slowly, covered, for 2½ hours, removing occasionally any
scum that has risen to the top. Add the leeks, carrots, and
turnips and continue to cook slowly about another 30 minutes,
or until the meat and vegetables are tender. Remove the kettle
from the stove. Take out and discard the bay leaves, cloves, parsley, and peppercorns. Remove the beef, beef bones, and chicken
wings. Keep the broth and vegetables warm over low heat. Cut
the beef into slices. Remove any meat from the beef bones and
chicken wings. To serve, put some of the beef, chicken, and
warm vegetables into individual soup plates; then cover with
some of the hot broth. Serve with toasted French bread and
grated cheese. Serves 8.

SWEDISH CHILLED FRUIT SOUP

Characteristic soups of northern Germany and Scandinavia are those made with such fruits as cherries, plums,
apples, or berries. They are served both hot and cold and

flavored with spices, fruit juices, and/or wine. Most are thickened with cornstarch and some are garnished with spoonfuls of whipped sweet cream or sour cream, and crumbled macaroons or other cookies. Visitors to these countries very often find that enjoyment of these soups is an acquired taste. This is a general recipe for a Swedish fruit soup, which may be made with any of the above-mentioned fruits.

2 pounds ripe fruit	1 teaspoon minced lemon peel
2 quarts water	Powdered cinnamon to taste
1½ to 2 cups sugar	1 tablespoon cornstarch
Juice of 1 lemon	

Clean the fruit by washing and removing any cores or seeds, but do not peel. Put in a large saucepan with the water and bring to a boil. Lower the heat and cook slowly, covered, until tender. The time will differ according to the kind of fruit. Put through a sieve or whirl in a blender. Mix with the sugar, lemon juice, lemon peel, and cinnamon. Stir the cornstarch with a little water and add to the mixture. Cook over low heat, stirring, about 5 minutes, until thickened. Serves 4 to 6.

COTRIADE OF BRITTANY

France's large coastal province of Brittany, surrounded on three sides by water, is a land of diverse contrasts, beloved for its rugged beauty. Its fishermen and farmers still carry on the traditions of yesteryear. Excellent native fare, particularly seafood dishes, are prepared as they have been for centuries. One of the most inviting specialties is a soup called *cotriade*, made with a variety of fish taken from the day's catch. Although it is sometimes referred to as the Breton *bouillabaisse*, it does not include shellfish. Its pungent flavor is derived from onions and herbs.

3 pounds mixed fish, cleaned	2 large onions, thinly sliced
(Suggestions include halibut,	1 large garlic clove, minced
haddock, sea bass, flounder, cod,	3 tablespoons butter or
mullet, and mackerel.)	margarine

6 medium potatoes, pared and
  quartered
2½ quarts water
2 medium bay leaves
1 teaspoon dried thyme

4 parsley sprigs
½ teaspoon dried marjoram
Salt, pepper to taste
Slices of crusty French bread

Cut the fish into chunks or slices of equal sizes. Sauté the onions and garlic in the butter in a large kettle. Add the potatoes, water, bay leaves, thyme, parsley, marjoram, salt, and pepper and bring to a boil. Add the prepared fish and lower the heat to moderate. Cook, covered, about 20 minutes, or until the fish are just tender and the potatoes are cooked. Ladle the broth over slices of bread in wide soup plates and serve the potatoes and fish separately on a platter. Serves 6 to 8.

DANISH GULE AERTER

Yellow pea soup has long been traditional winter fare in both Denmark and Sweden. In fact, it's the Swedish custom to eat *aerter med flask* every Thursday night for supper. The Danish version includes vegetables, but in each country the soup is made according to the preference of the cook. It is a hearty dish designed to offer nourishment and warmth during the long harsh winter months. Traditional accompaniments are mustard, dark bread, and *snaps* or *akvavit*.

1 pound yellow split peas,
  washed and drained
Water
2 pounds lean bacon or smoked
  pork in one piece
3 medium carrots, scraped
1 celeriac (celery root),
  washed, peeled, and
  quartered

4 medium leeks, white parts
  only, cleaned and washed
2 medium onions, peeled and
  cut into halves
½ teaspoon dried thyme
Salt, pepper to taste
1 pound pork sausage links,
  cooked and drained
  (optional)

Soak the peas in cold water according to the package directions, and then cook them slowly, covered, in 6 cups of water in a large saucepan until soft, about 1½ hours. Put the bacon, carrots, celeriac, leeks, onions, thyme, salt, and pepper in another large saucepan or kettle and cover with water. Cook slowly, covered, about 40 minutes, or until the vegetables and bacon are tender. Take out the bacon; slice and keep warm. Take out the vegetables and, if desired, cut up into smaller pieces. Add to the cooked peas some of the broth in which the vegetables were cooked to thin the soup; the soup may be very thick or somewhat thinner. Reheat, if necessary. Ladle the soup, including the vegetables, into wide soup plates and serve the sliced bacon and sausages separately on a platter. Serves 6 to 8.

BEER SOUPS

Beer has long been the common drink of northern European countries where the grapes for wine would not flourish. Over the years, the amber brew became very important also to the everyday life, folklore, and culture. A great deal has been written in literature about beer. Quite naturally the popular beverage was introduced into the cookery and a number of interesting beer dishes can be found in the various cuisines. Among these are several beer soups. Most of them have a quite different or strange taste for the uninitiated as they are heavily flavored with spices or other flavorings. Probably the country with the largest repertoire of them is Belgium. One Belgian beer cookbook lists 27 *consommés, crèmes, potages, soupes,* and *veloutés.* The following is but one version.

2 tablespoons butter or
  margarine
2 tablespoons flour
1½ quarts beer
1 to 2 tablespoons sugar,
  according to taste

½ teaspoon grated lemon rind
½ teaspoon each of ground
  cinnamon and ginger
Salt, pepper to taste
⅓ cup light cream

Melt the butter in a saucepan and add the flour. Cook, stirring, for 1 minute. Add the beer and bring to a boil. Add the sugar, lemon rind, cinnamon, ginger, salt, and pepper and lower the heat. Cook slowly, stirring frequently, for about 10 minutes. Add the cream and mix well. Remove from the heat. Serves 4 to 6.

SWISS CHEESE SOUP

In Switzerland, where a great variety of the best of cheeses made by the Alpine dairymen are readily available, there are of course a number of inviting dishes including them. Among the repertoire are several good soups and each district, or canton, has a favorite, made with a particular kind of cheese. This one, from the canton of Uri, includes Emmenthaler, a firm light yellow cheese with holes which we call Swiss cheese. A picturesque town in which to sample the soup is Altdorf, Uri's capital, where William Tell shot the apple from his young son's head and where there is an imposing statue of the Swiss hero.

1 tablespoon butter or margarine	1 garlic clove, cut in half (optional)
1/4 cup all-purpose flour	Salt, pepper, nutmeg to taste
4 cups cold water	1 cup grated Emmenthaler or Swiss cheese
1 tablespoon caraway seeds	1 cup hot milk

In a large saucepan melt the butter. Stir in the flour and cook over moderate heat until brown, but not burned. Remove from the stove. Have ready a cover for the saucepan in one hand and with the other quickly pour the cold water over the browned flour. Cover immediately. When the hissing and steaming stops, stir in the caraway seeds and garlic and mix rapidly so there will be no lumps. Season with salt, pepper, and nutmeg and return to the stove. Cook very slowly, covered, about 15 minutes. When almost finished cooking, combine the grated cheese and hot milk in a large soup tureen or bowl. Pour the hot soup over them and mix well. Remove and discard the garlic clove, if used. Serves 4 to 6.

3

Egg and Cheese Dishes

WE AMERICAN COOKS are indeed indebted to Western Europeans for devising numerous clever creations starring eggs and cheese, either separately or combined. Over the centuries, these basic nutritious and important foods have not been treated as ordinary fare but have been accorded great respect equal to that very often reserved for more exotic viands.

Eggs, for example, are not considered primarily as breakfast fare in Western Europe. True, the English enjoy them for their hearty morning repast, and the Germans often have an egg creation as a midmorning or second breakfast. But generally speaking, eggs are made into inventive specialties that are offered as separate courses of a dinner or entrées for luncheons or suppers. The repertoire of such dishes is indeed fascinating.

As we all know, most of the contemporary supply of eggs comes from hens; but Western Europeans have also been devotees of eggs of turkeys, ducks, geese, quail, and other fowl. A particular delicacy even today is the tiny plover egg. Eggs are important to all phases of cookery, as they are used in every type of dish. The basic methods for cooking eggs by themselves are limited to a very few; they are either boiled, baked, poached, scrambled, or fried.

Culinary experts have long been intrigued with perfecting egg cookery. Early French cookbooks dealt with the subject of how best to boil an egg, and there is still considerable disagreement about what the proper method is. In fact, fascinating controversies concern all of the basic egg cookery techniques. Thus one of our most common foods, which has been constantly extolled and studied, is still not completely understood by many cooks and therefore is often not properly prepared.

Thankfully, however, continuing attention to the improvement of cooking eggs and cooking with eggs led to the creation of a marvelous selection of Western European dishes starring them. In fact there are so many that it would not be possible even to begin to deal with them in one chapter of a book. By the early 1800s, a Parisian gastronome and food writer, Grimod de la Reynière, recorded that "they know in France 685 ways of dressing eggs. . . ." And in Alexander Dumas's *Dictionaire de Cuisine*, which appeared in 1872, he gives recipes for poached eggs with and without duck juice, mirrored eggs, eggs over eggs, and an Arabian omelet made with ostrich eggs, among others. By now the number of these dishes has increased to an uncounted, and possibly uncountable, total.

One of the best and most popular of the Western European contributions is the omelet or *omelette*, a word taken from an old French word for thin plate, *omelette*. The early Romans enjoyed a similar dish of eggs flavored with honey or a sweet-and-sour sauce. According to a story in the *Larousse Gastronomique*, however, the omelet was the creation of a peasant cook for a Spanish king. While taking a walk in the country, the king's hunger was appeased by some beaten eggs cooked in oil in a flat pan. They so pleased the king that he exclaimed "What an agile man!"

Whether this tale is true or not, we do know that it was the French who glorified and popularized the omelet and who have amassed a marvelous collection of recipes for it. In *Larousse*, to cite only one source, there are 106 suggested formulas for making unsweetened omelets. (Sweet ones are served generally as desserts.) Many of these have been adapted by other Western European cuisines. The Spanish, however, have a distinctive variation, which is flat and round, called a *tortilla*. In Italy a similarly shaped one is named a *frittata*.

Omelets and other classic egg dishes are flavored according to local taste in the various Western European cuisines. Scandinavians are devotees of dill, mushrooms, or lingonberries. The Spaniards and Portuguese favor onions, garlic, and tomatoes. In Germany and Austria there may be additions of sour cream, vegetables, or bacon. In Holland and Denmark eggs are often combined with another important dairy product, cheese, or mixed with the local ham or bacon. The Swiss also have many excellent egg-and-cheese dishes.

While eggs and cheese marry well to make many superb specialties, there is also a fascinating variety of innovative cheese dishes made with the local products of each country. The art of making cheese was known by the early Romans who are generally credited with giving it to other Europeans. Some authorities, however, have indicated that a great deal of the technical knowledge came originally from Switzerland to Rome during the reign of the Caesars.

After the fall of the Empire, cheese-making knowledge was kept alive and further advanced in the monasteries of Western Europe. Made with the milk of cows, goats, sheep, or buffalo, cheeses were developed into the great categories now universally known as very hard, hard, semisoft ripened, soft ripened, and soft unripened.

Some varieties are extremely old. Records reveal that gorgonzola was made in Italy's Po Valley as early as A.D. 879. Roquefort, another blue-veined cheese mentioned in writings of the tenth century, was discovered by accident. A shepherd left some bread and cheese in the caves of Roquefort and found several weeks later that his cheese had acquired not only a green mold but an inviting flavor. The monks of a nearby monastery at Conques developed the special technique of making Roquefort in the caves, so that it became a truly great treasure.

Many of the superb European cheeses took the names of the locales in which they were originally made. Thus there is Parmesan from Parma, Italy; Romano from Rome; Emmenthaler from Switzerland's valley of Emmenthal; Limburger from Limbourg, Belgium; Edam and Gouda from Holland; Cheddar from the village of Cheddar and Cheshire from Chester in England; Danish Samsoe from the island of Samsoe; and Spanish Roncal from the Roncal Valley.

Some cheeses, of course, are eaten uncooked, either plain or with other foods. In Scandinavia, Holland, and Denmark the local cheeses are standard breakfast foods. In other countries they are common snacks and desserts. Although many cheeses can be used in cookery, there are some that are more suitable, or adjustable to heat, than others. The best and most popular of these is Parmesan; another is Gruyère.

The repertoire of cheese dishes includes soufflés, rabbits, *quiches*, sandwiches, and fondues, among many others. Presented here is a representative collection of the best of egg and cheese specialties that Western Europeans have long enjoyed.

Quiches

French dishes made of pastry shells with egg-and-cream custard fillings are called *quiches* or sometimes *kiches*. Generally believed to have originated in the region of Alsace-Lorraine, *quiches* are made with the addition of such ingredients as ham, crabmeat, salmon, cheese, onions, etc. The best known, however, includes bacon and is called *quiche Lorraine*. A *quiche* is cooked traditionally in a simple metal *flan* ring placed on a cookie sheet. The pastry and filling are placed inside the ring, which is removed before serving. If a *flan* ring is not available, the dish can be made in a straight-sided cake pan with a removable bottom. Included here are recipes for two *quiches* which can be served as hors d'oeuvre, luncheon, or supper entrées. Although there are many recipes for these dishes, these are the traditional French ones.

QUICHE LORRAINE

Pastry for 1 8- or 9-inch pie
  shell
6 slices thin bacon
4 large eggs

2 cups heavy cream
Salt, freshly ground pepper and
  grated nutmeg to taste
2 tablespoons butter

Line a *flan* ring placed on a cookie sheet, or a straight-sided cake pan, with the pastry. Flute the edge of the shell and prick the bottom with a fork. Place a layer of aluminum foil or heavy brown paper over the pastry and fill with dried beans or rice to keep the pastry from shrinking while cooking. Bake in a preheated hot oven (400°F.) for 8 minutes. Take from the oven and remove the paper and beans. Prick again with a fork and return to the oven to cook about 2 minutes longer, or until done. Remove from the stove and cool.

Cook the bacon in a skillet and drain. Crumble over the bottom of the pastry shell, spreading evenly. In a large bowl beat the eggs. Mix in the cream, salt, pepper, and nutmeg. Pour over the bacon. Cut the butter into tiny pieces and distribute over the top. Bake in a 375°F. oven for 25 to 35 minutes or until the custard is set and a knife inserted into it comes out clean. Remove from the oven and let stand 2 or 3 minutes. Remove the ring and slide the *quiche* onto a warm plate. Cut into wedges. Serves 4 to 6.

QUICHE AU FROMAGE

Prepare the pastry as directed in the above recipe. Omit the bacon. Instead, mix together 2 cups (½ pound) grated Gruyère or Swiss cheese and 1 tablespoon of flour. Spread evenly in the pastry shell. Cover with the same ingredients as the above recipe (except that light cream may be substituted for the heavy) and cook and serve the same way.

SWEDISH ANCHOVIES AND EGGS

In the Scandinavian countries many interesting egg dishes are flavored with anchovies. These include simple preparations such as omelets and scrambled eggs as well as more intricate casserole combinations. This dish, *ansjovis-fräs* (literally, "anchovy hash"), is a piquant warm specialty of the *smörgåsbord* table. It may be served also as a brunch or luncheon dish.

1 medium onion, minced
2 tablespoons butter or
  margarine
8 to 10 flat anchovy fillets,
  minced

4 hard-cooked eggs, shelled and
  chopped
Black pepper to taste
Triangles of white toast

Sauté the onion in the butter in a skillet or saucepan until limp. Stir in the anchovies and eggs and sauté quickly over high heat until the flavors are blended and the mixture is hot. Season with pepper and serve at once on toast triangles. Serves 4.

CALZONE OF ITALY

This delectable filled pastry is a specialty of Naples and a gastronomic relative of pizza. Traditionally it is prepared with a buffalo-milk cheese, anchovies, and tomatoes. This is another popular version.

1 packaged dough mix (6¾
  ounces) or equivalent
  homemade yeast dough
About ¾ pound of sliced
  prosciutto or thinly sliced
  cooked ham, cut 2 by 2 inches
About 1 pound thinly sliced

mozzarella, cut 2 by 2 inches
About 1 tablespoon basil or
  oregano
Salt, pepper to taste
Olive oil, vegetable oil, or
  shortening for deep frying

Prepare the pizza dough according to the package directions. Roll out on a floured board as thin as possible and cut into 4-inch rounds. Place a slice of prosciutto on one half of each round. Top with a slice of mozzarella and another of prosciutto. Sprinkle with basil or oregano, salt, pepper, and a little olive oil. Dip the tip of a finger in cold water and run around the edge of each circle. Fold the other half of the round over the filling and press the edges to close firmly. Deep-fry a few at a time in moderately hot deep fat (375°F.) until golden and crisp, or cook in a hot (345°F.) oven about 20 minutes. If fried, drain on absorbent paper. Serve at once. Makes about 18.

SWISS CROUTE AU FROMAGE

A good open sandwich from Switzerland to serve at a
brunch or luncheon.

4 slices white bread	4 slices Swiss cheese
4 thin slices cooked ham	4 eggs, fried and kept warm

Cover the slices of bread with the ham and cheese. Slide
under the broiler until the cheese is bubbly and melted. Top
each sandwich with a hot fried egg and serve at once. Serves 4.

DANISH EGG AND BACON CAKE

Two of Denmark's best and most famous foods are bacon
and eggs, which they export in great quantity and use in
making many superb dishes. This simple one, *Aeggekage
med Bacon*, is good brunch or luncheon fare.

¼ pound thinly sliced bacon	2 tablespoons chopped chives
6 eggs	1 large tomato, peeled and
6 tablespoons cold water	sliced
Salt, pepper to taste	Brown bread

Fry the bacon in a medium-sized skillet until done. Remove to
a plate and keep warm. Leave enough bacon fat in the skillet to
cover the surface; drain off the remainder. Combine the eggs,
water, salt, and pepper so the yolks and whites are well mixed.
Turn into the skillet and cook until set. When done, place the
cooked bacon slices on the top and turn out onto a plate. Sprinkle
the top with chives and garnish with the tomato slices. Cut into
wedges and serve with brown bread. Serves 4 to 6.

SCOTCH WOODCOCK

The English have a unique gastronomic custom of partaking of savories at the end of the meal, after dessert.
The foods are unsweet, very often made with eggs and
cheese. This popular savory is said to have been created

when a clever Scottish cook did not have a woodcock to serve his guests. Instead, he gave them this dish. It has become an English favorite.

4 slices white bread
Butter
Anchovy paste
4 eggs

¼ cup light cream
Cayenne, salt, pepper to taste
3 tablespoons chopped fresh
  parsley

Toast the bread and spread one side of each slice generously with butter and lightly with anchovy paste. Keep warm. Beat the eggs to combine the yolks and whites. Mix with the cream, cayenne, salt, and pepper. Melt enough butter in a skillet to cover the surface and pour in the eggs. Cook, stirring, until done but creamy and not dry. Spoon over the toast. Garnish with the parsley. Serves 4.

BASQUE PIPERADE

A great egg and vegetable dish, *piperade*, believed to have originated in the Basque area of southern France, is often referred as an omelet, but is actually more similar to scrambled eggs. Always colorful and delicious, the creation varies as to ingredients but generally includes tomatoes and pimientos. *Piperade* is ever a welcome treat when one is traveling in the Basque area or in other southern regions of France. In America it can be served as a very good brunch dish.

½ cup olive oil
2 large onions, sliced thinly
1 or 2 garlic cloves, crushed
4 medium tomatoes, peeled and
  chopped
2 large green peppers, cleaned
  and chopped

2 canned pimientos, drained
  and chopped
½ teaspoon dried rosemary or
  marjoram
Salt, pepper to taste
8 eggs
¼ cup chopped fresh parsley
  or mixed fresh herbs

Heat the oil in a large skillet. Add the onions and garlic and sauté until tender. Mix in the tomatoes, green peppers, pimientos, rosemary, salt, and pepper and cook, stirring often, for several minutes, until the tomatoes are cooked. Add the eggs one at a time, stirring after each is added, and cook until the eggs are set but softly scrambled. Stir in the parsley. Serves 4.

FRITTATA GENOVESE

The Italian omelet is called *frittata* and is quite different from the French one. It is fried quickly on both sides and is served flat instead of folded over. Some are made only with beaten eggs but most varieties include other ingredients, such as chopped cooked meats, seafood, and especially vegetables—onions, potatoes, zucchini, spinach, asparagus, artichokes, mushrooms—with seasonings. This version is a specialty of Genoa.

1 cup finely chopped cooked spinach
1 or 2 garlic cloves, crushed or minced
2 tablespoons chopped fresh parsley
⅓ cup grated Parmesan cheese

1 tablespoon fresh basil or marjoram or ½ teaspoon dried herbs
8 eggs, beaten
Salt, pepper to taste
2 tablespoons butter or olive oil

Combine all the ingredients, except the butter, in a large bowl and mix well. Heat the butter in a heavy 9- or 10-inch skillet. Mix the other ingredients again and pour into the skillet. Cook about 2 minutes. Loosen around the edges with a spatula and tilt the pan to let any liquid run underneath. Put a plate over the skillet and invert the omelet onto it. Grease the skillet, if necessary. Return the omelet to it and cook on the reverse side. Lift onto a warm platter. Cut into wedges to serve. Serves 4 to 6.

WELSH RABBIT

There has been considerable gastronomical controversy concerning the proper name for this dish which originated in Wales but has long been a British and American favorite. We turn to *Webster's New World Dictionary* to settle the argument: "A dish of melted cheese, often mixed with ale or beer, served on crackers or toast: also, through faulty etymologizing, Welsh rarebit." In London a good place to enjoy this dish is the historic Ye Olde Cheshire Inn, where such personages as Dr. Samuel Johnson, Charles Dickens, and Oliver Goldsmith once dined. Located on Fleet Street the restaurant is still a gathering place for writers, especially journalists.

2 tablespoons butter or
  margarine
1 pound sharp Cheddar cheese,
  coarsely grated
½ teaspoon dry mustard
1 teaspoon Worcestershire
  sauce

Dash cayenne
Salt, pepper to taste
2 egg yolks, beaten
½ cup light beer or ale
4 slices toast

Melt the butter in a chafing dish or double boiler. Add the cheese and melt, stirring often in one direction. Add the mustard, Worcestershire, cayenne, salt, and pepper and continue to stir in the same direction. Combine the egg yolks and beer and gradually add to the cheese mixture, stirring as you do so. Cook over medium heat, never letting the mixture boil, and stirring almost continuously, until the mixture is smooth and velvety. Serve over slices of warm toast. Serves 4.

PORTUGUESE EGGS WITH TOMATO SAUCE

The Portuguese are extremely fond of eggs, *ovos*, which they use generously in a great number of interesting dishes. At some meals an egg creation is even served at the end of several courses, after dessert. This is one variation.

1 large onion, chopped
1 or 2 garlic cloves, crushed
2 tablespoons olive or
  vegetable oil
3 large tomatoes, peeled and

chopped
¼ cup almond slivers
⅓ cup chopped fresh parsley
Salt, pepper to taste
4 poached eggs

Sauté the onion and garlic in the oil in a skillet until tender. Add the tomatoes and cook slowly for 5 minutes. Stir in the almonds, parsley, salt, and pepper and cook a few minutes. Arrange the poached eggs in a buttered shallow baking dish and spoon the sauce over them. Put under the broiler for a minute or two. Serves 4 as a first course or 2 as an entrée.

EGGS BAKED IN SOUR CREAM FROM AUSTRIA

Austrians, like their neighbors the Hungarians, are devoted to such foods as mushrooms, sour cream, and paprika, which are combined here to make a flavorful egg dish excellent for a brunch or luncheon.

¼ cup minced green onions
3 tablespoons butter or
  margarine
½ pound fresh mushrooms,
  cleaned and thinly sliced
2 tablespoons fresh lemon juice
2 teaspoons paprika

2 cups sour cream, at room
  temperature
Salt, pepper to taste
6 eggs
3 tablespoons fine dry bread
  crumbs
3 tablespoons chopped fresh
  parsley

Sauté the onions in the butter in a skillet until tender. Add the mushrooms and lemon juice and sauté for 4 minutes. Stir in the paprika, sour cream, salt, and pepper. Remove from the stove and spoon into a shallow baking dish. Break the eggs into the mixture. Sprinkle the tops with bread crumbs and parsley. Dot with butter. Bake in a preheated moderate oven (350°F.) for about 10 minutes, or until the desired degree of doneness. Serves 4 to 6.

FRENCH OMELETTES

While traveling through France and partaking generously of superb but often rich fare, many an American visitor has found temporary respite by ordering a simple French *omelette*. Made with lightly beaten eggs and a minimum of seasoning, the dish is delicate and delicious. To a plain omelet may be added other ingredients such as cheese, minced onions, ham, mixed herbs, potatoes, fish, mushrooms, chicken livers, and cooked meats. Escoffier's *Le Guide Culinaire* lists recipes for 58 varieties ranging from simple combinations to more intricate creations. It is not difficult to make a French omelet, but there are some guidelines that might help someone who is just learning the technique. For example, many experts suggest that the pan is very important and preferably should be an omelet pan of enameled iron, aluminum, or copper with sloping sides and a long handle. They believe that it should not be used for cooking any other foods and that it should never be washed but wiped clean with paper toweling. They also suggest that the omelet be a small one, made up of a maximum of four eggs, as this size is easier to handle than larger ones. Minced ingredients may be combined with the egg mixture and poured into the pan at the same time. However, larger cut foods, such as potatoes, meats, and seafood, should be heated first and then spread on the omelette as it is cooking. The sides are folded over to enclose the ingredients.

3 eggs	Salt, pepper to taste
1 tablespoon cold water	Butter or margarine

Break the eggs, one at a time, into a bowl. Mix gently to combine the whites and yolks. Pour in the water and add the salt and pepper. Stir until well mixed but do not overbeat. Warm an omelet pan or skillet over low heat and brush the bottom of it with butter. When the butter is sizzling, stir the egg mixture again and pour quickly into the pan. Mix with a fork and shake the pan back and forth. When the mixture begins to set, put a knife around the edges and tilt the pan to let the runny mixture in the center run toward the sides and underneath. When all the mixture is set, fold over the sides toward the center. Turn out upside down onto a warm plate and serve at once. Brush the top with melted butter, if desired. Serves 2 as a first course or 1 as an entrée.

If desired, add to the egg mixture 1 or 2 tablespoons of minced green onions, fresh herbs, grated cheese, or chopped cooked spinach. Or sprinkle ⅓ cup of diced cooked potatoes, sautéed mushrooms, diced cooked ham, seafood, chicken livers, or vegetables over the eggs after they have set a little.

MOZZARELLA IN CARROZZA

Italy's southwestern region of Campania is dotted with scenic attractions. Who doesn't love Naples, Capri, Sorrento, and the Amalfi Drive? One of its great culinary specialties is mozzarella, made from the milk of water buffalo or cows in great quantity and exported around the world. The true cheese is made traditionally with only buffalo milk, and each step of the process is carefully done by hand. Most of the mozzarella sold in our stores is made with cow's milk. This dish, which in English means mozzarella in a carriage, is actually a fried cheese sandwich that can be served as a snack or entrée. As the latter, it is customarily garnished with an anchovy-butter sauce.

¼ cup butter or margarine
¼ cup olive or vegetable oil
4 flat anchovy fillets, minced
1 or 2 garlic cloves, crushed
1 tablespoon fresh lemon juice
1 tablespoon drained capers
   (optional)
¼ cup chopped fresh parsley
Pepper to taste

12 slices white bread
6 slices (about ½ pound)
   mozzarella cheese, ¼ inch
   thick
3 large eggs, beaten
½ cup milk
Shortening, butter or oil for
   frying

Prepare the sauce first. Melt the butter in a small saucepan. Add the oil, anchovies, garlic, lemon juice, capers, parsley, and pepper and heat 1 minute to blend the flavors. Remove the crusts from the bread and cut into 3-by-3½-inch pieces. Place on each of 6 slices of bread a slice of cheese the same size as the bread. Top with another slice of bread. Dip in the eggs and milk, mixed together. Heat enough shortening, butter, or oil to cover the surface of a large skillet. Fry the sandwiches on both sides until golden but not brown and the cheese begins to melt. Serve while still hot, with or without a little of the sauce. Serves 6.

SCALLOPED EGGS FROM HOLLAND

This is a flavorful dish, made with Holland's great Gouda cheese, which may be served as a first course or as a luncheon specialty.

4 large eggs	Salt, pepper to taste
2 slices thin bacon, minced	2 tablespoons flour
Butter	1 cup light cream or milk
1 medium onion, finely chopped	½ cup grated Gouda cheese
	Paprika
4 medium tomatoes, peeled and finely chopped	Fine dry bread crumbs

Hard-boil the eggs and shell them. Set aside. Put the minced bacon and 1 tablespoon of butter in a skillet and cook until the bacon is crisp. Add the onion and sauté until tender. Mix in the chopped tomatoes. Season with salt and pepper. Cook slowly for 5 minutes. Remove from the stove and set aside. In a small saucepan melt 1 tablespoon of butter. Stir in the flour and cook about 1 minute to form a *roux*. Gradually add the cream or milk and cook slowly, stirring, until the sauce is smooth and thickened. Stir in ⅓ cup of the cheese and season with salt, pepper, and paprika. Cook slowly until the cheese melts. Remove from the stove. Place each of the hard-cooked eggs in a scallop shell or ramekin. Spoon the onion-tomato mixture around the eggs, dividing evenly. Spoon the cheese sauce over and around the eggs. Sprinkle with fine dry bread crumbs, the remainder of the cheese and paprika. Dot the top with bits of butter. Put under the broiler for several minutes, until hot and bubbly. Serves 4.

SPIEDINI ALLA ROMANA

While strolling along the streets of Rome it is customary to stop at a sidewalk *rosticceria* for a snack, which might be this simple dish of skewered bread and cheese.

1 long loaf of Italian bread	10 flat anchovy fillets, minced
1 pound mozzarella cheese	1 tablespoon fresh lemon juice
¾ cup melted butter	

Cut the bread into slices about ½-inch thick. Trim off the crusts. Cut the cheese into slices the same size as the bread and about ¼-inch thick. Thread the bread and cheese alternately, beginning and ending with bread, on small skewers. Place in a shallow baking dish and cook in a hot oven (450°F.) about 15 minutes, turning once, until the bread is golden and the cheese is melting. Have ready the melted butter, anchovies, and lemon juice, heated in a saucepan. Spoon over the hot bread and cheese. Serve at once. It should be piping hot. Serves 6.

SPANISH HUEVOS A LA FLAMENCA

Eggs flamenco style are a colorful dish from Spain's Andalusia, the home of flamenco dancing, and they are served throughout the country. Generally the attractive and colorful ingredients are cooked and served in individual baking dishes.

1 large onion, chopped
¼ cup olive oil
1 cup diced *chorizo* (Spanish sausage) or cooked ham
2 large tomatoes, peeled and chopped
½ cup beef bouillon or chicken broth
Salt, pepper to taste

1 or 2 garlic cloves, crushed or minced
8 eggs
1 cup cooked green peas
16 cooked or canned asparagus tips
1 canned pimiento, julienne-cut
2 tablespoons chopped fresh parsley

Sauté the onion and garlic in the oil in a skillet until tender. Add the *chorizo* or ham and cook 1 or 2 minutes. Mix in the tomatoes, bouillon, salt, and pepper and cook about 5 minutes. Spoon into 4 individual baking dishes or ramekins (or 1 large shallow baking dish). Break the eggs over the ingredients in the dish. Arrange the peas, asparagus, and pimiento around the eggs. Sprinkle the parsley over the eggs. Bake in a preheated moderate oven (350°F.) about 15 minutes, or until the eggs are set to the desired degree of doneness. Serve as a dinner first course, or for brunch, luncheon, or supper. Serves 4.

SWISS RACLETTE

Raclette, originally from the canton of Valais, is known all over Switzerland as a traditional country dish. The name derives from the French verb *racler*, "to scrape." At first the dish was made by holding or putting a large piece of cheese in front of an open fire and, as the cheese melted, scraping the melted surface off onto a warm plate. It was then eaten with boiled potatoes, pickled onions, gherkins, and freshly ground pepper. Today, it is done in front of a special electric grill. In Switzerland the preferred cheeses are the semifirm kinds from Valais, such as Gonser, Bagnes, or *raclette*, since they melt easily. The recommended wine to serve with this dish is a chilled Valais Fendant. I recall first sampling *raclette* in an informal upstairs restaurant in Berne where the atmosphere was lightened with genial conversation sparked by lively interest in the preparation, service, and eating of the delicious dish. It is a dish that promotes conviviality.

The Swiss have improvised a substitute plan for anyone wishing to make *raclette* in the home, where an open fire or electric grill is not available. They suggest that a large piece of cheese be put in a hot oven (450°F.) until it begins to melt. It can be then scraped and served on hot plates with the accompaniments mentioned above, prepared beforehand. Or slices of cheese can be melted under the broiler and served in the same way. If the Swiss cheeses are not available good substitutes are muenster, Tilsiter, or jack.

FRENCH SOUFFLÉ DE CHAMPIGNONS

In French cookery there are two types of soufflés, the unsweetened, which is served as a dinner first course, for luncheon, or for supper; and the sweetened, which is eaten for dessert. The word soufflé is taken from the French for "puffed up" and each one is a lovely inflated light creation that has to be served immediately as it comes from the oven or it will quickly deflate. Unsweetened soufflés may be made with cheese, vegetables, seafood, or meat, but particularly inviting is this one, prepared with mushrooms.

4 eggs
1 additional egg white
1 tablespoon minced shallots
 or green onions
4 tablespoons butter
1 tablespoon lemon juice

1 cup finely chopped
 mushrooms
Salt, freshly ground pepper,
 and grated nutmeg to taste
3 tablespoons flour
1 cup milk

Before making the soufflé, remove the eggs from the refrigerator to attain room temperature. Separate, putting the yolks in a small bowl and, the whites—with the additional white—in a larger bowl. Sauté the shallots in 1 tablespoon of butter with the lemon juice until tender. Add the mushrooms and sauté about 3 minutes. Season with salt, pepper, and nutmeg and remove from the heat. In a saucepan, melt the remaining 3 tablespoons of butter. Stir in the flour to form a *roux*. Cook, stirring, 1 minute. Gradually add the milk, stirring as you do so, and cook slowly until thick and smooth. Remove from the heat and cool a little. Beat the egg yolks until creamy and mix into the white sauce. Stir in the mushroom mixture. Beat the egg whites until stiff. Carefully fold half of them into the mushroom combination. Then add the remaining half. Spoon the mixture into a buttered 1½-quart soufflé dish or casserole. Bake, uncovered, in a preheated moderate oven (375°F.) about 30 to 35 minutes, until puffed and golden. Serve at once. Serves 4.

ROMAN ARTICHOKE OMELET

A great specialty of Rome, *tortino di carciofi*, is a baked omelet made with tender young artichokes, which are particularly flavorful in Italy. This one is made with frozen artichoke hearts as a substitute.

1 package (9 ounces) frozen
 artichoke hearts
¼ cup olive or vegetable oil
1 garlic clove, crushed
Salt, pepper to taste

2 tablespoons fresh lemon juice
Butter or margarine
8 eggs, beaten
⅓ cup chopped fresh parsley

Defrost the artichoke hearts and cut each one lengthwise. Heat the oil in a skillet and add the garlic and artichokes. Sauté until fork tender. Season with salt and pepper. Add the lemon juice. Spoon into a well-buttered shallow baking dish. Combine the eggs and parsley and pour over the artichoke mixture. Tilt to spread evenly. Bake in a preheated hot oven (400°F.) about 15 minutes, or until the eggs are set. Cut into wedges to serve. Serves 4 to 6.

CROQUE MONSIEUR

This French ham and cheese sandwich can be either spread with butter and grilled or dipped in a batter and fried. It is a very popular snack or luncheon dish throughout Europe.

8 slices firm white bread	4 eggs
8 thin slices of Swiss or other cheese	4 tablespoons milk
4 thin slices boiled ham	Butter or margarine for frying

Cover each of 4 slices of bread with 1 slice of cheese, 1 slice of ham, and another slice of cheese. Top with the remaining 4 slices of bread. Mix together the eggs and milk in a shallow dish. Dip the sandwiches in the mixture and fry in melted butter on both sides in a skillet until golden brown. Serve at once. Serves 4.

LEEK AND CHEESE PIE FROM WALES

In Wales the leek is not only a favorite food but also the national emblem. Long ago a Welsh king, about to lead his men into battle against a neighboring foe, ordered his soldiers to wear leeks in their helmets so they could be distinguished from their enemies. Because they won the struggle, the leek was chosen to be Wales's symbol and has long had great significance in that small country. Of the many Welsh dishes made with leeks this is one of the best and can be served as a first course or luncheon or supper entrée.

3 large leeks
3 tablespoons butter or
  margarine
4 slices thin bacon
Standard pastry for 8- or
  9-inch shell, baked

4 large eggs
2 cups light cream
Salt, pepper, nutmeg to taste
⅓ cup grated Parmesan
  cheese

Wash the leeks well to remove all the dirt. Chop finely the white parts and some of the green. Sauté in the butter until tender. Remove from the heat and set aside. Cook the bacon by frying or broiling until done but not crisp. Cut into small pieces and put with the sautéed leeks into the pie shell. Put the eggs in a large bowl and mix to combine the yolks and whites. Add the cream, salt, pepper, and nutmeg and mix well. Stir in the cheese. When the ingredients are well combined, pour over the leeks and bacon. Bake in a preheated moderately hot oven (375°F.) for about 45 minutes, or until the blade of a knife inserted into the custard comes out clean. Remove from the oven and cool slightly before cutting. Serves 4 to 6.

SWISS CHEESE FONDUE

A delightful Swiss dish that has become very popular in our country during the past few years is cheese fondue. Particularly appealing is the idea of do-it-yourself cookery, as the dish is placed in the middle of the table and the participants dunk bread cubes in a previously prepared aromatic creamy cheese mixture. The Swiss make fondue in a heavy flat-bottomed round dish with a handle which is called a *caquelon*. It can be earthenware or made of cast iron or another metal, but it has to be heavy to hold the heat. Possible substitutes are chafing dishes, casseroles, or other round heat-proof dishes. The dish must be placed over heat such as a spirit-burner, candle, or other device that can be regulated while cooking. Also necessary are long-handled forks for spearing and dunking the bread cubes. Each piece of the French bread should have some crust on it so it will not slip off the fork. (If this happens, the loser of the bread must forfeit a kiss to the person to his or her right.) Wine is very important to the dish; it should be a dry white one with enough acid to help liquefy the cheese. Good Swiss wines are Fendant-Pétillant or Neuchâtel. The choice of cheese, of course, is of utmost significance, for in order to achieve the proper consistency and not lump or become stringy, the cheese should be well matured. Imported Swiss cheeses are the best. For a mild fondue, only Emmenthaler is used. A medium dish is made with half Emmenthaler and half Gruyère. The strongest is prepared only with Gruyère. The preferred drink to serve with fondue is kirsch; or you may serve the same kind of wine that was used in the dish. Generally speaking, it is best not to serve very cold or chilled drinks with the fondue. In Switzerland a course of smoked meats, followed by fresh fruit and tea, is served after this cheese dish. This recipe is for the traditional Neuchâtel fondue, which I recall first enjoying in that lovely Swiss city.

1 garlic clove, cut in half
2 cups dry white wine
1 or 2 teaspoons fresh lemon
  juice (optional)
½ pound (2 cups)
  Emmenthaler cheese, diced
  or shredded
½ pound (2 cups) Gruyère
  cheese, diced or shredded

1 tablespoon cornstarch
3 tablespoons kirsch, gin, or
  vodka
Salt, freshly ground pepper,
  and grated nutmeg to taste
Crusty French bread, cut into
  cubes

Rub the inside of the fondue dish, earthenware casserole, chafing dish, or skillet with the garlic clove. Add the wine, and lemon juice if used, and heat gradually over a low flame until the liquid begins to bubble. Gradually add the cheese, stirring constantly with a wooden spoon, until it melts. Dissolve the cornstarch in the kirsch and stir into the cheese mixture. Increase the heat to moderate and continue the cooking and stirring until the mixture is smooth and creamy. Season with salt, pepper, and nutmeg. Keep bubbling over low heat while serving. Each person serves himself by spearing a small piece of bread with a long-handled fork and then dipping it into the cheese mixture before eating. Serves 4.

If the mixture becomes too thick while cooking, gradually add some heated wine to it, stirring as you do so, until it reaches the desired consistency.

SWEDISH CHEESE-TOMATO CASSEROLE

One of the traditional dishes of the Swedish *smörgåsbord* is this casserole called *ostlada*. It may be also offered as a luncheon or supper specialty.

Butter
4 large tomatoes, peeled and
  sliced
4 hard-cooked eggs, sliced
Salt, pepper to taste

6 eggs
2 cups hot milk
½ teaspoon paprika
⅔ cup grated Swiss or Parmesan cheese

Butter a casserole on all the inner surfaces. Arrange the tomato and egg slices in it in layers. Sprinkle with salt and pepper. Beat the eggs in a bowl to combine the whites and yolks. Add the milk and paprika and pour over the ingredients in the casserole. Sprinkle the top with the cheese. Bake in a preheated hot oven (425°F.) for 25 minutes or until the mixture is set. Serves 4 to 6.

CROSTINI ALLA NAPOLITANA

A delectable cheese dish, *crostini*, which originated in Naples, is popular throughout Italy. Actually it is a flavorful open-faced sandwich, made with mozzarella cheese and various garnishes. It may be served as a snack or a luncheon dish.

24 2-inch rounds or squares of
  day-old firm white bread,
  ¼-inch thick
½ cup butter
4 tablespoons olive oil
24 2-inch rounds or squares of
  mozzarella cheese, ¼-inch
  thick

1 can (2 ounces) flat anchovy
  fillets, minced
3 or 4 garlic cloves, crushed
Freshly ground pepper
½ cup chopped fresh parsley

Fry the bread on both sides in butter and 2 tablespoons olive oil in a lightly greased skillet. Remove with a slotted spoon to a cookie sheet or shallow baking dish. Place a slice of cheese over each piece of bread. Combine the anchovies, garlic, pepper, and parsley with enough oil to make a fairly thick sauce and spoon a small amount over each slice of cheese. Put under the broiler until the cheese begins to melt. Serves 6 to 8.

For a variation, place a slice of tomato and anchovy fillet over the cheese. Sprinkle with oregano and olive oil.

SPANISH POTATO OMELET

The Spanish omelet called *tortilla* is a round and substantial one enriched with a wide variety of ingredients, such as seafood, vegetables, meats, or chickpeas. The simplest and most popular kind includes only potatoes. Eaten hot or cold, this national dish is a favorite luncheon dish in Spain. It is golden and crisp on both sides and as attractive to regard as it is delicious to eat.

1 large onion
1 large potato
About ¼ cup olive oil

Salt, pepper to taste
4 eggs, beaten

Peel and finely chop the onion and potato. Heat enough oil in a heavy 7- or 9-inch skillet to cover the surface. Add the vegetables and sauté over low heat, stirring and turning often, until soft. Do not brown. Add more oil while cooking, if necessary. Season with salt and pepper. Beat the eggs and pour half of them over the vegetables. Tilt the pan to spread them evenly. Cook over low heat, lifting up around the edges to let the wet mixture run underneath. Add the remaining half of the eggs and cook until golden and dry on top. Slide a spatula underneath to determine if the mixture is sticking to the pan and loosen. Remove from the heat and invert a plate over the omelet. Turn over. Oil the pan. Return the omelet to it and cook until golden and crisp on the other side. Serves 2.

GERMAN FARMERS' BREAKFAST

In Germany a favorite midmorning second breakfast is this hearty potato-egg combination called *Bauernfrühstück*. The dish appears frequently on German restaurant menus under the heading of *Eierspeisen*, egg specialties. I have particularly enjoyed it for luncheons in the attractive dining cars of the superb trains that whisk you quickly through Germany.

6 slices thin bacon, cut in
  small pieces
1 medium onion, chopped
3 medium-sized potatoes,
  cooked and cubed

Salt, pepper to taste
2 tablespoons chopped fresh
  parsley
6 eggs, beaten

Fry the bacon in a large skillet until crisp. Remove from the stove and drain. Pour off all except 3 tablespoons of the bacon fat. Add the onion and sauté in the fat until tender. Stir in the potatoes and cook until golden. While cooking, combine the cooked bacon, salt, pepper, parsley, and eggs in a bowl and mix well. Pour over the potato-onion mixture. Cook over low heat until the eggs are set. While cooking, slip a knife around the edges to let the wet egg mixture run under. When cooked, remove from the stove and cut into wedges. Serves 4.

4

Pasta, Rice, and Other Grains

EDIBLE SEEDS of the grass family, more commonly known as cereals or grains, have been so important to man's diet for so long that we generally do not appreciate the versatility of their gastronomic roles. In Western Europe, oats, wheat, barley, and rye and, to a lesser extent, rice and corn, provided necessary daily sustenance for the populace until modern times. But fortunately inventive cooks also utilized these foods in creating a wide selection of such culinary treasures as pasta, *paella*, and *risotto*, and pancakes, dumplings, and fritters, among others.

Wild grasses were first cultivated into crops of wheat, barley, and rye in the Mesopotamian Valley of the Near East. Such was their importance that we generally credit these foods as being the primary reason for nomadic tribes settling into permanent locations. The history of civilization became intertwined with the quest for rich grain-bearing lands and the crops they yielded.

In Western Europe the ancient Romans were fortunate in that their fertile plains provided an abundance of superb wheat. Even so, as the population swelled, it was also necessary to draw supplies from the rich granaries of their vast Empire. In those times, the average diet consisted of grain dishes of one form or another, including breads made with the important flour.

The Romans introduced the cultivation of grain crops to other Western European countries where these foods also became basic and essential fare. During and long after the Middle Ages, pottages, gruels, and soups, thickened and enriched with grains, were consumed three times daily. Since barley, rye, and oats were found to thrive in colder climates, they became important in the cuisines of Northern European countries. Wheat flourished in the more temperate areas.

Two other varieties, rice and corn, reached Western Europe from two opposite areas of the world and much later than the previously mentioned grains. Rice, native to India, was probably first brought to the eastern Mediterranean by Greek soldiers who had fought with Alexander the Great in Persia. It was introduced to the southern regions of Europe by the Moors of North Africa and became staple fare in Portugal and Spain, where the white seeds flourished and were used in making many inviting culinary creations, particularly *paella*. Italy, however, became—and is still—the largest producer of rice in Europe. Since the 1500s rice grown in the northern Piedmont area has been internationally renowned for its superior quality. Most of France's limited crop was not developed until after World War II, when it was found that rice could thrive in the marshy area of Camargue, west of Marseille.

One of the earliest of the great grain dishes was made with a particular hard durum wheat, called semolina, which, when mixed with water and rolled and dried, became what we term pasta. As early as 500 B.C. the Italians were making spaghetti, macaroni, noodles, and possibly other kinds of pasta. The Spaghetti Historical Museum in the tiny village of Pontedassio on the Italian Riviera contains displays and documents proving the ancient origin of this favorite food. Farther south, the ruins of Pompeii provide additional evidence of the early importance and popularity of pasta.

Over the years the Italians created many additional kinds of pasta, perhaps 100 different varieties, and by the 1500s their popularity had spread to other Western European countries. The chefs of the Italian princess Catherine de' Medici, who married France's King Henry II, prepared pasta dishes for elegant dinners in Paris. In 1599, the London dramatist and gourmet, Ben

Jonson, wrote about a friend: "He doth learne . . . to eat anchovies, macarone, bovoli, fagioli and cauiare." English cookbooks of the 1600s and 1700s included references to and recipes for macaroni dishes. Today, each of the European cuisines has several dishes that are versions of those inspired by the Italian creation.

Although rice dishes appear today on the menus of all Western European restaurants and are eaten in many of the homes, this grain never became staple or popular fare throughout the Continent. Rice truly belongs only to those southern countries where it is grown and relished as a great delicacy. Their varied preparations are well worth preparing and savoring.

Such great creations as pancakes, dumplings, and fritters, made with flour and other companionable ingredients, are also included here, as they were developed into such inviting creations by cooks who sought to vary the use of finely ground grains.

This characteristic and pleasing recipe collection reflects the many ways that the fruits of the field have been upgraded from basic fare to a position of esteem in Western European cuisines.

BASIC HOMEMADE EGG PASTA

A number of kinds of noodles can be prepared with basic egg pasta. Although some of them, such as *lasagne, cannelloni,* and *manicotti,* can be purchased, the homemade ones will be superior in quality. Once prepared, they can be boiled, drained, and used to make any favorite dish. To make good egg pasta takes time and considerable elbow grease for rolling, but the results are well worth the effort.

3 cups semolina or all-purpose white flour	¾ teaspoon salt
3 large eggs at room temperature	2 teaspoons olive or vegetable oil (optional)
	Lukewarm water

Sift the flour into a large bowl or onto a wooden surface to form a mound. Make a well in the center and break the eggs into it. Add the salt and oil, if used. Working with the tips of the fingers, mix the flour with the other ingredients to combine thoroughly. Add water, a little at a time, as needed, to make a stiff paste and form a compact ball. Leave, covered to rest for 15 minutes. Divide into halves. Roll each portion out on a lightly floured board, turning and rolling firmly often, and dusting with flour, if needed, until very thin, between 1/8 and 1/16 inch. Cut according to the following directions for which type of pasta is desired. Makes about 1 pound.

TAGLIATELLI:

Roll up each sheet of dough into a jelly-roll shape and, with a sharp knife, slice crosswise into strips ranging from 1/8 to 1/2 inch wide. Unroll each strip—quickly, so they do not stick together—and place on a clean towel to dry for one hour. Cook several at a time in a kettle of boiling salted water until just tender. Drain. Separate to keep from sticking. Serve at once.

FETTUCCINE:

Prepare and cook in the same fashion as for *tagliatelli* but cut 1/4 to 1/2 inch wide.

LASAGNE:

Cut the dough into 3-inch strips, about 6 inches long. Dry, covered, for 1 hour. Cook in boiling salted water, with a little oil added, until just tender. Drain and cool before using.

CANNELLONI:

Cut the dough into rectangles 4½ inches by 5 inches. Dry, covered, for 1 hour. Drop a few at a time into boiling salted water and cook until just tender. Remove carefully and drain. Allow to cool before filling and rolling.

MANICOTTI:

Cut the dough into 3-inch squares. Dry, covered, for 1 hour. Drop a few at a time into boiling salted water until just tender. Remove carefully and drain. Allow to cool before filling.

GREEN NOODLES

Spinach-flavored noodles, called green noodles, are one of the finest of the pasta creations. They may be mixed with melted butter and grated Parmesan or garnished with a sauce, and served as a first course or as an accompaniment to meats or seafood.

¼ pound cleaned fresh
  spinach
2 cups unsifted all-purpose
  flour

2 medium eggs at room
  temperature
½ teaspoon salt

Wash the spinach leaves and put in a saucepan with only the water remaining on the leaves from washing. Cook over very low heat until just tender, being careful not to burn, about 5 minutes. Remove from the heat and drain off any liquid and reserve it. Put the spinach through a food mill, sieve, or electric blender to purée it. Once again drain off any excess liquid and reserve. Cool the spinach.

Sift the flour into a large bowl or onto a wooden or marble surface to form a mound. Make a well in the center and break the eggs into it. Add the salt and puréed spinach. Working with the fingers, mix the flour with the other ingredients to combine well. Add as much of the spinach liquid as needed to form the dough into a stiff paste and form a compact ball. Knead the dough on a floured surface for 5 to 10 minutes, until smooth and elastic. Cover with a wet cloth or paper towel and leave for 15 minutes. Divide the dough into two portions and roll out with a rolling pin, preferably a long tapered one, into a large rectangle, as thin as possible, about 1/16 inch thick. Roll into a jelly-roll shape and slice crosswise into strips ⅛ to ¼ inch thick. Unroll each strip—quickly, before they stick together—and place on a clean towel to dry for at least one hour. When ready to cook, drop several at a time into a kettle of boiling salted water and cook until just tender, the exact time depending on the width of the noodles. Drain. Serve warm with melted butter and grated Parmesan cheese or a sauce. Makes 1 pound.

This dough may be used also for green lasagne noodles. Cut into 3 strips each 3 inches wide.

FETTUCCINE ROMANO

One of the best and most famous dishes made with the egg noodles is called *fettuccine*. Because it is served lavishly in two popular restaurants of Rome, each named Alfredo's, the dish is sometimes called by that name. For it, homemade *fettuccine* are preferable, but those sold fresh in Italian or specialty food stores or packaged dry medium egg noodles can be used.

1 pound *fettuccine* or medium
  egg noodles
½ cup soft butter
1 cup warm heavy cream

Freshly ground white pepper
2 cups grated Parmesan
  cheese, preferably freshly
  grated

Cook the *fettuccine* or noodles in salted boiling water until just tender, allowing about five minutes for the *fettuccine* and eight for the noodles. Drain. Spoon at once into a large skillet or chafing dish. Put the dish over very low heat. Add the butter and stir gently with the noodles until it melts. Add the cream and pepper and toss with two large forks. Add ½ cup of the cheese and continue tossing all the ingredients until they are well mixed and hot. Serve the remaining cheese separately to be sprinkled over the noodles at the table. Serves 6.

MACARONI AND CHEESE À LA SUISSE

Macaroni and cheese is a favorite combination in all the countries of Western Europe and has also become a popular American dish. This variation is excellent, as the macaroni is served with the traditional Swiss garnish of onions fried in butter and mixed with cheese. Noodles may be prepared the same way.

8 ounces elbow macaroni
6 tablespoons butter or
  margarine

2½ cups thinly sliced onions
1½ cups stale bread cubes
½ cup grated Swiss cheese

Cook the macaroni in boiling salted water until just tender and drain. Meanwhile, melt 3 tablespoons of butter in a skillet

and add the onions. Cook until deep golden and limp. Remove
with a slotted spoon to a plate. Add 3 more tablespoons of butter
and the bread cubes to the skillet. Sauté until golden. Combine
the drained, cooked macaroni and the onions with the bread
cubes in the skillet. Add the cheese and toss with two forks
to mix well. Serves 4.

ITALIAN SPAGHETTI WITH VEGETABLES

A typical Italian way of cooking pasta is with vegetables
such as eggplant, green peas, zucchini, or broccoli.

3 tablespoons olive oil
2 tablespoons butter or
  margarine
1 or 2 garlic cloves, crushed or
  minced
2 medium tomatoes, peeled and
  chopped
3 cups cubed eggplant or

zucchini, cut up broccoli, or
  green peas
½ cup chicken or beef bouillon
½ teaspoon dried basil
Salt, pepper to taste
1 pound spaghetti, cooked and
  drained
½ cup grated Parmesan cheese

Heat the oil and butter in a saucepan. Add the garlic and
tomatoes and cook 1 or 2 minutes. Add the vegetables, about ½
cup of bouillon, the basil, salt, and pepper. Cook slowly, covered,
until just tender. When cooked, toss with the spaghetti and
serve with the cheese. Serves 4.

DUTCH BAHMI GORENG

The Dutch cuisine is spiced with exotic flavors from the
East Indies, particularly dishes from Indonesia. Two of
the most popular are *nasi goreng* (made with rice) and
bahmi goreng (made with noodles) and the most delightful
place in Amsterdam to sample them is at the Bali Restaurant, where diners can indulge in an authentic 36-plate
rijstafel (rice table).

½ pound fine egg noodles or vermicelli
1½ pounds boneless pork strips, without fat
½ cup soy sauce
2 garlic cloves, crushed
6 green onions, with tops, chopped
2 eggs, beaten
About ½ cup peanut or vegetable oil

2 large onions, thinly sliced
2 teaspoons minced ginger root (optional)
1 cup drained bean sprouts
3 cups chopped Chinese cabbage
1½ cups cleaned, shelled, cooked small or medium shrimp
Freshly ground black pepper

Cook the noodles in boiling salted water according to the package directions, until tender. Drain and spread out on a large plate and cool. Put in the refrigerator for 2 hours.

Put the pork strips, ⅓ cup soy sauce, the garlic, and the green onions in a large bowl. Mix well and leave to marinate, stirring occasionally, for 2 hours.

Pour the eggs into a lightly greased skillet and tilt at once to spread evenly. Cook over a low fire until set. Remove to a plate and cool. Cut into strips. Set aside to use as a garnish.

When ready to cook the dish, heat 2 tablespoons of the oil in a large skillet. Add the pork mixture and sauté until the pork is cooked. Remove to a plate. Add 2 tablespoons of oil to the skillet. Add the onions and ginger root and sauté until limp. Remove to a plate. Add 3 tablespoons of oil and sauté the bean sprouts, Chinese cabbage, and shrimp until all the vegetables are just soft. Return the cooked pork, onions, and ginger root to the mixture. Stir in the remaining soy sauce. Season with pepper. Leave over low heat.

Melt 3 tablespoons of oil in another skillet. Add the chilled noodles and cook until golden and crisp. With a slotted spoon remove and mix with the pork-shrimp mixture. Serve on a large platter garnished with the cooked egg strips. Serves 4 to 6.

ENGLISH KEDGEREE

This favorite English breakfast dish originated in India, where it was made with lentils, rice, eggs, and spices. Adapted and popularized by the English, it has been customarily prepared by them with smoked or other fish, rice, hard-cooked eggs, and various seasonings. This is one of the many versions.

1/3 cup butter or margarine	2 teaspoons Worcestershire
1 or 2 tablespoons curry	sauce
powder	4 hard-cooked eggs, shelled and
2 tablespoons fresh lemon juice	chopped
2 1/2 cups cooked rice	1/2 cup chopped fresh parsley
2 1/2 cups flaked cooked fish (cod,	Salt, pepper to taste
salmon, or haddock)	

Melt the butter in a large saucepan. Stir in the curry powder and cook over low heat for 1 minute. Add the lemon juice, rice, and fish. Cook slowly, stirring, until the foods are heated. Mix in the remaining ingredients and leave on the stove long enough to heat them. Serve on a warm platter. Serves 6 to 8.

GERMAN BAKED NOODLES AND APPLESAUCE

The Germans enjoy sweet noodle dishes such as this one as dinner accompaniments to meats and poultry or for supper with sliced cold sausages.

1 package (8 ounces) wide egg	2 cans (1 pound each)
noodles	applesauce
2 eggs, slightly beaten	2/3 cup sugar
1/2 cup light cream or milk	1 teaspoon grated lemon rind
1/4 cup butter or margarine	1 teaspoon ground cinnamon
1 cup seedless raisins or	Fine dry bread crumbs
currants	

Cook the noodles in boiling salted water according to the package directions, until tender. Drain. Turn at once into a large bowl. Add the eggs, cream, butter, and raisins and mix well. In another bowl, combine the applesauce, sugar, lemon rind, and cinnamon. Arrange the noodle and applesauce mixtures in layers in a greased round baking dish. Sprinkle the top with bread crumbs and dot with butter. Bake in a preheated moderately hot oven (375°F.) for 30 to 40 minutes, or until cooked. Serves 6 to 8.

ARROZ À PORTUGUESA

An interesting rice dish from Portugal that could be served as an accompaniment to seafood or poultry.

1 large onion, finely chopped
1 garlic clove, crushed
3 tablespoons olive or
  vegetable oil
½ cup diced smoked pork or
  ham

2 large tomatoes, peeled and
  chopped
2½ cups water or broth
1 cup uncooked rice
1 cup shelled fresh green peas
  or other green vegetable
Salt, pepper to taste

Sauté the onion and garlic in the oil in a large saucepan until the onion is tender. Add the pork or ham and sauté 1 minute. Stir in the tomatoes and cook slowly about 5 minutes. Add the water and bring to a boil. Stir in the rice and peas and lower the heat. Season with salt and pepper. Cook slowly, covered, about 20 minutes, or until the rice grains are tender and most of the liquid has been absorbed. Serves 4 to 6.

ITALIAN GNOCCHI VERDI

Although Italians are not generally regarded as dumpling devotees, they do have a very popular kind called *gnocchi* which are made in interesting variety. Most are preparations of potatoes and flour, but some are made with such ingredients as flour and cheese or, like this one, spinach and cheese. They may be served like pasta, as a first course, or as an accompaniment to meats.

1 package (10 ounces) fresh
  spinach or 1 package (10
  ounces) frozen spinach

½ cup ricotta or cottage
  cheese
1 large egg, slightly beaten

½ cup freshly grated
Parmesan cheese
¼ to ⅓ cup flour

Salt, pepper, nutmeg to taste
¼ cup melted butter

If fresh spinach is used, clean, wash and chop it. If frozen, defrost and chop. Cook with only the water clinging to the fresh leaves (or add a small amount of water to the frozen) over low heat for a few minutes, until tender. Drain off all the liquid, pressing firmly with a spoon. Combine in a bowl with the ricotta, egg, ¼ cup of the Parmesan cheese, and ¼ cup of flour. Season with salt, pepper, and nutmeg and mix well. Add a little more flour, if necessary. The mixture should be quite thick. Chill in the refrigerator for 1 hour. With floured hands, form into 1½-inch balls and roll each in flour. Chill again for 30 minutes. Drop gently, a few at a time, into a saucepan of simmering salted water. Remove with a slotted spoon to a buttered shallow baking dish. When all are cooked, pour the melted butter and remaining ¼ cup of Parmesan over the *gnocchi*. Put in a hot oven (450°F.) for 5 minutes. Serves 4 to 6.

FRENCH CROQUETTES DE RIZ

Our word for croquette comes from the French *croquer*, "to crunch." In France croquettes are highly esteemed, beautifully made creations with savory fillings and crisp golden exteriors. They are served traditionally piled on a linen napkin in a pyramid or mound.

4 tablespoons butter
1 medium onion, minced
3 tablespoons flour
1 cup light cream or milk
Salt, white pepper to taste
⅛ teaspoon grated nutmeg
2 cups cooked rice

3 tablespoons chopped fresh
parsley
Fine dry bread crumbs
1 egg, beaten
1 tablespoon vegetable oil
Fat for frying

Melt 2 tablespoons of butter in a small skillet and sauté the onion in it until soft. Set aside. Melt the remaining 2 tablespoons of butter in a saucepan and mix in the flour to form a *roux*. Cook, stirring, about 2 minutes to blend well. Gradually add the cream while still stirring constantly. Bring to a boil and lower the heat. Simmer about 10 minutes, stirring frequently, until the sauce is slightly reduced, thick, and smooth. Season with salt, pepper, and nutmeg. Remove from the heat and mix well with the sautéed onion, the cooked rice, and the parsley. Spread evenly in a greased flat dish and chill. Shape the croquette mixture into any desired form. Roll in bread crumbs. Dip in the beaten egg mixed with the oil. Roll again in bread crumbs. Chill. Leave at room temperature for 1 hour. Fry in hot deep fat (375°F.) until golden brown. Drain on absorbent paper. Serve plain or with a warm tomato sauce. Serves 4 to 6.

ITALIAN POLENTA

Maize or corn from the New World became popular as a food in only one Western European area, northern Italy. There the staple food is *polenta,* the Italian name for corn meal and dishes made with it. Usually yellow, but sometimes white, either coarsely or finely ground, *polenta,* when cooked, may be eaten either soft and hot or cooled and firm. As the latter it is made into a number of inviting dishes. This is the basic recipe for *polenta.*

6 cups water	1½ cups finely ground *polenta*
1 teaspoon salt	or yellow corn meal

Put the water and salt in a large saucepan and bring to a boil. Slowly pour the *polenta* or corn meal into the boiling water, stirring as it is added to prevent lumping, and being sure the water continues to boil. When the mixture is smooth, lower the heat and cook, uncovered and with frequent stirring, about 30 minutes or until it is thick. A good test is to see if a wooden stirring spoon will stand without falling in the center of the mush. Serve at once while warm with butter and grated cheese. Or spoon into a buttered round or rectangular baking dish and chill for 1 hour or until very firm. Slice or cut into pieces. Fry, bake, or grill and serve with butter and cheese or a warm tomato or meat sauce. Serves 4 to 6.

GERMAN SPAETZLE

Tiny noodles called *Spaetzle*, served in soups or as accompaniments to meats, poultry, game, or stews, are homemade specialties of Germany's inviting region of Swabia. The little balls of dough are made in infinite variety and may include such ingredients as spinach or ham. When cooked, they are served in soups, mixed with gravy, or tossed with mushrooms. A good city in which to sample *Spaetzle* is Stuttgart, which has many atmospheric restaurants and a superb *Rathskeller* in the *Rathaus* (city hall).

2½ cups all-purpose flour
½ teaspoon salt

2 eggs, lightly beaten
Water

Sift the flour and salt into a bowl. Make a well in the center and add the eggs and ½ cup of water. Beat, adding more water as necessary, to make a stiff dough. Beat with a wooden spoon until soft and light. Let stand for 30 minutes. Dampen a wooden board or pastry board and turn out the dough on it. Roll out to a thickness of about ⅛ inch. Cut off small strips or slivers with a sharp knife and drop several of them at a time into boiling salted water. Cook until the noodles rise to the surface, 3 to 5 minutes. While cutting, dampen the board and dip the knife in boiling water as necessary. Remove from the water with a slotted spoon and drain. Makes about 4 cups.

CRÊPES AUX CHAMPIGNONS

Mushroom-filled pancakes may be served as a first course or as a luncheon entrée.

1 medium onion, finely
  chopped
Butter or margarine
1 pound fresh mushrooms,
  cleaned and chopped
2 tablespoons flour
½ cup sour cream at room
  temperature

2 tablespoons chopped fresh
  dill or parsley
Salt, pepper, freshly grated
  nutmeg to taste
1 cup milk
1 large egg, beaten
1 cup sifted all-purpose flour
Grated Parmesan cheese

Sauté the onion in 3 tablespoons of butter until tender. Add the mushrooms and sauté for 5 minutes. Mix in the flour and cook for 1 minute. Add the sour cream, dill, salt, pepper, and nutmeg. Cook slowly for 1 or 2 minutes to blend the flavors. Remove from the heat and cool.

Combine the milk, egg, and flour in a bowl and mix well. Season with salt. When the ingredients are thoroughly blended, pour 3 or 4 tablespoons of the batter into a heated lightly greased 7- or 8-inch skillet. Tlit at once to spread evenly. Cook until golden on one side. Turn and cook on the other side. Keep warm in a preheated 250°F. oven while cooking the other pancakes.

Put about 2 large spoonfuls of the mushroom mixture onto each pancake. Roll up and arrange, seam side down, in a buttered shallow baking dish. Dot the top with butter and sprinkle with cheese. Put in a preheated hot oven (400°F.) about 10 minutes before serving. Serves 4 to 6.

SUPPLI AL TELEFONO OF ITALY

"Croquettes on the telephone," made with cheese and rice, acquired this intriguing name as the melted cheese stretches into threads as thin as telephone wires. In Rome they are sold at sidewalk stands as snacks.

1 medium onion, minced
¼ cup olive oil or butter
1 cup short or medium-grain
  rice
½ cup dry white wine
2½ cups chicken broth
⅛ teaspoon powdered saffron
  steeped in hot water
  (optional)

Salt, pepper
⅓ cup grated Parmesan cheese
4 eggs
About ⅓ pound ½-inch cubes
  of mozzarella cheese
Flour
Fine dry bread crumbs
Oil or shortening for frying

Sauté the onion in the oil in a skillet. Add the rice and sauté until translucent, about 5 minutes. Pour in the wine and turn up the heat to high. Cook, stirring, until the liquid is absorbed. Lower the heat and add 1 cup of the broth. Cook slowly and add the rest of the liquid, ½ cup at a time. When the grains are tender and the liquid has been absorbed, add the saffron, salt, pepper, and Parmesan. Stir and remove from the heat. Cool. Slightly beat 2 of the eggs and stir into the rice mixture. Chill 30 minutes. Scoop up 2 or 3 tablespoons of the mixture in one hand. Place a mozzarella cube in the center and shape the mixture around it to form a ball. Be sure the mozzarella cube is completely enclosed. Roll each ball in flour. Dip in the remaining 2 eggs, beaten, and roll in bread crumbs. Chill 30 minutes. Fry in hot deep fat (375°F.) until golden brown. Drain on absorbent paper. Makes about 20 croquettes.

BREAD DUMPLINGS FROM GERMANY

The Germans are true devotees of dumplings which they make in great variety and consume daily in large quantity. *Knödel* are made with flour, potatoes, or bread, and can include such ingredients as bread cubes, fruit, or liver. They are eaten as accompaniments to meats and for dessert. This is an interesting version.

3 cups stale white bread cubes (½ inch each)
½ cup milk
3 slices bacon, finely chopped
1 small onion, minced

2 eggs, beaten
2 tablespoons chopped fresh parsley
About 1¾ cups sifted all-purpose flour

Place the bread cubes in a large bowl and cover with the milk. Fry the bacon and pour off all except 1 tablespoon of the fat. Add the onion and sauté in the fat until tender. Add the cooked bacon, sautéed onion, eggs, and parsley to the bread cubes and mix well. Stir in the flour, enough to make a stiff dough, and beat well. With floured hands, shape the dough into six balls. Drop into a large kettle of boiling salted water. Boil, uncovered, until the dumplings rise to the top. Cover and cook 10 to 15 minutes, or until done. Test by tearing one apart with two forks. Remove with a slotted spoon and drain. Serves 6.

PASTA WITH SALSA POMODORO

The word *pomodoro* ("golden apple") was given by the Italians to the tomato, probably because those first introduced into Europe from the New World were small and yellow. Today, bright red tomatoes are grown in great quantity in Italy and are used commonly in the cookery, particularly with pasta as in this dish.

3 tablespoons olive oil
1 cup chopped onions
2 small garlic cloves, crushed
  or minced
2 tablespoons chopped bacon
1 medium carrot, scraped and
  minced
1 medium stalk celery, cleaned
  and minced
3½ cups peeled and chopped
  fresh tomatoes or 1 large can
Italian-style plum tomatoes
  (28 or 29 ounces)

1 teaspoon dried basil
Salt, pepper to taste
⅓ cup chopped fresh parsley
1 pound cooked pasta
  (spaghetti, macaroni, or
  noodles), drained
⅓ cup butter
½ cup grated Romano or
  Parmesan cheese

Combine the oil, onions, garlic, bacon, carrot, and celery in a large saucepan or skillet. Cook slowly, stirring often, for 5 minutes. Add the tomatoes, basil, salt, and pepper. Mix well and simmer as slowly as possible, uncovered, for 1 hour, or until very thick. Stir in the parsley. Combine the pasta with the butter and cheese in a large serving dish and pour the warm sauce over it. Serves 4 to 6.

FRENCH BEIGNETS DE VOLAILLE

These chicken fritters may be served as a luncheon or supper entrée.

2 cups diced cooked chicken
1 tablespoon lemon juice
3 tablespoons vegetable oil

1 tablespoon minced onion
2 tablespoons minced fresh
  parsley

Salt, pepper to taste   1 cup water or milk
1 cup flour   1 tablespoon melted butter
2 eggs, beaten   Fat for frying

Put the chicken in a large bowl and add the lemon juice, oil, onion, parsley, salt, and pepper. Leave to marinate for 2 hours, stirring now and then.

Sift the flour and ½ teaspoon salt into another large bowl. Combine the eggs, water or milk, and melted butter and add to the flour. Stir until smooth. With a slotted spoon, take out the chicken pieces and add to the batter. Mix well. Drop by tablespoons into deep hot fat (375°F. on a frying thermometer) and fry until golden brown on all sides. Drain on absorbent paper. Serves 6.

PAELLA VALENCIANA

Spain's internationally famous dish, *paella*, derives its name from the two-handled large, round metal pan, *paellera*, in which it is traditionally cooked and served. Although now enjoyed throughout Spain, *paella* originated in the region of Valencia where a great deal of rice is grown and eaten. At first it was a simple dish made with fish, rice, and olive oil; over the years a number of other ingredients, such as seafood, chicken, and vegetables, have been added to it. Generally, it is seasoned with the expensive and exotic favorite Spanish spice, saffron, made from dried crocus stigmas. This adaptation is a good one, easy to prepare in an American kitchen. It may be prepared in a *paella* pan, an extra-large skillet, or a kettle.

8 chicken parts (legs, thighs, or breasts)
Olive or vegetable oil for frying
1 or 2 garlic cloves, crushed
1 pound raw shrimp, shelled and cleaned
2 medium onions, chopped

1 *chorizo* (Spanish sausage) or other garlic sausage, thinly sliced
3 large tomatoes, peeled and chopped
1½ cups raw long-grain rice
3 cups chicken broth
⅛ teaspoon powdered saffron

Salt, pepper to taste
1 package (10 ounces) frozen
   green peas

1 can (7½ ounces) minced
   clams
1 canned pimiento, cut into
   thin strips

Wash and dry the chicken. Fry in heated oil in a large skillet until golden on all sides. With tongs, remove to a large *paella* pan, skillet, or kettle. Add the garlic and shrimp, and more oil if necessary, to the drippings in the skillet. Sauté until the shrimp become pink. Spoon into the large dish with the chicken. Add the onions to the drippings and sauté until tender. Add with the *chorizo*, tomatoes, rice and chicken broth to the ingredients in the large dish. Bring to a boil. Add the saffron and season with salt and pepper. Lower the heat and simmer, covered, until half the liquid has been absorbed, about 25 minutes. Add the peas and clams and continue to cook about 10 minutes longer, or until the ingredients are tender and most of the liquid is absorbed. Spoon out some of the shrimp, sausages, and peas to arrange on the top as a garnish. Serve in the *paella* pan, if used, or on a large platter with the reserved garnishes and pimiento strips over the top. Serves 8.

ENGLISH YORKSHIRE PUDDING

This baked unsweetened batter called a pudding, which takes its name from Yorkshire, a county in northeastern England, is the traditional accompaniment for roast beef. The dish is cooked in drippings from the roast.

2 eggs
½ teaspoon salt
1 cup milk

1 cup all-purpose flour
3 tablespoons beef drippings
   or lard

Beat the eggs with a rotary or electric beater until well mixed. Season with salt. Gradually add the milk, beating while you do so. Slowly add the flour, still beating, and continue to beat until the mixture is smooth and creamy. Heat the drippings or lard and pour into a shallow baking pan (9 inches square). Mix the batter again and pour into the dish. Bake in a preheated hot oven (425°F.) for 10 minutes. Reduce the heat to 350°F. and cook until golden and puffy, about 15 minutes. Cut the pudding into squares and serve at once. Serves 6.

SWEET POPPY-SEED NOODLES FROM AUSTRIA

Austrians enjoy a sweet noodle dish such as this one for supper as an accompaniment to cold meats or poultry.

8 ounces fine egg noodles
¼ cup butter or margarine
3 tablespoons ground poppy
  seeds

3 tablespoons sugar
½ teaspoon grated lemon

Cook the noodles in boiling water until tender. Drain and turn at once into a warm bowl. Stir in the butter and mix with the hot noodles until the butter melts. Have ready the poppy seeds, sugar, and grated lemon and sprinkle them over the noodles. Serve at once. Serves 4.

Finely chopped nuts such as walnuts or hazelnuts may be substituted for the poppy seeds, if desired.

RISOTTO ALLA MILANESE

In northern Italy's thriving and most important city, Milan, several superb local specialties are worth seeking out. One of them is this well-known rice dish prepared with the fine grains grown in the nearby Po Valley of Lombardy. It is rich, creamy, and flavorful with saffron. One of the delightful places to savor it, and other good fare as well, is at a restaurant in the Galleria Vittorio Emanuele on the city's central square, Piazza del Duomo, across from the great Cathedral of Milan and near the famed opera house, Teatro della Scala.

8 tablespoons butter
1 cup finely chopped onion
2 cups short- or medium-grain
  rice

1 cup dry white wine
2 cups hot excellent
  well-seasoned chicken broth
Salt, white pepper to taste

⅛ teaspoon saffron, powdered   ⅓ cup freshly grated
  or crumbled   Parmesan cheese

Melt 6 tablespoons of butter in a large heavy pot or skillet. Add the onion and sauté until tender. Stir in the rice and sauté about 5 minutes, until the rice is well coated with butter. Turn the heat to high and pour in the wine. Cook, stirring often, over high heat until most of the wine has evaporated. Add 1 cup of the hot broth. Season with salt and pepper. Lower the heat a little and continue cooking, uncovered, stirring frequently, until most of the liquid has been absorbed. While cooking, add the remaining broth, ½ cup at a time, stirring to be sure the mixture does not stick to the pan. The whole cooking process will take about 30 minutes, possibly a bit longer. The resulting *risotto* should be creamy, with the grains tender. Steep the saffron in a little hot water for a minute or so. When the rice is cooked, mix in the remaining butter, the Parmesan cheese, and the saffron. Leave on the stove until the ingredients are well mixed and serve at once. Serves 8.

SWEDISH BACON PANCAKES

This is a good breakfast or brunch dish, which is served traditionally in Sweden with lingonberry sauce. Lingonberries are similar to cranberries but smaller. They are grown in northern Europe and are used frequently in the Scandinavian cuisines.

4 strips thin bacon, chopped   ¾ cups flour
2 large eggs, lightly beaten   1½ cups milk
½ teaspoon salt   Butter or margarine
1 teaspoon sugar

Fry the bacon until crisp and drain, reserving 3 tablespoons of the fat. In a bowl, combine the eggs, salt, and sugar. Mix well and add the flour, milk, and reserved bacon fat. With a whisk or fork, stir to thoroughly combine the ingredients. Add the bacon pieces. Heat a 7- or 8-inch skillet, lightly greased with butter, and add 3 tablespoons of the batter. Tilt the pan at once to spread evenly. Cook over medium heat until the underside of the pancake is golden. Turn over with a spatula and cook on the other side. If necessary, grease the pan again. Turn out onto a warm plate and keep warm in a preheated 250°F. oven. Continue cooking the other pancakes. Serve with ligonberry sauce. Serves 4 to 6.

SWISS CORN MEAL CHEESE CASSEROLE

The Swiss cuisine borrows from those of Germany, France, and Italy in the various regions neighboring these countries. Thus in Ticino, a vacation paradise south of the Alps, where tourists flock to Lugano, Locarno, and Ascona, there are many noteworthy specialties from Italy. One is *polenta*, an Italian word for corn meal and dishes made with the cooked product. The Swiss have created some individual ways of serving it such as this dish. It is a good accompaniment to meats, particularly pork or sausages.

6 cups water
1 teaspoon salt
1½ cups *polenta* or yellow
  corn meal

Melted butter
Grated Gruyère cheese
Tomato slices

Put the water and salt in a large saucepan and bring to a boil. Slowly pour the *polenta* or corn meal into the boiling water, stirring as you add it to prevent any lumping. The water should continue to boil. When the mixture is smooth, lower the heat and cook, uncovered and stirring often, about 30 minutes, or until the mixture is thickened and set. Let cool and cut into slices. Put in a buttered baking dish in layers covered with melted butter, grated Gruyère cheese, and tomato slices. Bake in a preheated moderately hot oven (375°F.) for 25 minutes. Serves 4 to 6.

SCOTTISH HAGGIS

The Scottish national dish, *haggis*, was rated by the noted poet Robert Burns as "the great chieftain o' the puddin' race." Made by stuffing a sheep's stomach with a variety of ingredients including the animal's innards, the dish is much beloved in its homeland but generally derided elsewhere. It is standard fare at all Scottish national holiday gatherings held around the world wherever Scots live. Anyone who has not tasted *haggis*, but has heard it described, approaches the dish timidly. The surprise at the goodness of the fare is a great delight to Scots. I was fascinated with my first sampling of *haggis* at the Café Royale restaurant in Edinburgh, and immediately became a devotee of the dish. This is the recipe presented by the restaurant to their patrons.

> 1 Sheep's Pluck; Liver, Lights and Heart.
> The Large Stomach Bag.
> ½ lb. Fresh Beef Suet.
> 1 Breakfast-cupful of Fine Oatmeal.
> 2 or 3 Onions.
> Salt and Pepper.
> Pinch of Cayenne.
> 1 Breakfast-cupful Stock or Gravy.

Clean the paunch or stomach bag thoroughly; wash first in cold water, then plunge into boiling water and scrape: then leave to soak overnight in cold salted water. In the morning put it aside with the rough side turned out. Wash the small bag and pluck, and put them on to boil in cold water to cover, letting the wind-pipe hang out over the pot to let any impurities pass out freely. Boil for an hour and a half, then remove and cut away the pipes and any superfluities of gristle. Mince the heart and lights, and grate half the liver. (The rest is not required.) Mince the onions and suet, and toast the oatmeal very slowly before the fire or in a warm oven. Mix all these ingredients together and season with salt, plenty of black pepper, and add a pinch of cayenne. Pour over this sufficient of the pluck bree to make the mixture sappy. Fill the bag rather more than half full—say five-eights. It needs plenty of room to swell. Press out the air and sew the bag up securely. Put it into a pot of fast boiling water, and prick it with a large needle when it first swells, to prevent bursting. Boil slowly but steadily for three hours, without the lid, adding more boiling water as required. Serve very hot without garnish.

At a Burns Supper the *haggis* is usually piped in and is served with "neeps" and "nips"—mashed turnips and nips of whisky—and, of course, potatoes.

Pancakes

One of the world's most ancient dishes is the pancake, made originally with a mixture of meal and water and cooked on hot stones. Over the centuries the popularity of this round, flat creation spread around the world and, enhanced with such additions, as eggs, milk, and butter, its form became more delicate. Each of the Western European nations has one or more of its own favorite versions. Prepared flat, rolled, or folded; filled or unfilled; sweetened or unsweetened; pancakes can be served as appetizers, snacks, entrées, or desserts. They are probably one of the most versatile and treasured Continental dishes.

In some Western European countries the pancake became associated with the Christian holiday of Shrove Tuesday. In pre-Reformation England all the forbidden foods of the strict Lenten fast had to be eaten before Ash Wednesday, so Tuesday became a day of feasting and merrymaking.

How the pancake became the honored food on this day is not certain. Some authorities point out that making them was a good way of using the forbidden Lenten eggs and dairy products. Evidently the pancakes did not please everyone. The author of a seventeenth-century English cookery book wrote that "there is a thing call'd wheaten floure, which the cookes do mingle with water, eggs, spices and other tragicall, magicall enchantments, and then they put it by little and little into a frying-pan of boiling suet, where it makes a confused dismall hissing, until at last by the skill of the Cook, it is transformed into the form of a Flip-Jack, called a Pancake, which ominous incantation the ignorant people do devour very greedily."

This uncomplimentary commentary, however, did not curtail the popularity of the pancake for Shrove Tuesday. Even the church bell that rang on that day to summon the penitent to confession became known as the Pancake Bell. An old rhyme sung in London went "Pancakes and fritters,/ Say the bells of Saint Peter's." The tossing of pancakes became a part of the general merrymaking. It is still the custom at Westminster College for a cook to toss a pancake over a bar into a group of selected students who vie with each other to get the largest piece of it and thus earn a reward.

From an old verse we can assume this frivolity was pretty general—it relates that each man and woman

> Doe toss their pancakes for fear they burn
> And all the kitchen doth with laughter sound,
> To see the pancakes fall upon the ground.

In 1445 at Olney, England, a colorful event called the Pancake Race was initiated and is still an annual competition. Housewives gather at the pumps of the village square and run a 415-yard course to the church, flipping pancakes as they run. The winner is warmly acclaimed and given an award. (A similar race is now held also in Kansas.)

In France, Shrove Tuesday became known as Fat Tuesday, or Mardi Gras, and pancakes are still favorite fare for the carnival celebrations. The custom also spread to other lands, but pancakes are relished on other days and for all meals as well. There are so many variations that it is not possible to give them here. With the basic French recipe below a number of tempting kinds of pancake creations can be evolved.

BASIC RECIPE FOR CRÊPES

3 large eggs, beaten
2 tablespoons melted butter
⅔ cup milk

⅓ cup water
1 cup all-purpose flour
¼ teaspoon salt

Put the ingredients in a large bowl and mix well to combine them thoroughly. Let stand in the refrigerator for 1 hour. Mix well again. Heat a 7- or 8-inch skillet, lightly greased with butter. Add 2 or 3 tablespoons of the batter and quickly tilt the pan to spread the batter evenly. Cook over medium heat until the underside of the pancake is golden. Turn over with a spatula and cook on the other side. Turn out onto a warm plate and keep warm in a preheated 250°F. oven. Continue cooking the other pancakes. Serve hot with melted butter and grated cheese or with a sauce. The pancakes may also be filled with chopped cooked poultry, seafood, meat, or vegetables mixed with an equal amount of a desirable sauce. Put 1 or 2 spoonfuls on each *crêpe*; roll up, arrange in a buttered shallow baking dish and dot with butter and sprinkle with cheese or cover with a sauce. Put under the broiler to heat until golden.

The crêpes may be prepared beforehand and frozen in stacks of 6, 8, or 10, wrapped in freezer paper. Thaw well before using.

5

Seafood

AMONG WESTERN EUROPE'S great gastronomic pleasures, none is more fascinating and delightful than the superb seafood. A varied and bountiful harvest of fish and shellfish from both fresh and salt waters is readily available and the cookery enhances the natural qualities and versatility of this marine treasure trove.

Since the beginning of time man has relied on the waters of sleepy streams, gurgling brooks, fast-running rivers, placid ponds, tepid and icy lakes, deep and mysterious seas and oceans, to provide necessary, nutritious, and inexpensive food. Without these resources he would not have survived. The waters in and around Western Europe have long been rich with seafood of all descriptions and qualities that could be caught at one time or another throughout the year. It is most interesting that through the centuries this bounty has been utilized to provide not only daily sustenance but notable and distinguished culinary creations.

An affinity for seafood began in Western Europe with the early Romans, who eagerly sought out the resources of inland waters and those of the neighboring seas. A mosaic uncovered in the ruins of Pompeii has revealed a wide number of local specialties, including eel, *langouste*, and octopus. Cooks devised a great number of recipes for cooking seafood, which was served in considerable variety at the daily lengthy banquets. Rulers thought nothing of dispatching ships to all parts of the Empire for particular favorites. One of the most sought-after delicacies, the oyster, was brought to Rome from the faraway waters of Britain. Such was the desire for oysters that in southern Italy they were cultivated on "farms" as early as 100 B.C.

During the Middle Ages seafood became an important food on the Continent; it was an essential supplement to the meager everyday diet. The church contributed greatly to the increasing consumption of "fysshe," as Christians were instructed to eat it on Fridays, for Lent, and on other fast days which, during the year, amounted to quite a large number. Little wonder that it became necessary to keep permanent stocks of freshwater fish in man-made ponds and even moats around the manors so that the masters and their minions could have a constant supply.

Quite understandably fishing became an important industry and fleets, departing daily from the coastal areas, operated farther and farther from the mainland in pursuit of the profusion of saltwater treasures. The quest for the small bony herring became so important that as late as the nineteenth century the French naturalist, Lacepède, remarked that "The herring is one of these productions which decide the destiny of Empires." Truly it did. Although the fish is no longer involved in political rivalries, it is still staple fare in all of the northern European countries.

Another very important fish, highly prized for its protein, was the cod taken from the cold waters of the North Atlantic and the Baltic Sea. Early Vikings learned that cod could be easily preserved; dried and salted, it not only provided nourishing food during the long winter months but also furnished sustenance for the lengthy sea voyages. From early times to the present day, this saltwater fish has also been an important element in the economies of the northern countries, particularly Norway. For the cod, after being dried on racks in the cold northern air, became a much desired food in the hot countries of southern Europe where it could withstand the heat and last for some time. Thus, paradoxically, in Spain, Portugal, Italy, and southern France, where fresh fish is in plentiful supply, the dried salt cod became favorite fare that inventive cooks transformed into some of their best dishes.

Throughout Scandinavia and the British Isles the dried salt cod was also used in making a number of unusual national favorites, including the Norwegian *lutefisk,* for which the cod is soaked in a lye solution before being cooked. But the fresh cod is even more highly prized as its flesh has a particularly appealing and delicate flavor. Simply boiled and served with butter or a sauce, it is a great delicacy. Also greatly appreciated are the cod's roe, tongue, cheeks, liver, and head, sometimes stuffed.

The eel has great appeal in all of the Western European countries where it is found both in salt and fresh waters. As mentioned in Chapter 1, "Appetizers," smoked eel is even more highly prized by many gastronomes, particularly the Germans, than is smoked salmon. In the English fish shops common snacks are eel soups, stews, pies, and a particular Cockney favorite, jellied eels. The French make fine eel stews and consider the fish an important ingredient of their famous soup-stew, *bouillabaisse.* In Belgium and Luxembourg eels served in a green sauce, made with a number of herbs, are in French called *anguilles au vert.* Southern Italians relish eel as their traditional Christmas Eve entrée and elsewhere in the country, particularly in coastal areas, eel is served with inviting sauces or, often, marinated in oil and vinegar. A specialty of the Spanish Basques is tiny baby eels, *angulas,* which are cooked in a spicy garlic-red-pepper combination. And in Portugal the river eel is added to the national mixed-fish stew, *caldeirada,* flavored with tomatoes, wine, and herbs.

There are too many of the other esteemed saltwater fish to mention them all. In Western Europe, good places to observe the great variety of seafoods are the lively and colorful fish markets where, among others, there will be swordfish, plaice, mackerel, turbot, haddock, mullet, hake, whiting, halibut, snapper, pollock, flounder, skate, tuna or tunny, lobster, *langouste,* rockfish, scallops, coalfish, anchovies, and sardines.

In addition, there might be three particular treasures which are luxury fare and rated among the world's greatest seafood treats. "The King Fish," salmon, taken from the Atlantic and famous northern rivers of the British Isles and Scandinavia, is sought after for its delicate flesh and superb flavor. Smoked, poached, baked, broiled, steamed, or, as in Sweden, cured with salt, sugar, pepper, and dill (see recipe for Swedish dill salmon, page 5), the salmon is truly a pleasurable repast. Another fish well worth savoring is the trout which throughout most of the Continent is taken from fresh water and is served most often either grilled, fried, *au bleu*, or *meunière*. An innovative treat, however, is the saltwater trout, called the sea or salmon trout, which is a little sweeter than that from fresh water.

Lastly, there is the English channel sole, listed on most restaurant menus as Dover sole, a true luxury that is superior to that of the North Sea, the lemon sole. Purists maintain that this delicate, well-flavored fish is best when grilled or broiled, and served with butter and fresh lemon juice. But there are also many elaborate preparations for sole. A fine selection of them is offered at the renowned London Wheeler's restaurants where 24 Dover sole dishes have been given such titles as Maryland, Egyptienne, Walewska, Cubat, Colbert, and St.-Germain.

Western Europeans are also devoted to the members of the mollusk family, which include snails, mussels, clams, oysters, and squid. The French, of course, have long been acknowledged fans of *escargots*, flavorful with garlic and butter, which are standard items on their menus, as well as those of other neighboring countries. Flavorful mussel stews have been long-time favorites in Belgium, France, and Italy, and are probably sampled more by Americans than the squid specialties that abound particularly in the Mediterranean locales.

Although saltwater seafood specialties are most important in Western European cuisines, the fine species from the inland lakes, rivers, and streams are also inviting fare. Carp, for example, is greatly valued on the Continent, and in Austria and Germany is traditional fare for many holiday meals. In Sweden and Finland, crayfish are considered a great delicacy and during the August season are featured boiled and garnished with fresh dill. The Swiss and French are devotees of *omble chevalier* (a kind of lake trout), and perch and pike appear frequently in other countries.

While it is impossible to include recipes for all the inviting seafood dishes of Western Europe, and indeed some of them cannot be duplicated elsewhere because some species are not available, this selection is representative of the fascinating repertoire.

ITALIAN PESCE AL CARTOCCIO

Fish cooked and served in paper is a great favorite in Italy as well as in some of the other Mediterranean countries. One of the best and most popular fish used in this type of cookery is the delicate red mullet, prized since ancient times for its particularly appealing flavor. Although there are many varieties of mullet, the two most common ones in Europe are the red and gray, both taken from salt water. In America we have both fresh- and saltwater mullets of varying sizes. Any of these or other white-fleshed fish may be used as a substitute for the red mullet. As for paper, Italians generally use parchment, but aluminum foil is also excellent.

Parchment paper or aluminum foil
2 medium onions, finely chopped
2 garlic cloves, crushed
3 tablespoons butter
Olive oil
2 medium carrots, scraped and diced
2 medium celery stalks, cleaned and diced
½ cup chopped fresh parsley
Salt, pepper to taste
4 small red mullets, or other white-fleshed fish, dressed, washed, and dried

Cut 4 pieces of parchment paper or foil that are large enough to completely enclose each of the fish. Sauté the onions and garlic in the heated butter and 2 tablespoons of oil until tender. Add the carrots and celery and sauté another 2 minutes. Stir in the parsley and season with salt and pepper. Remove from the stove. Place each fish on a piece of parchment or foil. Spoon the sautéed vegetable mixture over the fish, dividing it evenly. Sprinkle with olive oil, if desired. Fold over the paper to enclose the ingredients completely and crinkle the edges to secure them. Place on a baking sheet and cook in a preheated hot oven (450°F.) for about 15 minutes, until the fish is tender. Serve the fish in the paper, to be opened at the table. Serves 4.

BASEL SALMON WITH ONIONS

The favorite fish in Switzerland's northern port city of Basel is the salmon caught in the Rhine River. Once it was the custom to give one of the highly prized salmon as a gift to each visiting dignitary. Today, visitors to this inviting Swiss city can dine on the salmon in any of the superb restaurants. This is the special local way of preparing it.

2 medium onions, thinly sliced
9 tablespoons butter
4 salmon steaks, about 1 inch
  thick
Salt, pepper to taste

Flour
½ cup dry white wine
⅓ cup chopped fresh parsley
1 large lemon, sliced

Sauté the onions in 3 tablespoons of butter in a small skillet until tender. Remove from the heat and keep warm. Sprinkle the salmon with salt and pepper and dredge each steak on both sides with flour. Heat 6 tablespoons of butter in a large skillet and add the salmon. Pan-fry gently over medium heat about 10 minutes, or until fork tender. Remove to a platter and keep warm. Spoon the onions over the salmon. Pour the wine into the pan drippings. Scrape with a fork and bring quickly to a boil. Pour over the salmon. Sprinkle the parsley over the top and serve garnished with the lemon slices. Serves 4.

NORWEGIAN FISH-VEGETABLE STEW

This is an excellent winter supper dish that is easy to prepare.

4 medium potatoes, pared and
  cubed
3 medium carrots, scraped and
  sliced

2 cups cut-up green beans
3 medium onions, peeled and
  quartered
About 1½ cups milk

Salt, pepper to taste
1 pound codfish fillets
2 tablespoons butter

2 tablespoons flour
⅓ cup chopped parsley

Put the potatoes, carrots, green beans, and onions in a large saucepan. Add enough milk to cover them and season with salt and pepper. Cook slowly, covered, for 10 minutes. Place the codfish fillets in a colander that will fit over the saucepan and put it on the pan. Cover the fish and continue to cook until the fish and vegetables are tender. Remove the colander and cut the fish into small pieces. Drain the milk from the vegetables and reserve it. Combine the fish and vegetables and keep warm. Melt the butter in a saucepan and stir in the flour to form a *roux*. Gradually add the reserved milk and cook slowly until thick and smooth. Add more milk, if needed to make a thinner sauce. Season with salt and pepper and stir in the parsley. Spoon over the fish and vegetables. Serves 4.

FRENCH SOLE BONNE FEMME

This classic and very popular French fish dish has a name that means literally "good housewife." In gastronomic parlance, however, it refers to a dish that includes mushrooms and white wine.

1½ pounds sole fillets
Salt, pepper to taste
1 medium onion, minced
1 garlic clove, crushed
4 tablespoons butter
½ pound fresh mushrooms,
  cleaned and sliced

1 tablespoon fresh lemon juice
2 tablespoons chopped fresh
  parsley
½ cup dry white wine
1 teaspoon flour
¼ cup light cream

Sprinkle the fillets with salt and pepper and set aside. Sauté the onion and garlic in 3 tablespoons of butter in a small skillet until tender. With a slotted spoon, remove to a large skillet. Place the fillets over them. Add the mushrooms and lemon juice to the drippings in the small skillet and sauté them for 4 minutes. Spoon over the fish, adding the liquid also. Sprinkle with the parsley. Pour the wine around the fish and bring to a boil. Lower the heat and cook slowly, covered, about 7 minutes, or until the fish are just tender. Add the remaining tablespoon of butter to the pan. Stir in the flour. Gradually add the cream and cook slowly, stirring, until thickened. Serve at once. Serves 4.

ANDALUSIAN GRILLED HAKE WITH VEGETABLES

Hake, or *merluza*, is a very popular fish in Spain and is prepared in a number of interesting variations. It is a relative of cod and is caught in the Atlantic in great quantity. If not available, cod can be substituted for it.

2 pounds hake fillets
3 tablespoons fresh lemon
 juice
Olive oil
Salt, pepper to taste
Flour

1 pound asparagus, cooked and
 drained
6 medium potatoes, cooked,
 drained, and boiled
4 hard-cooked eggs, cooked,
 shelled, and sliced thickly
¼ cup chopped fresh parsley

Sprinkle the fillets with the lemon juice, 3 tablespoons of olive oil, salt, and pepper, and leave for 20 minutes. Dredge in flour on both sides. Grease a grill or large skillet with oil and fry the fillets on both sides until tender and golden. Serve on a large platter surrounded by the asparagus and potatoes and garnished with the eggs and parsley. Serves 4 to 6.

GERMAN BAKED MUSHROOM-STUFFED PIKE

This is an interesting way of preparing pike that I enjoyed at the home of a German friend.

1 whole pike (4 to 5 pounds),
 cleaned and washed
Salt

½ cup minced green onions,
 with tops

3 tablespoons butter or
  margarine
1 pound fresh mushrooms,
  cleaned and sliced
2 tablespoons fresh lemon juice
Pepper, nutmeg to taste

2 cups stale white bread cubes
3 tablespoons chopped fresh
  dill or parsley
1 cup dry white wine
1 cup sour cream at room
  temperature

Sprinkle the pike inside and out with salt. Sauté the onions in the butter in a skillet until tender. Add the mushrooms and lemon juice and sauté for 4 minutes. Season with salt, pepper, and nutmeg. Stir in the bread cubes and dill and remove from the heat. Spoon into the cavity of the fish. Close with small skewers and place in a buttered shallow baking dish. Pour the wine over the fish. Bake in a preheated moderate oven (350°F.) for about 40 minutes, or until the flesh is fork tender. Remove to a warm platter and keep warm. Scrape the drippings and add the sour cream to them. Leave on the stove long enough to heat through. Spoon over the fish and serve. Serves 4 to 6.

SWEDISH JANSSON'S TEMPTATION

This piquant potato dish, flavored with onions and anchovies, called Jansson's *Frestelse*, is a favorite hot *smörgåsbord* specialty in Sweden. It can also be served as an accompaniment to meat or poultry.

1 can (2 ounces) flat anchovy
  fillets
2 medium onions, thinly sliced
Butter
6 medium potatoes, pared and
  cut into small strips

Pepper
1½ to 2 cups light cream or
  milk
Buttered bread crumbs
  (optional)

Drain the anchovies, reserving the liquid. Chop the anchovies into small pieces. Sauté the onions in 3 tablespoons of butter until tender. In a buttered shallow baking dish, arrange the potatoes and onions in layers, sprinkled with the chopped anchovies and pepper, and dotted with butter. Slowly pour the cream or milk over the ingredients, using enough to cover them.

Pour also the reserved anchovy liquid. Sprinkle the top with buttered crumbs, if desired, or dot with butter. Bake, covered, in a hot over (400°F.) for 30 minutes. Uncover and continue to cook several minutes longer until the potatoes are tender and the top is golden. Serves 6 to 8.

FLEMISH FISH WATERZOOI

This is a flavorful fish stew which is a great favorite of the Flemings who live in the north of Belgium and have their own distinctive cookery.

2 pounds white-fleshed fish
  fillets (cod, haddock, flounder)
1 quart water
2 cups dry white wine
2 medium carrots, scraped and
  sliced
2 medium leeks, white parts
  only, cleaned and sliced

1 medium bay leaf
½ teaspoon dried thyme
¼ teaspoon ground cloves
4 parsley sprigs
Salt, pepper to taste
1 lemon, sliced
3 tablespoons chopped fresh
  parsley

Cut the fish into good-sized chunks and put in a large kettle with the water, wine, carrots, leeks, bay leaf, thyme, cloves, parsley, salt, and pepper and bring to a boil. Lower the heat and simmer the fish, covered, about 20 minutes. Add the lemon slices 5 minutes before the stew is finished cooking. Remove and discard the bay leaf and parsley sprigs. Serve garnished with the chopped parsley. Serves 6.

SCOTTISH FINNAN HADDIE

Smoked haddock, a Scottish national dish, derived its name from the village of Findon in Scotland, and is popularly called by a corruption of the name, finnan haddie. The English and Scots enjoy it as a breakfast dish.

2 tablespoons butter
1 pound smoked haddock or
 finnan haddie, skinned and
 cut into small pieces

Pepper to taste
2 teaspoons cornstarch
1 cup milk
4 hot poached eggs

Heat the butter in a skillet and add the pieces of haddock. Sprinkle with pepper. Cook over low heat for 5 minutes. Combine the cornstarch with a little of the milk and add to the haddock. Pour in the remainder of the milk and cook another 5 minutes. Serve with the poached eggs placed over the fish mixture. Serves 4.

AUSTRIAN FISH GOULASH

The Austrians have borrowed a well-flavored fish stew, or goulash, from their neighbors, the Hungarians. In Austria an assortment of freshwater fish is used to make the dish.

2 pounds white-fleshed fish
 fillets
Salt, pepper to taste
2 large onions, thinly sliced
1 garlic clove, minced
2 tablespoons butter
2 tablespoons vegetable oil

1 to 2 tablespoons paprika
2 large tomatoes, peeled and
 chopped
6 medium potatoes, pared and
 cubed
Water or fish broth

Cut the fish into cubes and season with salt and pepper. Set aside. Sauté the onions and garlic in a large saucepan in the butter and oil until tender. Stir in the paprika and cook 1 minute. Stir in the tomatoes and cook until mushy, 3 or 4 minutes. Add the potatoes and water or broth to cover. Cook over medium heat, covered, for 10 minutes. Add the chunks of fish and continue to cook until they are tender, about 10 minutes. Do not stir while the mixture is cooking but shake occasionally if the ingredients are sticking to the pan. Add a little more water while cooking, if needed. Serves 4 to 6.

GERMAN BLUE TROUT

In several Western European countries a favorite way of preparing fish is to marinate it briefly or cook it in a vinegar solution, which turns the skin to a vivid blue (*blau*). Trout, preferably freshly caught, prepared in this manner have a particularly appealing flavor. A restaurant which specializes in trout dishes, the *Forellengut*, is situated in a lovely forest setting about two miles from Bad Hamburg, famous for its spas.

4 trout, dressed	2 tablespoons chopped onion
1 cup vinegar	1 bay leaf
3 cups water	Salt, pepper to taste
2 parsley sprigs	

Wash the trout under running water. If desired, form each fish into a ring by tying the head to the tail with a strong thread. Bring the remaining ingredients to a boil in a kettle. Plunge in the trout and simmer 4 to 6 minutes, just long enough to cook. Drain well. Serve garnished with parsley and lemon wedges, if desired. Serves 4.

DANISH PLAICE GRATINÉ

In northern Europe a very popular fish is the plaice, flat, brown, and spotted, somewhat similar to the flounder. The Danes poach, fry, and grill the *Rodspaette* and serve it with sauces or cold with mayonnaise. In Copenhagen two good restaurants noted for their seafood, both facing the docks and located next to each other, are the Fiskehusets and Krogs Fiskerestaurant. Their plaice specialties are superb.

1 pound plaice or flounder fillets	3 whole peppercorns
2 lemon slices	Water
1 bay leaf	3 tablespoons butter
3 sprigs parsley	½ pound sliced fresh mushrooms

2 tablespoons flour
Salt, pepper, nutmeg to taste
¼ cup dry sherry

Fine dry bread crumbs
Grated Parmesan cheese

Put the fish fillets in a large saucepan. Add the lemon slices, bay leaf, parsley, and peppercorns. Pour in 2½ cups of water. Bring to a boil. Reduce the heat and cook slowly, covered, about 10 minutes, or until the fish is just tender. Remove them and keep warm. Strain the broth and reserve. Melt the butter in a saucepan and add the mushrooms. Sauté 4 minutes. Stir in the flour and cook for 1 minute. Gradually add 2 cups of the strained broth and cook slowly, stirring, until the sauce is thickened. Season with salt, pepper, and nutmeg. Stir in the sherry and remove from the heat. Put the cooked fish into a buttered baking dish. Spoon the mushroom sauce over them. Sprinkle the top generously with bread crumbs and cheese. Dot with butter. Cook in a preheated hot oven (425°F.) for about 12 minutes, or until the top is golden. Serves 4.

SHRIMP CROQUETTES FROM HOLLAND

In Holland the shrimp, or *garnalen,* are very tiny and thus very time-consuming to shell and clean. They are treasured, however, for their delicate flavor. This typical dish can be served as a luncheon or supper entrée.

3 tablespoons butter
¼ cup flour
1 cup light cream
Salt, pepper, freshly grated
  nutmeg to taste
2 eggs

2 cups chopped, cleaned,
  cooked small shrimp
2 tablespoons chopped fresh
  parsley
Juice of 1 lemon
Bread crumbs
Fat for deep frying

Melt the butter in a saucepan. Stir in the flour and cook 1 minute to form a *roux.* Gradually add the cream and cook slowly, stirring, until the sauce is smooth and thick. Season with salt, pepper, and nutmeg. Separate 1 egg. Beat the yolk with a fork and mix some of the hot sauce with it. Return to the sauce. Add the shrimp, parsley, and lemon juice. Mix well and take off the stove. Beat the egg white until stiff and fold carefully into the mixture. Spoon into a flat dish, spreading evenly, and cool. Divide the mixture into 12 equal parts. Form each into a 2-inch ball. Chill for 1 hour. Beat the remaining egg lightly. Roll each croquette in bread crumbs, then in beaten egg, and again in bread crumbs. Refrigerate for 1 hour. Fry in deep fat (390°F. on a thermometer) until golden. Drain and serve. Serves 4 to 6.

BELGIAN COQUILLES SAINT-JACQUES

In France there is a type of scallop called *coquille Saint-Jacques* and a well-known dish, made with the mollusks in a rich cream sauce, has been given the same name. This Belgian version includes champagne.

1 cup dry champagne
2 tablespoons minced shallots
  or green onions
3 sprigs parsley
1/8 teaspoon dried thyme
Salt, freshly ground pepper to
  taste
1 pound sea scallops, washed
  and diced
4 tablespoons butter

Juice of 1 lemon
1/2 pound fresh mushrooms,
  cleaned and sliced
Freshly grated nutmeg
2 tablespoons flour
1 cup heavy cream
1/3 cup buttered bread crumbs
2 tablespoons grated
  Parmesan cheese

Combine the champagne, shallots, parsley, thyme, salt, and pepper in a saucepan and bring to a boil. Add the scallops and lower the heat. Cook slowly, covered, until the scallops are tender, about 5 minutes. Remove from the stove and spoon out the scallops. Strain the liquid and set aside.

Melt 2 tablespoons of butter in a skillet. Add the lemon juice and mushrooms and sauté for 4 minutes. Season with nutmeg, salt, and pepper. Remove from the heat and spoon out the mushrooms, adding to the scallops. Add the drippings to the champagne broth and bring to a rapid boil. Cook until the liquid is reduced to 1 cup.

Melt 2 tablespoons of butter in a saucepan. Stir in the flour and cook 1 minute. Pour in the reduced liquid and cook slowly, stirring, until it is a thick and smooth sauce. Add the cream and bring to a boil. Remove at once from the heat. Add the scallops and mushrooms. Spoon into six individual shells (*coquilles*) or ramekins. Sprinkle with the buttered crumbs and grated cheese. Put under the broiler and leave about 5 minutes, or until bubbly and golden on top. Serves 6.

TUNA FISH, ITALIAN-STYLE

If fresh tuna steaks are not available, the piquant sauce may be served over heated canned tuna fish.

1 large onion, finely chopped
1 large garlic clove, crushed
2 tablespoons olive oil
3 large tomatoes, peeled and
   chopped
1 cup tomato juice
1 tablespoon fresh lemon juice

4 flat anchovies, chopped
½ teaspoon dried oregano or
   basil
Salt, pepper to taste
2 pounds fresh tuna steaks, cut
   into serving pieces

Sauté the onion and garlic in the oil in a large skillet until tender. Add the tomatoes and cook, stirring, for 5 minutes. Add the tomato and lemon juices, anchovies, oregano, salt, and pepper and cook slowly, uncovered, for 15 minutes. Put the tuna steaks over the sauce and cook slowly, covered, about 15 minutes, or until tender, the exact time depending on the thickness of the steaks. Serve with the sauce spooned over the tuna steaks. Serves 4 to 6.

SCOTCH TROUT FRIED IN OATMEAL

This is a favorite breakfast dish in Scotland.

Wash and dry a cleaned trout, allowing 1 per person. Dip each in milk and dredge on both sides with oatmeal. Season with salt and pepper. Fry quickly in heated lard or other fat until golden on both sides and the flesh is fork tender. Serve at once, garnished with a cube of butter and a lemon wedge.

VENETIAN SAUTÉED SCAMPI

One of the great gastronomic treats in Venice is to dine on *scampi*, which are something like shrimp but are distinctive and come only from the nearby Adriatic Sea. At the convivial Al Colombo *trattoria* I enjoyed a large plate of *scampi* that had simply been grilled. This is the best way to appreciate their delicate flavor. They are also made into good dishes such as this one.

¼ cup olive oil
2 garlic cloves, crushed or
  minced
½ cup minced green onions,
  with tops

2 pounds shelled and cleaned
  raw large shrimp
1 tablespoon drained capers
½ cup chopped fresh parsley
Salt, pepper to taste

Heat the oil in a large skillet. Add the garlic and green onions and sauté until tender. Add the shrimp and sauté until they become pink, a few minutes. Stir in the capers, parsley, salt, and pepper and cook gently for 5 minutes. Serves 4.

COSTA BRAVA ZARZUELA DE MARISCOS

The name of this dish is literally "musical comedy of shellfish" and is a specialty of the Catalan region of Spain. The selection of local denizens of the sea will vary but they will always be served in a rich flavorful sauce in which they slowly cook. A delightful locale to savor this dish is the lovely Costa Brava which has innumerable seaside restaurants featuring it.

2 pounds fish (halibut, bass,
  flounder), cut into chunks
2 small squid, cleaned and cut
  up

Flour
About ½ cup olive oil
2 dozen large shrimp, shelled
  and deveined

1 large onion, chopped
1 or 2 garlic cloves, minced
3 large tomatoes, peeled and
  chopped
1 bay leaf
Salt, pepper to taste

Dry white wine
1 canned pimiento, chopped
⅓ cup chopped fresh parsley
2 tablespoons brandy or
  Pernod

Dust the fish and squid with flour. Heat the oil in a kettle. Fry the seafood in it on both sides. Remove to a warm platter. Add the shrimp and sauté in the drippings until pink. Add more oil if necessary. Remove to a platter. Add the onion and garlic to the drippings and sauté until soft. Mix in the tomatoes and bay leaf and cook 2 minutes. Return the fish, squid, and shrimp to the kettle. Add the salt, pepper, and white wine to cover. Cook over a moderate fire about 10 minutes, until the ingredients are tender. Add the pimiento, parsley, and brandy. Cook another minute or so. Serves 4 to 6.

VIENNESE BAKED FISH WITH SOUR CREAM

As an inland country, Austria's primary sources of fish are the Danube River, mountain lakes, and streams, from which are taken a good supply of three favorite kinds— trout, carp, and pike. The latter, called *hecht*, is very often baked and flavored with sour cream. I recall eating a dish similar to this one in a small restaurant on a mountainside overlooking Innsbruck, the capital of the Tyrol and considered by many persons to be one of the world's most beautiful cities. The view was exhilarating and the fare inviting.

2 pounds pike or whitefish,
  cleaned and washed
3 tablespoons butter or
  margarine
2 medium onions, sliced
2 cups sour cream at room
  temperature

2 tablespoons drained capers
Salt, pepper to taste
2 tablespoons chopped fresh
  dill or parsley
1 lemon, sliced
Paprika

Leave the fish whole or cut into serving pieces. Place in a buttered shallow baking dish. Melt the butter in a skillet. Add the onions and sauté until tender. Add the sour cream, capers, salt, pepper, and dill and mix well. Spoon over the fish. Top with the lemon slices and sprinkle with paprika. Bake in a preheated moderate oven (350°F.) about 20 minutes, or until the fish is fork tender. Baste occasionally while cooking. Serves 4 to 6.

ENGLISH FISH AND CHIPS

There are certain foods and dishes that have such significance in certain countries that they cannot be referred to merely as national or favorite fare. Their importance extends to so many aspects of everyday living that they are more comparable to an institution. Such is the case with England's fish and chips.

"The Good Companions," as the late Sir Winston Churchill affectionately called fish and chips, have surpassed roast beef and Yorkshire pudding as the country's most popular gastronomic duet. Cooking and selling them is a sizable industry involving over 16,000 enterprises that utilize more than 300,000 tons of fish, 1 million tons of potatoes, and 80,000 tons of oils and fats annually. They are flown to Englishmen living abroad, and the craze has spread to other countries where businesses in "English Fish and Chips" have been springing up like mushrooms.

Profit-making aside, what is most important about these foods is that the English dearly love to go to a bar, shop, or restaurant, very often a family-run neighborhood establishment, to place an order for "fish 'n' chips," sprinkled with salt and malt vinegar and wrapped traditionally in a newspaper cornucopia. Workers and socialites, young and old, singles and couples can be observed at all hours of the day or night sauntering off nibbling the simple food, picked from the paper with the fingers.

So, what are fish and chips? Simply, they are strips of fish and potatoes fried in deep fat until golden and crisp. There are various stories of how these two foods were combined to make this popular combination. As early as the 1700s, probably because they were readily available and inexpensive, each was a favorite street snack, sold by vendors, generally women, and at shops. Some authorities point out that during the industrial revolution the two were offered together as easy and cheap hot meals for factory workers. However, Pierre Picton, author of *A Gourmet's Guide to Fish and Chips*, speculates about another idea. He suggests that perhaps "around 1855 there was a chipper run by a woman whose husband was a fishmonger, and suppose he had a load of cod waiting to be used before it went bad."

However the marriage of the fish and potatoes occurred, it is true that by far the favorite kind of fish used to make it is cod. Actually, any firm, white-fleshed fish will suffice, but in England certain areas and individuals have their favorites. Many an argument has taken place over the merits of hake, haddock, skate, plaice, halibut, whiting, sole, or rock salmon (another name for dogfish) as the best choice.

It is not difficult to start debates also over the selection of newspaper. The idea of the traditional wrapping is indeed as utilitarian as it is inexpensive—it keeps the food warm, soaks up the fat, provides a "napkin," and, if anyone wishes, serves as something to read. Some connoisseurs of fish and chips, perhaps with tongue in cheek but also with seriousness, claim that a particular newspaper imparts such a particular flavor to the fare that it can be detected. In the late 1960s, however, the Ministry of Health ruled that the newspaper wrapping is not hygienic and that a sterile white paper must enclose the food. So now the newspaper is placed outside the hygienic wrapper

The British not only eat fish and chips as street snacks but also pick them up, or send out for orders, to eat in the home. In recent years it has even become fashionable to serve these humble companions at aristocratic parties. Fish and chips are simple to prepare, delectable to savor, and fun to serve. This is one recipe for preparing them.

2 pounds white potatoes
2 pounds firm white-fleshed
  fish (cod, haddock, flounder,
  sole)
1 cup flour
Salt

1 egg beaten
⅓ cup milk
About ⅓ cup water
Shortening or vegetable oil
  for frying
Malt vinegar (optional)

Peel and slice the potatoes and cut into strips about 2½ inches long and 2 inches wide. Leave in cold water until ready to cook. Wash the fish and wipe completely dry. Cut into strips or pieces about 3 by 3 inches. Meanwhile, combine the flour, ½ teaspoon salt, the egg, milk, and water in a bowl, and mix with a whisk or fork until the batter is smooth. (The batter will be better if it remains at room temperature for 30 to 40 minutes.)

When ready to cook, heat the shortening or oil in a deep-fat fryer to a temperature of 375°F. on a frying thermometer. Wipe dry the potato strips and deep-fry them, several at a time, until golden and crisp. Drain on absorbent paper and keep warm in a preheated 250°F. oven. Dip the pieces of fish in the batter and fry them, several pieces at a time, in the hot fat until golden and crisp. Keep warm in the oven while cooking the other pieces. Serve the potatoes and fish together and pass salt and malt vinegar to be sprinkled over them. Serves 4.

NORWEGIAN FISKEPUDDING

A very special Norwegian dish, this delicate steamed fish pudding is eaten each week in most homes. It is always made with absolutely fresh fish, generally cod or haddock. The pudding may be served hot with a shrimp or lobster sauce or in cold slices on bread.

2 pounds fresh white-fleshed
  fish fillets (cod, halibut,
  flounder, sole)
2 teaspoons salt
3 tablespoons cornstarch
½ teaspoon ground mace or
  nutmeg

1½ cups light cream
½ cup milk
Butter
2 tablespoons fine dry bread
  crumbs

Wash, dry, and cut up the fillets. Put through a food chopper or meat grinder or whirl in a blender. Add the salt, cornstarch, and mace and put through either of the previously mentioned implements 3 more times. Turn into a large bowl. Gradually add the cream and milk, mixing vigorously after each addition, until the ingredients are well combined and do not separate.

Butter a loaf pan, 9¼ x 5¼ x 2¼ inches, or a mold, and sprinkle the bread crumbs over the surface, tilting to spread evenly. Cover the dish with aluminum foil and set it in a shallow pan or baking dish partially filled with hot water. Bake in a pre-heated moderate oven (350°F.) for about 50 minutes, until the pudding is set and a knife inserted into it comes out clean. Unmold onto a warm serving plate and serve hot with melted butter or with Shrimp Sauce (page 211). Serves 6.

This same mixture can be used to make another great Norwegian favorite, fish balls or *fiskefarse*. When the ingredients are mixed, spread in a flat dish and chill for 30 minutes to 1 hour. Shape into 1½-inch balls. Drop into lightly salted simmering water and cook about 20 minutes. Drain and serve with Shrimp Sauce (page 211).

PORTUGUESE COD WITH POTATOES AND ONIONS

This flavorful and attractive dish, *Bacalhau a "Gomes de Sa,"* is one of the many Portuguese combinations made with their favorite salted dried codfish. It could be served for a brunch or a buffet.

1 pound salted dried codfish
4 medium potatoes, peeled and
  cut into halves
½ cup olive oil
2 large onions, sliced thinly
1 or 2 garlic cloves, crushed

16 pitted black olives
Pepper to taste
4 hard-cooked eggs, shelled
  and sliced thickly
¼ cup chopped fresh parsley

Soak the codfish in cold water to cover overnight. Change the water 2 or more times. Drain the fish and put in a saucepan with fresh water to cover. Bring to a boil. Lower the heat and cook slowly, covered, until the fish is tender, about 12 minutes. Remove from the stove and, with a slotted spoon, take out the fish. Put the potatoes in the liquid in which the fish was cooked and cook, covered, until just tender, about 20 minutes. Drain, discarding the liquid. Cut the potatoes into cubes and flake the fish. Heat the oil in a large skillet and add the onions and garlic. Sauté until the onions are tender. Add the potatoes, fish, and

olives. Season with pepper. Mix well and cook, turning over
the ingredients now and then, until the combination is heated
through the golden. Serve on a platter garnished with the egg
sliced and parsley. Serves 4.

FISHERMEN'S MUSSEL STEW FROM BELGIUM

The Belgians are devotees of mussels, which they cook in
a number of interesting dishes such as this one, *matelote
de moules*.

4 dozen mussels in shells
2 medium onions, sliced thinly
1½ cups dry white wine or red
   wine
1 teaspoon sugar
1 bay leaf
½ teaspoon dried thyme
2 tablespoons chopped fresh
   parsley

Salt, pepper to taste
¼ pound fresh mushrooms,
   cleaned and quartered
¼ cup butter or margarine
Juice of ½ lemon
2 tablespoons flour
Toast triangles from 4 slices
   white bread

Scrub the mussels well and rinse one or more times under running water to remove all the dirt. Combine the mussels with
the onions, wine, sugar, bay leaf, thyme, parsley, salt, and
pepper in a large kettle. Cook over low heat, covered, until the
mussel shells open, about 10 minutes. Shake the kettle occasionally while cooking. Remove the mussels from the shells and cut
off the beards. Strain the mussel liquid and reserve.

Sauté the mushrooms in 2 tablespoons of butter and the lemon
juice in a skillet for 4 minutes and set aside. Melt the remaining
2 tablespoons of butter in a saucepan and stir in the flour to
form a *roux*. Add the strained liquid and cook slowly, stirring,
until the sauce is smooth. Add the cooked mussels and mushrooms and leave on the stove long enough to heat. Serve on toast
triangles. Serves 4 to 6.

6

Poultry and Game Birds

WESTERN EUROPEANS have long been ardent devotees of their great variety of poultry and game birds, which are still accorded places of honor on their dining tables. Fanciers of chicken, turkey, duck, goose, pheasant, partridge, woodcock, thrush, quail, or grouse, to name only a few, can discover a treasure trove of innovative dishes featuring them. Both domesticated and wild species are deeply respected and sought-after fare in all of the countries.

From ancient times poultry and game birds have had a very particular gastronomic status in Western Europe. Some were even worshiped. Others became important in folklore and literature. The early Romans, for example, considered geese sacred. Ducks were so revered that they were given a daily diet of figs and dates. Chicken and other fowl were especially fattened in the dark and "force fed" with grain to enlarge their livers.

Just about every available kind of poultry and bird was served at the lavish daily meals in a fascinating variety of preparations. In the cookbook of Apicius we find recipes for an intriguing number of sauces to adorn ostriches, cranes, ducks, partridges, turtledoves, wood pigeons, pigeons, hazel hens, flamingos, and geese. The selection of chicken concoctions ranged from one made with white sauce to another stuffed with a complicated spicy meat combination.

At the Roman banquets and for centuries thereafter, however, the most important bird was the peacock. During the Middle Ages every special occasion meal starred this prized food, and no dish was more handsomely and ceremoniously presented than the peacock. The bird, after being stuffed and cooked, was brought to the table in full plumage, with head and feet intact, and lighted spirits flaming from its beak. Magical powers were also assigned to the peacock. Knights, before setting out on daring missions, took an oath to the beautiful bird. "I vow to God, the Holy Virgin, Ladies, and the Peacock to accomplish my mission," was the solemn pledge of the warrior at a raucous farewell celebration.

We can acquire an idea of the popularity of poultry and game birds for European meals from a fourteenth-century verse discussing the "menu" of a holiday celebration. After mentioning "chickens grilled . . . quartered swans . . . wild fowl . . ." the anonymous author advised:

> Save a hen unto him that the house owneth;
> And ye will have basted birds broach'd on a spit,
> Barnacle-geese and bitterns, and many billed snipes,
> Larks and linnets, lapp'd in sugar,
> Woodcock and woodpeckers, full warm and hot.

For Catherine de' Medici's welcoming banquet given by the city of Paris in 1549, the guests dined on 30 peacocks, 33 pheasants, 21 swans, 9 cranes, 33 ducks, 33 ibises, 33 egrets, 33 young herons, 99 young pigeons, 99 turtledoves, 13 partridges, 33 goslings, 3 young bustards, 13 young capons, 90 quails, 66 boiling chickens, 66 Indian chickens, 30 capons, 90 spring chickens in vinegar, and 66 chickens "cooked as grouse."

As queen of France, however, Catherine did a great deal to advocate a more varied menu with less emphasis on the above-mentioned fare and more versatility and creativity in preparation. French chefs thereafter devised and inspired innumerable superb poultry and game-bird preparations that ranged from humble country kitchen casseroles to the most complex, elegant offerings.

Chicken gained considerable publicity when France's King Henry IV declared: "I want there to be no peasant in my kingdom so poor that he is unable to have a chicken in his pot every Sunday." The French would develop many fine preparations for *poulet au pot*, and every region has its own favorite version. Generally speaking, however, until the end of World War II chicken in France and other Continental countries was a special treat. Chickens were kept in the back yard or purchased at an open market and were often scrawny and tough. In recent years the bird has become more available, less expensive, and more flavorful. Now exceptionally interesting chicken preparations are popular in all the Continental cuisines.

A wild bird from the New World, the turkey, did not reach Europe until the sixteenth century, when Spanish conquistadors introduced it to the Mediterranean countries. The origin of its curious name is not certain. Some authorities claim that it was used because a similar bird had been brought to England from the Near Eastern country of the same name. In French it would become known as *dinde*, a name taken from *coq d'Inde* ("chicken from India"), as America was then known as the West Indies. No matter, the turkey was quickly accepted by the Europeans and paid a fine tribute by the French gastronome, Brillat Savarin, who wrote, "It is surely one of the prettiest presents the Old World has received from the New."

Western Europeans have always been partial to duck and geese. Both wild and domesticated ducks are prized as delicacies. The Danes stuff them with apples and/or prunes. In Germany and Austria they are cooked with red cabbage or sauerkraut. The Portuguese and Spanish make them into flavorful stews, whereas in France there is the famous *caneton à l'orange*, *caneton en salmis*, and *caneton à la bigarade*, always excellent in restaurants. The most famous *caneton* specialty is the pressed duck of Paris' La Tours d'Argent, which is presented with a number indicating how many have been served before it.

While duck is a favorite for some holidays, such as those in Scandinavia, the goose is a traditional food in several countries for the most important occasions. England long ago observed the autumn celebration of Michaelmas with the eating of a roast goose. stuffed with sage and onions, and, along with turkey, it has been featured on the Christmas dinner table. In Germany and Austria roast goose is a must for Christmas, and throughout northern Europe it is traditional for the feast of Martinmas. The liver of the goose provides the internationally famous French *pâté de foie gras*, and goose fat is used for cooking and is eaten as a spread on bread by many Europeans.

It is fortunate for devotees of wild game birds that in Western Europe there are still ample supplies of them that are available in season in the markets and made into excellent dishes at restaurants. Long ago the pursuit of feathered game became very important for everyday meals. Each head of the household understood the art of shooting particular local varieties and brought home considerable numbers for the housewife to prepare. Thus the skill of bagging them and the requisite culinary techniques were passed from one family to another. Small birds were made into savory combinations flavored with such seasonings as juniper, onion, leek, herbs, and wine.

Over the years, as available supplies began to dwindle, each country established stringent laws concerning the shooting of birds; these are rigidly maintained. But shooting as a sport continues throughout the Continent. One of the most sought-after birds is the delicious plump partridge, which was brought originally from Italy to France and thereafter to the rest of Europe. Long ago in the famous English carol, "The Twelve Days of Christmas," it was heralded as "the partridge in a pear tree." It also remains a gastronomic joy served in imaginative preparations. Another great bird, bagged in large numbers, is the pheasant, beautiful to regard and most flavorful to savor. It has long been sought after for the tables of nobility and is still a regal food, however offered.

For many gastronomes the greatest treasure of all the birds is the grouse. In northern Europe there are several species of grouse—the capercailzie or wood, ptarmigan or white, the black, and the red. Although all are appealing to eat, the most highly prized is the red grouse, called in Britain simply grouse or Scotch grouse, which is found on the moorlands of Scotland. Attempts to raise any of them on the Continent have failed. The first grouse that falls each year on August 12 heralds the opening of the British shooting season, and ardent guns come from around the world to bag them, a sport reserved for the privileged, well-heeled participants. These grouse have a particular gamy individual flavor achieved from dining on heather and are most often cooked stuffed with a handful of whortleberries or cranberries. As is also the case with pheasant, they are made into superb pies.

The British have traditionally favored pies made with game or birds such as pigeons or blackbirds. We all recall the nursery rhyme, "Four and Twenty Blackbirds, Baked in a Pie." Unfortunately, many of these Western European national favorites utilizing such Continental birds are not easy to duplicate elsewhere. Thus this collection of recipes includes dishes that can be easily prepared in American kitchens, with particular emphasis on poultry.

GERMAN BRAISED DUCK WITH RED CABBAGE

One of the great joys of dining in German restaurants is that most of them have a number of superb game-bird dishes on the menus. An excellent one is the Jagdschloss Kranichstein, a sixteenth-century hunting castle outside Darmstadt, a small city near Frankfurt. This is a typical German duck dish, which is most often prepared with a wild bird.

1 wild duck or duckling, about
    5 pounds, cut up
Salt, pepper to taste
1 medium head red cabbage,
    washed
⅓ cup lemon juice

¼ pound salt pork, diced
1 large onion, chopped
1 tablespoon flour
About ½ cup dry red wine
1 teaspoon sugar

Wash the duck or duckling and pat dry. Season with salt and pepper. Place in a shallow pan and roast in a preheated moderately hot oven (375°F.) for 30 minutes. Meanwhile, blanch the cabbage in boiling water. Drain. Remove center core and any wilted leaves. Sprinkle with lemon juice. Shred. Brown the salt pork in a large saucepan or kettle. Add the onions and sauté until tender. Mix in the flour. Add the cabbage, red wine, and sugar. Season with salt and pepper. Cook slowly, covered, for 30 minutes. Put the partially cooked duck pieces and some of the drippings from the pan over the cabbage. Continue to cook slowly, covered, for 1 hour, or until the duck is done. Add more red wine while cooking, if needed. Serves 4 to 6.

CIDER-FLAVORED CHICKEN FROM IRELAND

In an Irish cookbook this dish was called "Chicken Hibernia." Hibernia is the Latin name for Ireland.

1 frying chicken, about 3
  pounds, cut up
Salt, pepper
Flour
3 tablespoons butter or
  margarine
1 thin slice bacon, diced

1 medium leek, white part
  only, cleaned and chopped
1 cup sliced fresh mushrooms
1 cup heavy cream
½ cup apple cider
Watercress

Wash and pat dry the chicken. Pull off the skin and discard. Season with salt and pepper and coat with flour. Brown in butter on all sides over moderate heat in a large skillet or casserole. Remove with tongs and keep warm. Add the bacon and leeks to the drippings and cook until tender. Add the mushrooms and sauté 3 minutes. Return the chicken to the cooking dish and add the cream and cider. Cook over low heat, covered, about 35 minutes, or until the chicken is just tender. Check the seasoning. Serve with watercress. Serves 4.

SWEDISH CHICKEN SALAD

This piquant salad, called *hönssallad*, is a specialty of the cold table of *smörgåsbord*. It can be served also as a luncheon entrée.

3 cups diced cooked cold
  chicken
½ cup mayonnaise
¼ to ⅓ cup sour cream

2 to 3 teaspoons curry powder
Salt, pepper to taste
Lettuce leaves

Garnishes:

wedges of hard-cooked eggs, capers, olive slices, finely chopped dill pickle.

Combine the chicken with the mayonnaise, sour cream, and curry powder. Season with salt and pepper. Spoon onto lettuce leaves on a platter and serve decorated with the garnishes. Serves 6.

PARISIAN SUPRÊMES DE VOLAILLE

One of the glories of French cooking is a boneless raw breast of chicken, *suprême de volaille,* which is sautéed briefly in butter until just tender. It should be white and juicy and served with a rich cream sauce such as this one.

4 half chicken breasts	1½ cups sliced fresh
Salt, white pepper to taste	mushrooms
¼ cup fresh lemon juice	¼ cup chicken broth
¼ cup butter	¼ cup dry white wine
1 small onion, minced	1 cup heavy cream

Take off the skin from each chicken breast. Loosen the flesh from the bone of each. Pull out the bone and pieces of cartilage. Cut the meat away from the bone. Pull out the white tendons. Sprinkle the chicken with salt, pepper, and 1 tablespoon of lemon juice. Melt the butter in a skillet and sauté the chicken in it for 6 to 8 minutes, until white or, if pressed with the finger, it is soft but springy. Do not overcook. Remove from the heat and keep warm. Add the onion and mushrooms to the drippings and sauté for 4 minutes. Season with salt and pepper. Add the broth and wine and cook over high heat until syrupy. Stir in the cream and cook until the mixture thickens slightly. Season with salt and pepper and add the remaining lemon juice. Pour over the chicken and serve. Serves 4.

SMALL GAME BIRDS PORTUGUESA

In Portugal there is an abundance of wild birds, such as pheasant, partridges, quail, or woodcock, which provide inviting dishes for everyday meals. This is a typical manner of cooking them that can be also used for chicken.

4 small game birds or 4 pounds chicken pieces
2 large onions, chopped
1 or 2 large garlic cloves, minced
¼ pound lean ham or bacon, diced
2 medium carrots, scraped and diced
3 tablespoons olive oil
2 tablespoons fresh lemon juice
4 large tomatoes, peeled and chopped
⅓ cup fresh coriander or parsley
Salt, pepper to taste
About 1 cup dry red or white wine

Wash the birds or chicken and wipe dry. Combine the onions, garlic, ham, carrots, and oil in a large skillet or kettle. Sauté for 5 minutes. Add the lemon juice, tomatoes, coriander, salt, and pepper and cook slowly, uncovered, for 10 minutes. Place the birds or chicken over the sautéed mixture and pour in enough wine to cover them. Cook slowly, covered, until the ingredients are tender, about 35 minutes. Serves 4 to 6.

GERMAN ROAST GOOSE WITH SAUERKRAUT STUFFING

Favorite fare in northern European countries is flavorful roast goose, traditionally served on certain holidays, particularly Christmas. Although most common stuffings are made with chestnuts or a combination of dried fruit such as prunes with apples, this is an interesting variation.

1 fresh or frozen ready-to-cook goose, 8 to 10 pounds
Salt, pepper to taste
Juice of 1 lemon
1 large onion, finely chopped
2 pounds sauerkraut, drained
½ teaspoon crushed juniper berries or caraway seeds
½ cup dry white wine

Wash and wipe dry the goose. Remove any fat from the cavity and reserve. Rub inside and out with salt and pepper. Prick the skin in several places and rub with lemon juice. Sauté the onion in 2 tablespoons of the goose fat in a saucepan until tender. Add the sauerkraut and sauté 1 minute. Add the juniper berries or caraway seeds and wine. Season with salt and pepper. Bring to a boil and remove from the heat. Stuff lightly into the goose. Close the cavity. Place in a roasting pan and roast, uncovered, in a preheated slow oven (325°F.) for 3 hours or longer, until tender. Spoon off the fat as it accumulates in the pan. Serves 6 to 8.

If any of the stuffing is left over, heat and serve with the goose.

POULET MARENGO

After Napoleon defeated the Austrians in a battle at Marengo in Italy's Piedmont region in 1800, he asked his chef to create a special dish. Since they were away from the supply wagons, it was necessary to hunt for provisions from the ravaged countryside. According to the story, the scouts found a scrawny chicken, three eggs, four tomatoes, six crayfish, and some seasonings. Napoleon was delighted with the dish that was invented with these foods. Mushrooms and wine were later additions.

2 frying chickens, about 2½
  pounds each, cut up
Salt, pepper to taste
6 tablespoons olive oil
3 tablespoons butter
1 pound medium fresh
  mushrooms, cleaned
2 garlic cloves
1 cup chopped onions

⅓ cup tomato purée
1 cup dry white wine
4 medium tomatoes, peeled,
  seeded, chopped
1 *bouquet garni* (bay leaf,
  parsley, thyme tied together
  in a small muslin or
  cheesecloth bag)

Garnishes:

8 eggs, deep-fried in olive oil; 4 slices French bread, fried in oil and cut into triangles; 16 cooked, shelled, deveined, large shrimp

Wash the chicken and pat dry. Season with salt and pepper. Heat the oil and butter in a large heavy casserole or skillet. Add the chicken pieces and fry until golden brown on all sides. Remove to a warm platter. Carefully pull the stems from half the mushrooms. Reserve the caps. Slice the stems and the other ½ pound of mushrooms. Sauté in the drippings for 4 minutes. With a slotted spoon, remove to a plate. Add the garlic and onions to the drippings and sauté until tender. Stir in the tomato purée and wine. Bring to a boil. Cook over high heat for 5 minutes. Return the chicken pieces to the kettle. Add the tomatoes, *bouquet garni,* and season with salt and pepper. Cook slowly, covered, for about 35 minutes, until the chicken is tender. Add the reserved sautéed sliced mushrooms and mushroom caps 10 minutes before the cooking is finished. Remove and discard the *bouquet garni.* To serve, arrange the chicken pieces on a large platter. Spoon the sauce, including the sliced mushrooms, over them. Arrange the fried eggs, each on a toast triangle, and the shrimp around the chicken. Serves 8.

NORTHERN SCANDINAVIAN PTARMIGAN

A highly esteemed wild bird in northern Scandinavia and Scotland is the ptarmigan, a member of the grouse family. The two most common kinds are known as the willow and the rock, and both have strong-flavored flesh that the Scandinavians prefer to serve with a tart sauce made with lingonberries or red currant jelly. Grouse may be used as a substitute.

4 ptarmigan or grouse, dressed	Salt, pepper to taste
4 thin slices bacon	2 tablespoons flour
⅓ to ½ cup butter or	1½ cups light cream
margarine	3 or 4 tablespoons red currant
1½ cups broth or stock	jelly

Wash and pat dry the birds. Wrap a slice of bacon around each ptarmigan and secure with a toothpick. Fry in butter in a large skillet. Add the broth and season with salt and pepper. Cook slowly, covered, until tender, about 30 minutes; the exact time depends on the age of the birds. Remove the ptarmigans to a warm platter and keep warm. Scrape the drippings. Add the flour and mix well. Pour in the cream and cook over high heat, stirring, until the mixture is smooth and thickened. Stir in the jelly and season with salt and pepper. Cut the birds into halves and pour some of the sauce over them. Serve the rest of it in a gravy boat or bowl. Serves 4.

DUCKLING WITH OLIVES FROM SPAIN

Two of Spain's favorite foods, duckling and olives, are combined in this dish. Traditionally, however, it would be prepared with wild duck.

1 duckling, 4 to 5 pounds, cut up
1 tablespoon olive oil
2 large onions, sliced thinly
3 medium carrots, scraped and sliced thinly
1 can (8 ounces) tomato sauce

About 1 cup dry red or white wine
2 tablespoons chopped fresh parsley
Salt, pepper to taste
12 large pitted green olives

Wash the duckling and pat dry. Heat the oil in a large skillet or heavy casserole and brown the duckling in it. Cook over moderate heat, covered, for 30 minutes. Remove the duckling and pour off all the fat except 3 tablespoons of it. Add the onions and carrots and sauté for 5 minutes. Return the duckling to the cooking dish and add the remaining ingredients, except the olives. Cook slowly, covered, about 1 hour, or until the duckling is tender. Add more wine while cooking, if needed. Stir in the olives just before serving. Serves 4 to 6.

POULET EN COCOTTE

One of the best French methods of preparing poultry is to cook it in a tightly closed casserole on top of the stove or in the oven, as the flavor is enhanced by the slow steaming process. This is an excellent one-dish meal.

1 roasting chicken, about 3½
  pounds
Salt, pepper to taste
4 sprigs fresh tarragon or ½
  teaspoon dried tarragon
About 3 tablespoons butter or
  margarine
About 2 tablespoons olive oil
18 small white onions, peeled
½ cup tomato sauce

1 *bouquet garni* (parsley,
  thyme, bay leaf tied together
  in a small muslin or
  cheesecloth bag)
Salt, pepper to taste
16 small new potatoes, peeled
1 pound medium fresh
  mushrooms, cleaned
1 package (9 ounces) frozen
  artichoke hearts, defrosted

Wash the chicken and pat dry. Season inside and out with salt and pepper. Put the tarragon in the cavity. Truss the chicken. Heat the butter and oil in a heavy casserole. Add the chicken and brown on all sides, turning carefully with two spoons so the skin is not broken. Remove to a platter or pan. Add the onions to the drippings and more butter, if needed, and sauté them about 5 minutes, until translucent. Stir in the tomato sauce. Return the chicken to the casserole and add the *bouquet garni*. Season with salt and pepper. Cook on the top of the stove, tightly covered, for about 1 hour, or put in a preheated slow oven (325°F.) and cook about 1½ hours, or until the chicken is just tender. Add the vegetables after the dish has been cooking for 30 minutes. Take off the heat or out of the oven. Take out and cut up the chicken. Serve surrounded with the vegetables. Serves 4.

GERMAN HASENPFEFFER

Rabbit is not actually poultry or a game bird but I've included it in this chapter because it can be prepared in many ways that chicken is.

This flavorful well-known German specialty, which means "hare pepper," is made also with rabbit, which can be purchased frozen in our supermarkets. Chicken could be used as a substitute.

2 fresh or frozen rabbits (2½
  to 3 pounds each), cut into
  serving pieces

Equal parts of wine vinegar
  and water to cover the rabbit
  pieces

2 medium onions, sliced
2 medium bay leaves
4 juniper berries
4 whole cloves
2 tablespoons sugar
6 peppercorns, bruised

Salt
Flour
Pepper
Butter or margarine
½ cup sour cream, at room
  temperature

Put the rabbit pieces in a large crock or kettle and add the vinegar, water, onions, bay leaves, juniper berries, cloves, sugar, peppercorns, and salt. Let stand, covered in a cool place for 2 days. Turn over the rabbit pieces 1 or 2 times daily. When the marinating is finished, take out the rabbit and strain the marinade, reserving it. Wipe dry the rabbit and dust with flour, seasoned with salt and pepper. Fry in butter until golden on all sides. Add some of the strained marinade and cook very slowly, covered, until the rabbit is tender, about 1 hour. Add more marinade as needed while cooking. Mix in the sour cream and remove from the stove. Serves 6 to 8.

CHICKEN SAUTÉ À LA BORDELAISE

The sauce in this dish takes its name from the magnificent port city of Bordeaux in southwestern France, famous for its splendid heritage, architecture, theater, wines, and cookery. Bordeaux is truly one of the country's leading gastronomic capitals and many of its superb dishes include one of the fine wines from the nearby vineyards.

1 frying chicken, 2½ to 3
  pounds, cut up
About 2 tablespoons butter
About 1 tablespoon olive oil
Salt, pepper to taste
1 tablespoon minced shallots
  or green onions

1 large garlic clove, crushed
  and minced
⅓ cup tomato sauce
1 cup dry red wine
2 tablespoons chopped fresh
  herbs (parsley, tarragon,
  basil)

Wash the chicken and wipe dry. Heat the butter and oil in a large skillet or heavy casserole until foaming. Add the chicken pieces, a few at a time, and brown until golden over moderate heat on all sides, turning carefully with tongs. Season with salt and pepper. Cook slowly, covered, about 25 minutes or until just tender. Check while cooking to see if more butter and oil are needed and turn over occasionally. Take out the chicken and keep warm. Spoon off all the butter and oil except 3 tablespoons of it. Add the shallots and garlic and sauté for 1 minute. Stir in the tomato sauce and then add the wine. Bring to a boil and cook a few minutes to reduce. Stir in the herbs and season with salt and pepper. Serve with the sautéed chicken. Serves 4.

VIENNESE FRIED CHICKEN

One of the appealing specialties available in all the local restaurants in Vienna is the tender fried chicken called *Backhende*. It is always served immediately after frying.

2 frying chickens (about 2½ pounds each), cut up	Fine dry bread crumbs
Salt	Lard or other fat
Flour	Chicken liver, gizzard, and
2 or 3 eggs, beaten	heart (optional)
	Lemon wedges

Wash the chicken and pat dry. Sprinkle with salt. Dredge with flour and dip in beaten egg. Roll in bread crumbs. Shake to remove any excess crumbs. Fry in hot lard or fat over a fairly high flame until golden on one side. Turn over and fry on the other side. Reduce the heat and fry uncovered about 15 minutes on each side. When done, remove with tongs and keep warm in a preheated 250°F. oven. If the liver, gizzard, and heart are to be used, dip them in flour, egg, and bread crumbs and fry also in hot lard until brown, a few minutes. Serve with lemon wedges. Serves 6 to 8.

ITALIAN CHICKEN BREASTS
WITH HAM AND CHEESE

This specialty, *petti di pollo alla bolognese,* is a superb example of the Italian deftness in creating some of the world's most imaginative chicken creations. The dish is easy to prepare yet a praiseworthy entrée.

4 single chicken breasts
Salt, pepper to taste
Flour
5 tablespoons butter
4 thin slices of cooked ham

½ pound sliced fresh
  mushrooms
4 tablespoons grated
  Parmesan cheese

Take off the skin from each chicken breast and remove the flesh from the bone with the tip of a sharp knife. Pull out the white tendons. Sprinkle with salt and pepper and coat with flour. Heat 2 tablespoons of butter in a skillet and sauté the chicken in it, about 5 minutes on each side. Remove to a shallow baking dish and top each with a slice of ham cut to be about the same size as the chicken. Sauté mushrooms in remaining 3 tablespoons butter for 3 minutes and arrange, dividing evenly, over the ham. Sprinkle 1 tablespoon of cheese over the top of each of the chicken breasts and dot with butter. Cover the pan and cook just until the cheese melts. Serves 4.

COQ AU VIN

This famous French dish, chicken cooked in wine, is a very old one originally thickened with the blood of the chicken. The modern version is a marvelous entrée when entertaining as it can be prepared beforehand and is attractive to serve.

1 frying chicken, about 3
  pounds, cut up
Salt, pepper to taste
5 tablespoons butter
About 2 tablespoons olive oil
1 small piece lean bacon, diced
1½ pounds small white onions,
  peeled
¾ pound medium fresh
  mushrooms

¼ cup brandy
2 cups dry red wine
¼ teaspoon dried thyme
1 medium bay leaf
2 sprigs parsley
2 medium garlic cloves,
  crushed
2 tablespoons flour
3 tablespoons chopped fresh
  parsley

Wash the chicken and pat dry. Season with salt and pepper. Heat 3 tablespoons of the butter, the oil, and the bacon in a large kettle or casserole. Add the onions and sauté about 10 minutes, depending on their size, a little less if very small. With a slotted spoon, take out the onions and set aside. Add the mushrooms to the drippings and sauté 5 minutes, adding more oil if needed. Remove and set aside. Add the chicken pieces to the drippings and fry until golden on all sides. Pour in the brandy and ignite it. Let burn, shaking the pan, until the flames subside. Return the onions to the kettle. Add the wine, thyme, bay leaf, parsley, and garlic. Season with salt and pepper. Bring to a boil. Lower the heat and cook slowly, covered, about 30 minutes, or until the chicken is tender. Add the mushrooms during the last 5 minutes of cooking. Blend together 2 tablespoons of softened butter and the flour. Shape into tiny balls and add to the liquid; stir with a whisk until well blended. Arrange the chicken, onions, and mushrooms on a platter. Cover with the sauce. Garnish with the parsley. Serves 4 to 6.

SPANISH POLLO A LA CHILINDRÓN

In Spain dishes that are cooked in a flavorful sauce made with onions, garlic, tomatoes, ham, and peppers are called *chilindrón*. This type of cookery is native to the region of Aragon in northeastern Spain.

1 frying chicken, 3 to 3½ pounds, cut up
Salt, pepper to taste
⅓ cup olive oil
1 large onion, sliced
1 garlic clove, crushed

3 small hot red or green peppers, seeded and minced
¼ pound smoked ham, diced
4 large tomatoes, peeled and chopped
2 canned pimientos, chopped
12 pitted black olives

Wash and pat dry the chicken pieces. Season with salt and pepper. Fry in the heated oil in a skillet over moderate heat until golden on all sides. Remove to a plate. Put the onion, garlic, peppers, and ham in the drippings and sauté them for 5 minutes. Add the tomatoes and pimientos and cook over medium heat for 5 minutes. Return the chicken pieces to the kettle. Cook over very low heat, tightly covered, for about 30 minutes or until tender. Add a little water while cooking, if needed. Stir in the olives just before serving. Serves 4 to 6.

DANISH BRAISED CHICKEN WITH PARSLEY

In Copenhagen one of the most inviting places to dine is in any of the lovely restaurants of the gay Tivoli Gardens, one of the world's most wonderful amusement parks in the heart of the city, with every conceivable enticing entertainment. This typical chicken dish is one of the delights to order.

1 roasting chicken, about 4
  pounds
Salt, pepper
½ cup butter

1 large bunch parsley with
  stems removed
1 cup heavy cream
2 tablespoons flour

Wash and pat dry the chicken. Sprinkle on the inside and out with salt and pepper. Put ¼ cup of butter and the parsley in the cavity of the chicken. Melt ¼ cup of butter in a large casserole or kettle and add the chicken. Braise on all sides over moderate heat until golden, turning caerfully with 2 large wooden spoons so the skin will not be pierced. Pour in a little water and cook slowly, covered, for 45 minutes to 1 hour, until tender, turning over once while cooking. When done, remove the chicken to a warm platter and keep warm. Add the cream to the juices, and after scraping up the drippings, quickly bring to a boil. Mix the flour with a little water and stir into the cream. Cook over high heat, stirring, until smooth. Season with salt and pepper. Take the parsley from the chicken cavity and serve it with the chicken. Serve the gravy separately in a gravy boat or bowl. Serves 4 to 6.

SWISS CHICKEN AND MUSHROOM VOL-AU-VENT

The cuisine of western Switzerland has definite culinary similarities to that of its neighbor, France. The menus of many of the great restaurants of Geneva include a number of French specialties, including *vol-au-vent,* which I once enjoyed filled with a rich combination of chicken and morels in a wine sauce. This is an adaptation of the dish. In French *vol-au-vent* means "flying in the wind," the term probably referring to the lightness of the pastry made from puff paste.

1 tablespoon minced shallots
  or green onions
½ pound fresh mushrooms,
  cleaned and sliced thinly
¼ cup butter
1 tablespoon fresh lemon juice
3 tablespoons flour
Salt, pepper to taste

2½ cups light cream
½ cup dry white wine
3 cups diced cooked chicken
2 egg yolks
¼ cup grated Gruyére or
  Parmesan cheese
6 warm patty shells

Sauté the shallots and mushrooms in the butter and lemon juice for 4 minutes. Stir in the flour and season with salt and pepper. Cook several seconds. Gradually add the cream and cook slowly, stirring, until thickened. Add the wine and chicken and leave over low heat long enough to heat through. Spoon some of the hot mixture into a small bowl to mix with the egg yolks. Stir well and return to the chicken mixture. Add the cheese and cook over low heat, stirring, until the cheese melts. Spoon into and around the patty shells, dividing evenly. Serves 6.

ENGLISH ROAST TURKEY WITH SAUSAGE STUFFING

The traditional Christmas bird in England has long been the goose, but in recent years turkey has been gracing more and more holiday tables. The two most popular stuffings for the turkey are made with chestnuts or sausage.

1 turkey, about 12 pounds
Salt
1 pound sausage meat
1½ cups chopped celery
1½ cups chopped onion

2 cups chopped fresh parsley
2 quarts soft stale bread
  cubes
Pepper
Butter

Wash the turkey and wipe dry; sprinkle the cavities lightly with salt. Set aside. Fry the sausage in a skillet until all the redness disappears. Separate with a fork. Pour off the fat, reserving ⅓ cup of it. Put the sausage in a large bowl and, if necessary, separate again with a fork. Add the celery, onion, parsley, and bread cubes. Mix well and season with salt and pepper. Add the reserved sausage fat and mix again. Spoon the stuffing into the cavities and fasten with skewers or sew. Fold the wings under the back; tie the legs. Place, breast side up, in a roasting pan and rub lightly with butter. Cover with foil. Roast in a slow oven (325°F.) for 3 hours or longer, until the turkey is cooked. Baste occasionally with the drippings. Remove the foil during the last 30 minutes of cooking. Cut and discard the string. Let rest 30 minutes before carving. Serves about 12.

If there is any leftover stuffing put it in a shallow baking dish and cook in a moderate oven (350°F.).

POLLO ALLA CACCIATORA

Italian chicken "hunter's style" is a flavorful and attractive creation cooked in a colorful sauce made of a medley of ingredients.

1 frying chicken (about 3 pounds), cut up
3 tablespoons olive oil
2 tablespoons butter
2 medium onions, sliced
1 or 2 garlic cloves, crushed
4 medium tomatoes, peeled, seeded and chopped
1 can (8 ounces) tomato sauce
½ cup dry white wine
2 tablespoons chopped fresh parsley
½ teaspoon dried basil
Salt, pepper to taste

Wash the chicken pieces and pat dry. Heat the oil and butter in a large skillet and brown the chicken on all sides. Remove and keep warm. Add the onions and garlic to the drippings and cook until tender. Add the remaining ingredients and cook slowly, uncovered, for 10 minutes. Return the chicken pieces to the skillet and cook slowly, covered, about 30 minutes, or until the chicken is just tender. Serves 4 to 6.

AUSTRIAN CHICKEN PAPRIKA

Paprikahühn, chicken pieces with a paprika sauce, is a dish I recall from the colorful restaurant Bosnia in Vienna that specializes in Balkan dishes. It is popular throughout Austria.

2 frying chickens, about 2½ pounds each, cut up
Salt, pepper to taste
About ⅓ cup butter or margarine
2 medium onions, chopped
1 to 2 tablespoons paprika

2 medium tomatoes, peeled and chopped (optional)
About 1 cup chicken broth
2 tablespoons flour
2 cups sour cream at room temperature
3 tablespoons chopped fresh parsley

Wash and pat dry the chicken. Season with salt and pepper. Heat the butter in a large skillet and brown the chicken in it on both sides, over moderate heat, until golden. With tongs remove and keep warm. Add the onions to the drippings and more butter, if needed. Sauté until tender. Stir in the paprika and cook 1 minute. Add the tomatoes, chicken broth, and chicken pieces. Cook slowly, covered, until the chicken is tender, about 35 minutes. Add more broth while cooking, if needed. Take out the chicken with tongs and keep warm. Scrape the drippings and stir in the flour. Gradually add the sour cream and cook, stirring, until thickened and smooth. Spoon the sauce over the chicken. Sprinkle with the parsley. Serve with dumplings or noodles. Serves 6 to 8.

BELGIAN JUGGED HARE WITH PRUNES

The word "jugged" is used for dishes that are marinated or cooked in a jug, crock, or large dish. In Belgium the strong-flavored hare, the cousin of the rabbit, is tenderized by leaving it in a flavorful marinade for two or more days. Hare is not available in America, but rabbit can be used as a substitute.

1 hare or rabbit, about
  3 pounds, cut up
Red wine
Wine vinegar
1 bay leaf
½ teaspoon dried thyme

4 peppercorns, bruised
Salt
3 tablespoons butter
2 tablespoons flour
2 cups pitted prunes,
  previously soaked in cold water

Put the hare or rabbit pieces in a large bowl, crock, or kettle and cover with a liquid combination of ⅔ red wine and ⅓ wine vinegar. Add the bay leaf, thyme, peppercorns, and salt and leave to marinate for 2 days. Turn over the pieces once or twice each day. Remove the hare and wipe dry. Strain the marinade and reserve. Brown the hare on both sides in the butter in a large skillet or casserole. Mix in the flour and then add the marinade. Bring slowly to a boil, stirring, and then cook slowly, covered, until the hare is tender, about 1 hour, depending on the size. Add more red wine while cooking, if needed. Add the prunes 20 minutes before the cooking is finished. Serves 4.

POULET VALLÉE D'AUGE

This dish, called also *poulet à la crème*, derives from the valley of Auge in France's northwestern region of Normandy. This is the heart of the great cider and Calvados (apple brandy) country where fruit production is very important and the apples are rated highly. Characteristic dishes of Normandy are rich with butter and cream and flavored with cider or Calvados. American applejack can be used as a substitute for the Calvados. The dish may be prepared with a cut-up chicken or, as in this recipe, with chicken breasts.

6 single chicken breasts
Salt, pepper to taste
⅓ cup butter
⅓ cup Calvados or applejack
2 tablespoons finely chopped
  shallots or green onions
½ teaspoon dried thyme

2 tablespoons chopped fresh
  parsley
About ½ cup chicken broth or
  dry white wine
2 egg yolks
1 cup heavy cream

Wash and pat dry the chicken breasts. Season with salt and pepper. Brown on both sides in the butter in a heavy skillet. Add the Calvados and ignite it with a match. When the flames subside add the shallots, thyme, and parsley and mix well. Add the broth or wine and cook slowly, covered, about 25 minutes, or until the chicken is just tender, adding more broth or wine while cooking, if needed. Remove the chicken to a warm platter and keep warm. Scrape the drippings and bring the juices to a boil. Combine the egg yolks and cream in a bowl and stir with a whisk until smooth. Pour in some of the hot juices and mix well. Return to the skillet and cook over low heat, stirring until the sauce begins to thicken. Correct the seasoning. Spoon over the chicken. Serve garnished with parsley. Serves 6.

7

Meats

IT IS EXCEEDINGLY DIFFICULT to deal with the marvelous meat creations of Western Europe in one chapter as the subject could easily fill a lengthy encyclopedia. The diverse selection of excellent and innovative national favorites made with pork, veal, lamb, beef, and variety meats is particularly noteworthy for its endless appeal to all tastes. Meat in one form or another is the cornerstone of each country's cookery.

Western Europeans have been dedicated meat eaters since earliest times, and have been ingenious in using not only the flesh but all parts of animals, together with other compatible ingredients, in the creation of distinctive national dishes.

We have only to look at the menus of the ancient Romans to discover what could be done even so long ago with whole or cut-up carcasses, their innards, feet, and even udders. Some animals were roasted over open fires; others were cooked in cauldrons, made into fricassees, stews, and ragouts, braised in frying pans, or baked in ovens. Banquets included a fascinating variety of sausages, meat loaves, and meatballs, as well as such dishes as spice and honey-flavored pork with apricots, ham cooked with dried figs and served with wine sauce, roast meat with dill sauce, pine-nut–herb-stuffed kidneys, and suckling pigs filled with "fig-peckers, oysters and thrushes."

The Romans were the first to pay carving experts handsome salaries for their services. Such was the preoccupation with meats that Emperor Claudius is said to have astonished the Senate by asking: "Tell me, would it be possible to live without salt pork?" To appease the ruler, they officially declared that it would not. On another occasion, while presiding at the Tribunal, the Emperor interrupted the proceedings to state: "How wonderful are meat pies. We shall have them for dinner." Presumably they did.

Perhaps the Romans introduced some of their exotic meat dishes to other Europeans; however, after the fall of the Empire, the diet was far more meager. During the Dark Ages, poor folk subsisted on what they could find by foraging, and meat was a luxury for them. Feudal estates, however, gradually became well stocked with swine and herds of cattle, and there were always wild animals in the surrounding forests. Banquets were lengthy feasts of great haunches of meat that had been roasted over open fires or on spits in fireplaces. Eating them was done with knives and the fingers.

The Romans introduced to the other Europeans the art of flavoring and preserving meats, and this became very important. Sometimes the fare was so "high" that the undesirable flavor had to be camouflaged with pepper, cinnamon, cloves, nutmeg, or other aromatics. More importantly, the meat slaughtered in the fall had to be cured to keep for several months. Thus, Western Europeans became experts in several processes of preserving meats; and sausage, bacon, and ham, among other meats, were most important to the various diets and were eaten in considerable quantity. Among the hams still rated as great culinary treasures are Italy's prosciutto, Switzerland's *Bundnerfleisch*, Belgium's Ardennes ham, England's York ham, France's *jambon de Bayonne*, and Spain's Asturias ham.

The cookery of meats began to improve in some parts of Europe, particularly in France, during the fourteenth century. The noted French chef Taillevent gave instructions for making several superb meat dishes, including inviting stews and ragouts, in his 1375 cookbook, *Le Viandier*. Thereafter, chefs strove to dispense with the excessive and heavy seasonings of medieval days and devised dishes that enhanced the natural flavor of the particular foods and provided more variety in the menu.

One can get some notion of the diversity of Western European meat creations from the story of a popular dish offered in the first Parisian restaurant. In 1765 one Boulanger opened an establishment that sold soups, advertised as restoratives. Wishing to expand his menu, the owner faced difficulty, as the laws of the time prohibited the selling of meat in less than whole cuts, thus protecting the monopoly of the *traiteurs*, a sort of union of food dealers. The dish he wished to sell was sheep's feet in a white sauce, and he went to court to win his right to do so. Because of the widely advertised lawsuit, the dish became the rage of Paris and his business prospered.

Over the years the most favored meat in Western Europe has been pork, both fresh and cured. Since everything but "the oink" was edible and made into one creation or another, pork very often provided the main meat supply in a large part of Western Europe. European pigs were crossbred with those of China during the Middle Ages, and the flesh of the animal was greatly improved. Pig-killing time in November and the processing of the various parts became an important and festive annual event. Such was the demand for the meat that the trade of slaughtering, butchering, and selling the various cuts flourished. Every small town still has one or more shops well stocked with ample supplies of the local varieties. A *charcuterie* in France, for example, has such an unbelievable array of pork products that it takes a well versed buyer to choose among them.

Great and interesting pork dishes are found in all the cuisines of Europe. In Denmark, the pig is a treasured national symbol, and Danes proudly point out that their country has three times as many hogs as people. Pork is the national meat and is valued also as the Danish primary export. In Germany, too, the most widely used of all meats is pork, and there are a great number of good recipes for cooking both the fresh and cured products. Pork is greatly adored in Spain, and one of the finest dishes to enjoy there is suckling pig. At the lovely restaurant Casa Candido in Segovia, with a spectacular view of an ancient Roman aqueduct, the crisp roast suckling pig is so tender that the waiter cuts it with a plate.

Although beef appears frequently and in great variety on all the menus in Western Europe, it is the preferred meat in only one country—England. Over the years, some of the world's finest cattle were raised on the Island. England became known as a "nation of Beefeaters," and the English are justifiably proud of

their great roasts and joints of beef. A cherished national dish
and favorite Sunday dinner is roast beef served with Yorkshire
pudding and roast potatoes and accompanied by mustard and
freshly grated horseradish. The English also have superb beef
pies and puddings made with flaky pastry enclosing the meat
and a thick broth.

Unlike their neighbors across the Channel, the French are
not fond of large beef roasts but prefer to braise the meat in
the oven or on top of the stove. One of their great dishes is
boeuf à la mode, which is served garnished with vegetables. The
French and American methods for cutting meat differ remarkably, so it is often difficult to understand the various items in a
shop or on a menu. As one example, French steaks are of four
cuts from the tenderloin—*Châteaubriand, filet, tournedos,* and
filet mignon.

Throughout Western Europe there are great beef dishes, such
as the thick rich stews of the northern countries, and meatball
and meat loaf variations, which utilize cuts other than roasts
and steaks. A particular specialty in Austria is boiled beef. Despite the popularity of beef, a meat that is much preferred in
such countries as Italy, France, Switzerland, Germany, and Austria is the tender veal, always a superlative treat, and made
into some of the Continent's most imaginative and luxurious
creations. These range from the humble *osso buco* of Italy to
the noble *blanquette de veau* of France.

Herds of sheep or lamb are a common sight in the southern
European countries, and the dishes made with them are imaginative and delicious. Tiny baby lamb, sometimes called spring
lamb, is a delightful Italian Easter specialty, flavored traditionally with anchovies and rosemary. In Provence there are a
number of roast *gigot* variations and superb flavorful stews. A
specialty at Madrid's Casa Botin is tiny roast lamb, *cordero
asado,* well flavored with aromatic herbs.

Lamb is also important to the cuisines of Great Britain and
Scandinavia. The English raise superb lamb, including the
Down, which is bred on hills and downs and thus acquires a
good salt and aromatic herb diet. There are excellent lamb
crowns, saddles, and chops that are always esteemed fare. Other
cuts are used to make such famous dishes as shepherd's pie,
Lancashire hot pot, and Irish stew. The Scots also prepare mutton pies and use the meat innards to make their famous *haggis.*
In Norway and Sweden there are numerous good mutton- or

lamb-and-vegetable combinations, and the Finns have a favorite hot pot that includes lamb, as well as veal and pork.

Special mention must be made of such Continental favorites as tripe, brains, kidneys, sweetbreads, tongue, and liver, which are highly esteemed delicacies, often preferred to other cuts. Since these are, unfortunately, often shunned by Americans, not much space is allotted to recipes for them.

The meat of wild animals has long been important to the cuisines of Western Europe and is still relished in many homes and restaurants. In Norway and Sweden reindeer is a common food. Central Europeans are fond of venison, and in southern locales boar meat is sought after. Because these meats are not commonly available in America, recipes are not given for their preparation.

Included here is a selection from the Western European culinary repertoire that reflects the fascinating diversity of these delectable dishes.

SAUERBRATEN OF GERMANY

The best known of all the German meat dishes, *Sauerbraten* ("sour pot roast"), bears a misleading name. For although the meat is marinated in a tart liquid, the resulting richly flavored dish is a pleasure to savor. In Germany there are many recipes for preparing *Sauerbraten*, some of which differ according to their region of origin. Northern Germans, for example, marinate the meat in buttermilk, which gives a unique and pleasing flavor. In olden times it was necessary to leave the tough meat, either oxen or beef, in the marinade for several days in order to tenderize it. Nowadays, with excellent pot roast meat available, it is not necessary to marinate the meat so long. According to the grade of meat selected, the marination can vary from 24 to 72 hours. Gingersnap crumbs are used as a substitute for the German honey cake or cookies.

4- to 5-pound boneless beef roast (bottom round, rump, or chuck), trimmed of fat

1 cup dry red wine
1 cup red wine vinegar
2 cups cold water

1 large onion, peeled and
  thinly sliced
1 medium bay leaf
8 peppercorns, bruised
4 whole cloves
4 parsley sprigs
Salt to taste

2 tablespoons flour
Pepper to taste
3 tablespoons lard or other fat
1 cup finely chopped onion
1 medium carrot, scraped and
  diced
8 gingersnaps, crumbled

Put the beef in a large kettle or bowl. Combine the wine, vinegar, water, onion, bay leaf, peppercorns, cloves, parsley, and salt in a saucepan and bring to a boil. Pour over the beef and cool. Cover and leave in the refrigerator for 1 to 3 days, depending on the quality of the meat, longer for chuck than for bottom round. Turn the meat at least once each day. Take the meat from the marinade and pat dry. Strain the marinade and reserve. Rub the meat with flour seasoned with salt and pepper. Melt the lard or fat in a Dutch oven or heavy kettle and brown the meat in it on all sides. Remove with 2 spoons. Add the onion and carrots to the drippings and sauté for 5 minutes. Add 3 cups of the reserved marinade and bring to a boil. Return the meat to the kettle. Simmer, covered, for 2 hours or longer, until the meat is tender. Take the meat from the kettle and put on a warm platter. Bring the remaining liquid and drippings to a boil and add the gingersnaps. Cook 1 or more minutes until thickened. Remove from the heat. To serve, slice the meat and pour the sauce over it or serve separately. Serves 6 to 8.

DUTCH KALE AND SAUSAGES

The Dutch are devotees of this typical country dish called *stamppot*, a name that derives from the thorough mixing together of the ingredients.

2 packages (10 ounces each)
  frozen kale
4 cups warm mashed potatoes
2 tablespoons finely chopped
  onion

1/4 cup butter
1/8 teaspoon freshly grated
  nutmeg
Salt, pepper to taste
16 cooked beef sausages such
  as mettwurst

Cook the kale in a little salted water until tender. Drain and chop finely. Mix with the warm potatoes, onion, butter, nutmeg, salt, and pepper and beat until smooth. Spoon into a mound and place the cooked sausages over it. Serves 8.

VENETIAN LIVER AND ONIONS

This dish, served throughout Italy but particularly associated with Venice, is called *fegato alla veneziana*. The authentic preparation is made only with very tender liver, cut as thin as possible.

1½ pounds calf's liver	3 tablespoons olive oil
Salt	1½ pounds onions, peeled and
Freshly ground pepper	thinly sliced
¼ cup butter	¼ cup chopped fresh parsley

Wash the liver and wipe dry. Cut into very thin slices. Season with salt and pepper. Heat the butter and oil in a skillet. Add the onions and sauté until golden but do not brown. This will take several minutes. Add the liver and sauté on both sides until just tender. Sprinkle with the parsley. Serve at once. Serves 4.

PORK CHOPS A LA ARAGONESA

Spain's inland northeastern region of Aragon is not frequently visited by foreigners, but it has many interesting attractions. Its cuisine generally is not outstanding but does include some unique dishes. Many are typically flavored with such Spanish favorites as garlic and/or red peppers. An interesting creation is a tongue specialty enriched with a touch of chocolate in the sauce. This dish also has an individual taste, achieved by combining a number of local seasonings.

6 boneless pork chops, about	⅔ cup olive oil
½ inch thick	2 garlic cloves, crushed

½ teaspoon ground cloves   1 medium onion, finely
1 teaspoon paprika   chopped
Flour   2 tablespoons red wine vinegar
                       About ⅓ cup dry red wine

Garnishes:
   hard-cooked egg wedges and olives

Cut off and discard any fat from the chops. Combine ⅓ cup of olive oil, the garlic, cloves, and paprika and rub on both sides of the chops. Arrange on a large plate and leave at room temperature for 2 hours. Take the chops from the plate and cut them into narrow strips. Wipe dry and dust with flour. Brown in the remaining ⅓ cup of oil in a heavy skillet. Remove to a plate. Add the onion to the drippings and sauté until tender. Pour in the vinegar and bring to a boil. Cook over high heat until the liquid evaporates. Return the pork to the skillet. Add a little red wine to cover the meat and cook slowly, covered, for about 1 hour, or until the pork is tender. Add a little more wine while cooking, if needed. Serve garnished with the eggs and olives. Serves 4 to 6.

AUSTRIAN WIENER SCHNITZEL

In Austria it is always possible to dine on a superb selection of mouth-watering national specialties. Outstanding among them are schnitzels. In Germany, a *Schnitzel* means a cutlet of pork or veal; in Austria it generally refers to the latter. On restaurant menus there are customarily several schnitzels such as *natur, pariser, champignon, paprika,* and *holsteiner,* as well as the most popular of them all, the *Wiener schnitzel.* This specialty of Vienna can be and is described simply as a fried breaded veal cutlet, but such a noble dish should not be dismissed so lightly. The making of a perfect schnitzel requires careful attention and expertise. To begin with, the veal should be only the best. The coating of flour, egg, and bread crumbs must be artfully added, and when cooked, should be golden and not dark. It is also important that a schnitzel be served immediately after cooking and never reheated. In Vienna one of the most fascinating places to enjoy any of the various schnitzels is the Rathauskeller, a colossal restaurant establishment of three large underground rooms in the basement of the imposing city hall. The central dining area is richly embellished with wooden paneling, decorated walls and ceilings, ornate chandeliers, and well-appointed tables. Diners may choose from a wide number of menu items, including several *Spezialität des Hauses*, but I always like to order a Wiener schnitzel, almost as large as the plate on which it is served and garnished simply, as it should be, only with lemon wedges.

4 large veal cutlets, 1½ to 2 pounds	Fine dry bread crumbs
Flour	Lard
Salt, pepper to taste	Oil
2 eggs, beaten	4 lemon wedges

Trim each cutlet neatly and make slits slantwise along the edges. Beat well with a wooden mallet or the edge of a plate, being careful not to tear the flesh. Have ready three bowls filled with the following: flour seasoned with salt and pepper, the beaten eggs, and fine dry bread crumbs. Dip each cutlet first in flour and shake off any surplus. Then dip in beaten egg; and lastly in bread crumbs. Again shake off any surplus. Heat enough lard and oil of equal proportions to be ½ inch deep in a skillet. When hot, add the cutlets and fry, 1 or 2 at a time, until golden brown on both sides. Add more lard and oil as needed. Serve at once garnished with lemon wedges. Serves 4.

DANISH FRIKADELLER

One of the most beloved of the Danish dishes is this one, meatballs. The Danes point out, however, that they are very special meatballs. No two cooks will agree about their recipes, and each Dane has his own favorite version. Generally the meat is a combination of pork and veal. *Frikadeller* are served traditionally with boiled potatoes and pickled beets or red cabbage. This is one recipe version.

5 tablespoons butter
1 large onion, finely chopped
1 cup soft bread crumbs
½ cup milk
1 pound ground veal or beef
1 pound ground pork

2 eggs, beaten
½ teaspoon allspice
Salt, pepper to taste
2 tablespoons vegetable oil
¼ cup chopped fresh parsley

Heat 2 tablespoons of butter in a small saucepan and sauté the onion in it until tender. Remove from the heat and spoon into a large bowl. Soak the bread crumbs in the milk and add to the onion. Stir in the veal and pork and mix thoroughly. Add the eggs, allspice, salt, and pepper and combine well. Shape into 2-inch balls, slightly flattened. Heat the remaining 3 tablespoons of butter and oil in a large skillet and brown the meatballs on all sides. Continue the cooking, turning occasionally, for several minutes on each side until they are thoroughly cooked. Serve garnished with the parsley. Serves 8.

OSSO BUCO MILANESE

This culinary gift from the northern Italian city of Milan is now a favorite in many other parts of the country and beyond. The name means "hollow bones" and one of the best aspects of the dish is the marrow of the bones, which is extracted and eaten. After the primary ingredients have been cooked they are sprinkled with what the Italians call *gremolata,* a combination of chopped garlic, parsley, and grated lemon peel. This dish traditionally is served with *Risotto alla Milanese* (page 94).

7 to 8 pounds veal shank or
  shin with marrow in the bone,
  cut into 2½-inch pieces
Salt, pepper to taste
Flour
About ⅓ cup butter or olive oil
1 cup chopped onion
2 large garlic cloves, crushed
1 cup dry white wine

3 cups canned Italian plum
  tomatoes, drained and
  chopped
1 cup beef stock or bouillon
1 *bouquet garni* (parsley,
  thyme, bay leaf tied together
  in a small muslin or
  cheesecloth bag)
1 tablespoon grated lemon peel
3 tablespoons chopped fresh
  parsley

Wipe the pieces of shank and sprinkle them with salt and pepper. Dust with flour. Heat the butter or oil in a heavy casserole or Dutch oven and brown the shank pieces on both sides, a few at a time, over moderate heat. As they are cooked, transfer them to a platter. Sauté the onions and 1 clove of garlic in the drippings, adding more butter if needed, until tender. Arrange the shanks to stand upright over the onions. Pour the wine over them. Spoon the tomatoes on top and add the stock and *bouquet garni*. Bring the mixture to a boil. Reduce the heat and cook slowly, covered tightly, for 1½ to 2 hours, until the meat is tender. When the dish is cooked, combine the remaining clove of garlic, the lemon peel, and the parsley and sprinkle over the ingredients. Remove and discard the *bouquet garni*. Serves 4 to 6.

NORWEGIAN LAMB AND CABBAGE STEW

Two favorite Scandinavian foods, lamb (or mutton) and cabbage, are combined to make this easy-to-prepare stew, which in Norway is called *far i kal*. It is a good family winter dish.

2 pounds shoulder or breast of lamb	Salt to taste
1 medium green cabbage	1 medium bay leaf
About ¼ cup butter or margarine	8 peppercorns
2 tablespoons flour	About 1 cup bouillon or water
	⅓ cup chopped fresh parsley

Remove any excess fat from the lamb and cut into 2-inch cubes. Cut the center core from the cabbage. Remove and discard any wilted leaves. Cut the cabbage into wedges. Brown the lamb cubes and the cabbage separately in the butter, adding more if necessary, in a large skillet or saucepan. Arrange in layers in a large saucepan with each layer sprinkled with flour and salt. Add the bay leaf and peppercorns. Pour in the bouillon or water, enough to cover the ingredients. Bring to a boil. Skim off any fat. Cover and cook slowly for about 1½ hours, or until the ingredients are tender. Remove and discard the bay leaf and peppercorns. Serve sprinkled with parsley and accompanied by boiled potatoes. Serves 6.

FRENCH PEPPER STEAK

Steak au poivre is a celebrated dish throughout Europe, although it originated in France. In restaurants it is very often served with flaming brandy. I recall first sampling this dish, without the fascination of flames, in a *brasserie* of Arles, once one of France's most important cities and now known for its Roman ruins. Therefore I prefer the simpler version such as this one.

1 steak (chuck, club, rib, sirloin), about 2½ pounds, cut 1 inch thick	4 tablespoons butter
	2 tablespoons vegetable oil
	Salt
2 tablespoons peppercorns	⅓ cup Cognac or brandy

Crush with a rolling pin or in a mortar with a pestle. Wipe dry the steak. Using the heel of the hand, press the crushed peppercorns into both sides of the steak. Leave to rest 1 hour or longer. Heat 2 tablespoons of butter and the oil in a heavy skillet and brown the steak in it for about 4 minutes on each side, or until the desired degree of doneness. Remove to a warm plate and keep warm. Season with salt. Scrape the juices in the pan. Add the remaining 2 tablespoons of butter and the Cognac or brandy and bring to a boil. Pour over the steak and serve at once. Serve 4 to 6.

DANISH ROAST PORK

One of the most cherished Danish national dishes is roast pork, served for holidays and special occasions. *Flaeskesteg* is generally cooked with the rind on so that the roast has a crisp skin. To do this it is necessary to have a fresh shoulder or loin of pork with the skin on. The skin is then scored with a sharp knife, cutting lengthwise about ⅛ inch apart, and rubbed with salt. Cook the roast in a preheated slow oven (325°F.), allowing 35 to 40 minutes per pound, or until the meat thermometer registers 185°F. Do not baste while cooking. Cut the roast into slices and serve with Carmelized Potatoes (p. 195) and Red Cabbage (p. 186).

Another favorite Danish way of preparing a pork roast is to stuff it with peeled apples and scalded pitted prunes before cooking.

SWISS ÉMINCÉ DE VEAU

The German name for this dish is *Kalbfleisch geschnetzelt*. Small strips of tender veal in a flavorful cream sauce is a Swiss creation that has also become an international favorite. In Zurich's esteemed restaurant, Kronenhalle, which boasts a magnificent art collection as well as a fine menu, the veal is flamed with Cognac. Very often *émincé* also includes mushrooms. It is served traditionally with *Rösti* (page 183).

2 pounds veal scallops or cutlets
About 6 tablespoons butter
2 tablespoons minced shallots or green onions

1 cup dry white wine
1¼ cups heavy cream
Salt, pepper to taste

Trim any fat from the escallops and discard it. Cut the veal into slivers about ¼ inch wide and 2½ inches long. Heat 3 tablespoons of the butter in a skillet and when foaming add half the veal slivers. Sauté, mixing about with a fork, about 2 minutes, or until tender. Remove to a plate and keep warm. Add 3 more tablespoons of butter to the skillet and heat. Add the remaining veal and cook in the same way. Remove to a platter. Add the shallots to the drippings and include more butter, if necessary. Sauté for 1 minute, or until tender. Pour in the wine and bring to a boil. Cook over high heat to reduce almost to half. Add the cream and turn down the heat, stirring slowly 1 minute. Add the veal and any juices and leave on the stove long enough to heat through. Season with salt and pepper. Serves 4 to 6.

BIFE À PORTUGUESA

This is one variation of a popular Portuguese dish, served traditionally with fried potatoes placed in a ring around the meat.

1 medium onion, finely
  chopped
1 garlic clove, crushed
6 tablespoons butter
1 tablespoon olive oil
1 bay leaf, crumbled
7 tablespoons chopped fresh
  parsley
2 tablespoons tomato purée

1 cup port wine
Salt, pepper to taste
4 club, chuck, or rib steaks,
  about ¾ pound each, cut
  about ¾ inch thick
Juice of 1 large lemon
8 slices prosciutto or other
  thinly smoked ham

Sauté the onion and garlic in 2 tablespoons of butter and the oil in a small saucepan or skillet until tender. Stir in the bay leaf and 3 tablespoons of parsley and then the tomato purée. Cook, stirring, for 1 minute. Add the wine, salt, and pepper and cook slowly, uncovered, for 15 minutes. Meanwhile, fry the steaks in the remaining 4 tablespoons of butter and the lemon juice for about 4 minutes on each side, or to the desired degree of doneness. To serve, place the slices of ham over the hot steaks and pour the sauce over them. Sprinkle with the remaining 4 tablespoons of parsley. Serves 4.

BRATWURST IN BEER, BERLIN-STYLE

Although this dish is a specialty from the famous German city of Berlin, the small whitish pork sausages called *Bratwurst* originated in Nuremberg where they are still featured in all the restaurants. Grilled over a beechwood fire that permeates the meat, the crisp spicy sausages, served with pepper-flavored sauerkraut and freshly grated horseradish on pewter plates, are always a welcome repast. One of the places they taste best is at the ancient city's annual *Christkindlesmarkt* ("Christ Child's market"). During the cold December days and evenings they are served by the thousands on crusty rolls with sharp mustard. The *Markt* is permeated with their tantalizing aroma, as well as that of other native fare sold to the hungry visitors. Throughout the year the sausages are a specialty at Bratwurst Herzle, a restaurant established in 1515.

12 *Bratwurst*
1 tablespoon butter or
  margarine
2 medium onions, chopped
1 cup beer

Salt, pepper to taste
1 tablespoon flour
3 tablespoons chopped fresh
  parsley

Place the *Bratwurst* in a saucepan and cover with boiling water. Cook 3 minutes; drain. Melt the butter in a skillet and add the *Bratwurst* to brown. Remove to a warm plate. Pour off all except 2 tablespoons of the fat. Add the onions and sauté until tender. Return the sausages to the skillet. Add the beer, salt, and pepper. Cook slowly, covered, for 15 minutes. Remove the *Bratwurst* to a warm platter. Mix the flour with a little cold water and stir into the hot liquid. Cook, stirring, until a thick sauce. Add the parsley and pour over the *Bratwurst*. Serve with mashed potatoes. Serves 4.

ITALIAN VEAL BIRDS

These small filled "packets" of veal are sometimes called "poor men's birds," as they were served as a substitute for roasted small birds. They are, however, not poor fare but elegant and delicious creations.

8 thin veal scallops, sliced thin
8 slices prosciutto or other
  thinly cut smoked ham
8 slices mozzarella cheese

⅓ cup butter
Salt, pepper to taste
⅓ cup Marsala wine
⅓ cup chopped fresh parsley

With a wooden mallet flatten out the veal scallops, making them as thin as possible but being careful not to tear the meat. Arrange a slice of prosciutto and mozzarella on each scallop. Fold over to have the veal enclose the prosciutto and cheese. Fasten with toothpicks. Fry in heated butter to brown on all sides. Season with salt and pepper. Remove to a warm plate.

Add the Marsala to the drippings. Heat and pour over the birds. Sprinkle with the parsley. Serves 4.

ALSATIAN CHOUCROUTE GARNIE

One of the glories of the cookery of delightful Alsace in northeastern France is sauerkraut, *choucroute*, served by itself or in a variety of interesting dishes such as this one, garnished with a variety of meats. I first enjoyed this native specialty on a rainy autumn day in the restaurant of Savern's Hotel Geiswiller where the platter of hearty sauerkraut, with local beer, made a welcome repast. This is an excellent dish for an informal winter meal.

2 pounds sauerkraut
3 medium onions, finely
  chopped
2 tablespoons bacon or pork fat
2 medium tart apples, peeled,
  cored, and chopped
6 peppercorns, bruised

10 juniper berries
2½ cups dry white wine
12 pork link sausages
6 thick slices cooked ham
6 smoked pork chops or slices
  of pork
6 frankfurters

Soak the sauerkraut in cold water to cover for 15 minutes. Drain thoroughly. Sauté the onions in the fat in a large saucepan or kettle until tender. Add the sauerkraut and toss with a fork. Cook for 5 minutes, stirring occasionally. Add the apples, peppercorns, juniper berries, and wine. Cook slowly, covered for 1 hour. Meanwhile, fry the sausages. Drain off the fat and put the sausages on absorbent paper. Add with the ham, pork chops, and frankfurters to the sauerkraut and cook 30 minutes longer. Remove and discard the peppercorns and juniper berries. To serve, pile the sauerkraut on a platter and place the meats and sausages around and over it. Serve with boiled potatoes and mustard. Serves 6.

FABADA A LA ASTURIANA

One of Spain's great regional dishes is a bean-sausage stew from the northwest region of Asturias along the Bay of Biscay. The name derives from the local large white bean, *faba*, traditionally used in it. The dish, however, cannot be authentically made outside of Spain, as such ingredients as *longaniza* sausage, local black sausage and ham, as well as pigs' feet and ears, are either not available or easily obtainable. *Fabada* is cooked and served in a large earthenware casserole and accompanied by corn bread and cider. This version is an adaptation.

1 pound large white beans, washed and drained	½ pound smoked bacon in one piece
2 medium onions, coarsely chopped	4 smoked ham hocks
2 garlic cloves, minced	½ pound blood sausage
3 tablespoons olive oil	½ pound *chorizo* (Spanish sausage), or other garlic
1 can (6 ounces) tomato paste	sausage, sliced and cooked
Salt, pepper to taste	⅛ teaspoon ground saffron

Cover the beans with water and bring to a boil. Boil for 2 minutes. Remove from the heat. Cover the pan and let stand for 1 hour. Meanwhile, sauté the onions and garlic in the olive oil in a large casserole or heavy kettle until tender. Stir in the tomato paste and season with salt and pepper. When the beans are through standing, put them and the liquid in the casserole over the onions. Mix well. Add the bacon. Pour in enough water to completely cover the ingredients. Bring to a boil. Lower the heat and cook as slowly as possible, tightly covered, for 1 hour. Add the ham and blood sausage and continue cooking slowly for about 1 hour longer, or until the ingredients are cooked. Add the *chorizo* and saffron 30 minutes before the dish is finished cooking. If it is needed, add more water to the dish while cooking. Serves 6.

ENGLISH TOAD IN THE HOLE

This traditional English dish with a curious name was originally made with slices of bacon coated with batter. Today it is generally prepared with slices of leftover cooked beef or with pork sausages.

1 cup all-purpose flour	Salt, pepper to taste
1 cup milk	1 pound pork sausages or slices
2 medium eggs, beaten	of cooked beef

Combine the flour, milk, eggs, salt, and pepper in a bowl and mix well to form a batter. Leave for 30 minutes. If sausages are to be used, cook and drain them. Place the sausages or beef in a shallow baking dish and cover with the batter. Bake in a preheated hot (400°F.) oven about 30 minutes, or until cooked. Serves 4.

GERMAN ROULADEN

Braised stuffed beef rolls, *Rouladen,* are one of the great German favorites for a midday meal. Traditionally they are served with red cabbage and dumplings or potatoes and are accompanied by a stein of beer. In Germany, thinly sliced beef, specially prepared for *Rouladen,* is sold at most meat markets. In America, round steak is a good substitute, but it should be sliced thinly and pounded with a mallet.

2 pounds round steak,	Flour
trimmed of fat	3 tablespoons butter or
Hot prepared mustard	margarine
4 slices thin bacon, diced	2 cups beef bouillon
3 tablespoons minced dill	Salt, pepper to taste
pickle or relish	3 tablespoons chopped fresh
1 large onion, finely chopped	parsley

Cut the meat into 4 thin rectangles, each about 4 inches wide and 8 inches long. Pound with a mallet or the edge of a plate to make as thin as possible. Arrange the beef slices on a flat surface and spread the top side of each one with mustard. Combine the bacon, pickle, and onions and place a large spoonful of the mixture on each slice of meat. Roll up carefully and secure with toothpicks, being sure that the filling is completely enclosed. Dust each beef roll with flour. Melt the butter in a skillet and brown the *Rouladen* on both sides in it. Add the bouillon and season with salt and pepper. Cook slowly, covered, about 1 hour, until the meat is cooked. Stir in the parsley and serve. Serves 4.

PROVENÇAL BEEF DAUBE

The French have several marvelous country dishes, made with meat, poultry, or game as well as other ingredients, which are cooked slowly to make flavorful stews. Traditionally each is cooked in a *daubière*, a special earthenware pot.

3 pounds stewing beef, cubed and trimmed of fat
1 cup dry white or red wine
¼ cup brandy
6 tablespoons olive oil
2 large onions, thinly sliced
4 medium carrots, scraped and diced
2 medium bay leaves
1 teaspoon dried thyme
½ cup chopped fresh parsley

Salt, freshly ground pepper to taste
½ cup diced thick bacon
2 garlic cloves, crushed
3 medium tomatoes, peeled and chopped
1 cup sliced fresh mushrooms
1 small strip orange peel
½ teaspoon dried rosemary
12 pitted black olives

Put the beef, wine, brandy, ¼ cup olive oil, 1 sliced onion, 2 diced carrots, the bay leaves, thyme, and 2 tablespoons parsley in a large bowl. Season with salt and pepper and leave to marinate for 2 to 3 hours. Mix about the beef now and then.

When ready to cook, put the bacon, garlic, remaining 2 tablespoons of oil, 1 sliced onion, and 2 diced carrots in a kettle and sauté for 5 minutes. Remove the meat from the marinade, reserving the marinade. Wipe dry. Brown a few pieces at a time in the oil drippings, pushing the vegetables aside. When all the meat is browned, mix in the tomatoes, mushrooms, orange peel, and rosemary. Season with salt and pepper. Pour in the reserved marinade, including the vegetables. Cook slowly, covered, for 1 hour. Stir in the olives after cooking for 30 minutes. When the cooking is finished, add the remaining parsley. Remove and discard the bay leaves. Serves 6 to 8.

BERNER PLATTE OF SWITZERLAND

A national Swiss specialty, made with sauerkraut and a wide variety of meats, is sometimes called the local version of French *choucroute garnie*. There are similarities in the hearty platters, but the one enjoyed in Switzerland includes several native sausages and sometimes pigs' ears, feet, and tongue. It is always fascinating to order as the ingredients will very often be different—and always good. In Berne, Switzerland's charming and carefully preserved medieval capital, a good place to order the local specialty is the Kornhauskeller. Now an amazing expanse of restaurant, reached by a wide descending staircase, the establishment was used during the eighteenth century as a granary. For many years, however, the old building has been very much alive with the chatter of animated diners, a band playing festive songs, and the bustling of buxom waitresses toting large, heavily laden trays. Beer, dispensed from a famous barrel said to contain some 10,000 gallons of the foaming brew, flows freely into gigantic mugs. Although this is truly a convival atmosphere in which to enjoy the *berner Platte*, the specialty may be also served for any informal home meal. This is one version of it.

2 pounds sauerkraut
2 tablespoons bacon or pork fat
2 medium onions, chopped
8 peppercorns
10 juniper berries
Salt to taste
2½ cups dry white wine
½ pound bacon in one piece
6 smoked pork chops
1 pound pork sausage links, cooked and drained

6 *Bratwurst* or *Knockwurst*, braised and drained
6 thick slices cooked ham
3 cups cooked and drained hot green beans
3 tablespoons butter
1 garlic clove, minced
Pepper to taste
6 medium potatoes, boiled, drained, and peeled

Rinse the sauerkraut and drain well to remove all the liquid. Heat the fat in a large kettle. Add the onions and sauté until tender. Add the sauerkraut and sauté about 5 minutes, mixing with a fork. Add the peppercorns, juniper berries, salt, wine, and bacon. Cook slowly, covered, for 1 hour. Add the pork chops, sausage, *Bratwurst,* and ham and continue cooking for another 30 minutes, or until all the ingredients are cooked. Remove and discard the peppercorns and juniper berries. Combine the hot green beens, butter, and garlic and season with salt and pepper. To serve, spoon the sauerkraut onto a large platter and surround with the meats. Put the potatoes in a bowl and the green beans in another and serve with the *Platte.* Serves 6 to 8.

SWEDISH KALDOLMAR

The custom of wrapping ground meat and other foods in cabbage leaves was adapted in Sweden after King Charles XII returned from captivity in Turkey during the eighteenth century. He had evidently enjoyed the Turkish *dolmas* wrapped in grape leaves. In Stockholm this specialty is particularly delicious at the Operagrillen Restaurant, one of the city's finest, where it is served with lingonberries and mashed potatoes.

1 large head green cabbage, 2½ to 3 pounds	2 tablespoons minced onion
	½ teaspoon ground allspice
Salt	Pepper
¾ pound lean ground beef	3 tablespoons butter or
¼ pound ground veal	margarine
⅔ cup cooked rice	½ cup corn syrup
¼ cup milk	2 tablespoons flour

Cut out the center core of the cabbage. Remove and discard any wilted leaves. Place in a large kettle of lightly salted boiling water and cook over moderate heat, covered, for 10 minutes or until the outer leaves are soft. Take out of the kettle and drain. Remove all the leaves that are soft enough to be pliable. Return the cabbage to the kettle and continue to cook until all the remaining leaves are soft. Drain and take off all the leaves. Cut any hard sections from them and leave on a flat surface. Cut the larger leaves in halves, if smaller rolls are desired.

Meanwhile, combine the beef, veal, rice, milk, onion, allspice, and pepper in a large bowl and stir together until the ingredients are thoroughly mixed. To fill the leaves, place 1 or 2 spoonfuls, depending on the size of the leaf, on each one and roll up. Tuck in the ends so the filling is completely enclosed and secure each roll with a toothpick. Keep filling and rolling until all the ingredients are used. (If any leaves are left over, use them for something else.) Sauté the stuffed rolls in butter, turning once, in a heavy kettle or casserole until golden on each side. Drizzle the corn syrup over them and add 1 cup of water. Cover the dish and bake in a preheated hot oven (400°F.) for 1 hour. Take out the rolls and keep warm. Stir the flour into the drippings and cook briskly, stirring, until thickened. Add more water if a thinner gravy is desired. Pour over the cabbage rolls and serve hot. Serves 8 to 10.

BISTECCA ALLA FIORENTINA

One of the great Italian dishes, and Florence's most famous, is this steak, a product of the superb Tuscan beef cattle called *chianinas*. A delightful place to enjoy the steak is the Buca San Ruffillo on the Piazza dell' Olio, an atmospheric restaurant specializing in Florentine cookery. *Buca* is an Italian word meaning "hole," and a restaurant with *buca* in its name is generally an intimate, informal, below-the-street place with exceptional food.

1 steak, porterhouse, or sirloin, about 3 pounds, cut 1½ inches thick
⅔ cup olive oil
Juice of 1 large lemon
1 or 2 garlic cloves, minced

3 tablespoons chopped fresh parsley
Salt, freshly ground pepper to taste
Butter

Marinate the steak in the oil, lemon juice, garlic, and parsley at room temperature for 4 hours. Turn it over now and then. Remove from the marinade and pat dry. Place under a preheated broiler and cook on both sides to the desired degree of doneness, 5 to 8 minutes on each side. Put on a warm plate. Season with salt and pepper and put a large pat of butter on top. Serve at once. Serves 4.

ENGLISH STEAK, KIDNEY, AND MUSHROOM PIE

The English have long been devotees of great meat pies and puddings that are prepared in various forms and then baked or steamed. One of the most traditional and commonly served is steak-and-kidney pie, sometimes also made with mushrooms.

1 beef kidney
1½ pounds round steak, cut
 into 1-inch cubes
⅓ cup all-purpose flour
Salt, pepper to taste
¼ cup butter or margarine
1 small onion, minced

3 cups beef bouillon
½ pound fresh mushrooms,
 cleaned and sliced thickly
2 tablespoons dry sherry
Standard pastry for a 1-crust
 9-inch pie, unbaked
1 egg, beaten

Remove the outer membrane of the kidney. Split open and remove any fat and white veins. Cut into 1-inch pieces. Soak in salted cold water to cover for 30 minutes. Drain and wipe dry. Dredge the kidney and steak cubes with the flour, seasoned with salt and pepper. Melt the butter in a large saucepan. Add the onion and sauté until tender. Push aside. Add the dredged meats and brown on all sides. Season with salt and pepper. Add the bouillon and stir, cooking until thickened. Cook slowly, covered, about 1 hour, or until the meats are tender. Add the mushrooms and sherry. Turn into a 2-quart casserole. Roll out the pastry to fit the top and place over the dish. Flute the edges and brush the top with beaten egg. Bake in a preheated hot oven (450°F.) for about 20 minutes, or until the pastry is cooked and golden. Serves 6.

The pastry may be decorated with "leaves" made with pastry and placed on the top crust.

PORTUGUESE PORK-CLAM STEW

This unusual and inviting stew is typical of the humble but flavorful fare devised by Portuguese fishermen. It combines two favorite foods—pork and clams.

2 pounds lean boneless pork,
  cut into small cubes
About ¼ cup olive oil
2 large onions, thinly sliced
1 or 2 garlic cloves, crushed
4 large tomatoes, peeled and
  chopped

1 can (6 ounces) tomato paste
Dry white wine
½ teaspoon paprika
Salt, pepper to taste
2 dozen hard-shelled clams,
  scrubbed and washed
½ cup chopped fresh parsley

Brown the pork cubes in the oil in a large saucepan or kettle.
Remove with a slotted spoon. Add the onions and garlic to the
drippings and more oil, if needed, and sauté until tender. Return the meat to the pan. Add the tomatoes and sauté 2 or 3
minutes. Stir in the tomato paste. Add enough white wine to
cover the ingredients and the paprika, salt, and pepper. Stir
well and bring to a boil. Lower the heat and cook slowly, covered, about 1½ hours, or until the meat is tender. Add more
wine during the cooking, if needed. Add the clams about 15
minutes before the cooking is finished, or until the shells open.
Mix in the parsley. Serves 4.

SPANISH LAMB COCHIFRITO

A common sight on the high plateau of Spain's northern
region of Old Castile is herd after herd of sheep and lambs,
which will be featured later as local specialties in a number of inviting dishes. This fricasseed lamb preparation,
enhanced by the combination of lemon juice and parsley,
is one of the best of the native creations.

2 pounds lean lamb shoulder,
  cut into 1-inch cubes
¼ cup olive oil
2 medium onions, chopped
1 or 2 garlic cloves, minced
1 or 2 teaspoons paprika

Juice of 1 medium lemon
3 tablespoons chopped fresh
  parsley
Salt, freshly ground black
  pepper

Brown the lamb in the oil in a large heavy skillet. Remove
to a plate. Add the onions and garlic to the drippings and sauté
until tender. Stir in the paprika. Return the lamb to the skillet.

Add the lemon juice, parsley, salt, and pepper. Cook very slowly, covered, about 1 hour, or until the lamb is cooked. Serves 4.

SALTIMBOCCA ALLA ROMANA

This favorite Italian dish is found on restaurant menus throughout the country, though generally it is associated with Rome. The name literally means "jump into the mouth." It is traditionally made with fresh sage leaves, which impart a most desirable flavor to the veal.

8 thin veal escallops
Salt, pepper
16 fresh sage leaves or 1
  teaspoon dried sage

8 paper thin slices of prosciutto
  or other smoked ham
About ¼ cup butter
¾ cup dry white wine

Put the veal escallops between wax paper and pound with a wooden mallet or edge of a plate to make as thin as possible, being careful not to tear the meat. Sprinkle them with salt and pepper and place the sage over them. Arrange a slice of ham on each one. Roll up and enclose each with a toothpick. Melt the butter in a skillet and add the rolled-up veal slices. Brown on both sides over fairly high heat. Lower the heat and simmer until the meat is tender. Carefully remove with tongs to a plate and keep warm. Add the wine to the drippings and boil up to reduce. Pour over the veal and serve. Serves 4.

DUTCH HUTSPOT

In northern Europe there are several thick soups or stews that have similar names but are made of various ingredients. The French and Belgians have *hotch potch;* in Holland there is *hutspot.* In the latter, the vegetables are mashed together.

2 pounds beef chuck or flank
1 teaspoon salt

1½ pounds carrots, scraped
  and sliced

2 pounds (about 6 medium)
  potatoes, peeled and
  quartered
2 large onions, chopped

2 tablespoons light cream or
  milk
2 tablespoons butter or
  margarine
Salt, pepper to taste

Cut any fat from the chuck or flank and, if the flank is used, take off any membranes. Put in a large saucepan with the salt and 1 quart of water. Bring to a boil. Remove any scum that rises to the top. Lower the heat and simmer, covered, about 1½ hours. Add the carrots, potatoes, and onions and simmer another hour, or until the vegetables are tender. Remove the meat to a warm platter and cut into strips. If flank is used it should be cut across the grain. Take out the vegetables and mash with the cream, butter, salt, and pepper. Add some of the broth to thin the mixture, if desired. To serve, spoon the vegetables onto a platter and surround with the meat slices. Serves 4 to 6.

BELGIAN CARBONNADE FLAMANDE

This beer stew featuring beef and onions is a specialty of the northern Flemings and has an innovative flavor. Since beer is the Belgian national beverage, it is only natural that the brew is used in the cookery also.

3 pounds lean boneless
  beef chuck or round steak,
  cut into 1-inch cubes or
  2-inch strips
Flour
Salt, pepper to taste
½ cup lard or butter
6 medium onions, thinly sliced

1 garlic clove, crushed
1 *bouquet garni* (bay leaf,
  parsley, thyme tied together
  in a small muslin or
  cheesecloth bag)
2 tablespoons brown sugar
About 2½ cups light beer
2 tablespoons red wine vinegar

Dredge the meat cubes or strips with flour seasoned with salt and pepper. Set aside. Heat the lard or butter in a large saucepan or kettle and sauté the onions and garlic in it until tender. Push aside and add the meat. Brown on all sides. Add *bouquet garni.* Mix in the sugar and beer. Season with salt and pepper. Cook, tightly covered, over low heat for about 1½ hours, or until the meat is tender. Add more beer during the cooking, if necessary. (The liquid should cover the ingredients while cooking.) Remove and discard the *bouquet garni.* Add the vinegar just before serving. Serve with boiled potatoes. Serves 6.

LANCASHIRE HOT POT

Although native to northern England's Lancashire, this humble stew, resembling somewhat the famous Irish stew, is eaten throughout the country. Oysters are traditionally added to it, a contribution of the local fishermen. The dish was so important for everyday meals that a special pot, tall enough to hold the long mutton chops that stood upright in it, was devised for it. Left in the oven during the day, the hot pot was ready when the working family returned home at night. Now it is generally made in a heavy casserole.

2 pounds neck of lamb, sliced
3 tablespoons lard or
  margarine
1 large onion, sliced
½ pound fresh mushrooms,
  cleaned and sliced
  lengthwise
3 lamb kidneys, sliced

6 shucked oysters (optional)
2 pounds potatoes, peeled and
  sliced thickly
1½ cups beef bouillon
2 teaspoons sugar
Pinch mace or nutmeg
Salt, pepper to taste

Brown the lamb slices in the lard on both sides in a large skillet and then put in a large casserole or pot. Add the onions to the drippings and sauté until just tender. Spoon over the lamb. Arrange over them the mushrooms, kidneys, and oysters in layers. Place the potato slices, overlapping each other, to cover the top. Combine the bouillon, sugar, mace, salt, and pepper and pour over the ingredients. Bake, covered with foil or a lid, in a moderate oven (350°F.) for 1½ to 2 hours, until the ingredients are cooked. Remove the cover during the last 30 minutes so the top will become golden. Serves 6.

CARRÉ DE PORC À LA PROVENÇALE

This pork roast is traditionally made with fresh sage leaves, which are inserted into it several hours before cooking. If available, use in this recipe. Otherwise it is flavorful with only thyme and bay leaves.

1 roast loin of pork, 7 to 8 pounds
4 garlic cloves, cut into slivers
2 teaspoons dried thyme
2 medium bay leaves, crumbled

Salt, freshly ground pepper to taste
3 to 4 tablespoons olive oil
½ cup dry white wine
½ cup chopped fresh parsley

Trim any excess fat from the roast. With the point of a sharp knife make small incisions in the flesh and insert the garlic slivers into them. Rub the pork with the thyme, bay leaves, salt, and pepper. Put in a large bowl or kettle and sprinkle with olive oil and wine. Leave 4 to 5 hours. Arrange on a rack in a shallow roasting pan. Pour any liquid over the pork. Roast, uncovered, in a preheated slow oven (325°F.), allowing 35 to 40 minutes per pound, or until the meat thermometer registers 185°F. When cooked, sprinkle parsley over the roast. Serves 8 to 10.

ITALIAN VITELLO TONNATO

This excellent Italian cold dish, superb for summer entertaining, is made traditionally with tender milk-fed veal, *vitello,* and a rich tuna sauce.

1 boneless veal roast, 3 to 3½ pounds, tied securely
4 flat anchovy fillets, chopped
1 medium onion stuck with 4 whole cloves
2 celery stalks, chopped

2 medium carrots, scraped and cut up
2 medium bay leaves
5 parsley sprigs
8 whole peppercorns
Salt to taste

With the point of a sharp knife make several small slits in the veal. Insert the pieces of anchovy into the slits. Place the roast in a kettle. Add the onion with the cloves, and the celery, carrots, bay leaves, parsley, peppercorns, and salt (only a little because of the anchovies). Pour in enough water to cover the ingredients. Bring the water to a boil. Reduce the heat and cook slowly, covered, for about 1½ hours, or until the meat is tender. Carefully take out the meat and cool. Discard the cooking liquid. Meanwhile, prepare the tuna sauce (recipe below). When the meat is cool cut into thin slices and arrange them attractively on a platter. Spoon the tuna sauce over them and refrigerate 2 or 3 hours or until ready to serve. Serve garnished with drained capers, chopped fresh parsley and lemon slices, if desired. Serves 6 to 8.

TUNA SAUCE

2 cans (about 7 ounces each)
  tuna fish, drained
6 flat anchovy fillets, diced
1 cup olive oil
Juice of 2 medium lemons

2 tablespoons drained capers
2 tablespoons chopped fresh
  parsley
Freshly ground pepper to taste

Combine all the ingredients and mix well, preferably in an electric blender, to make a smooth but fairly liquid sauce.

GERMAN MEATBALLS IN CAPER SAUCE

These flavorful meatballs, *Königsberger Klopse*, are always made with ground pork but may include another meat such as beef or veal. Piquant with capers and lemon juice, they originated in the eastern port city of Königsberg, once an important fortress of Prussia. Now the city is a part of the U.S.S.R., and its name has been changed to Kaliningrad. The meatballs remain, however, great German favorites.

1½ cups stale white bread
  cubes
Milk

2 pounds ground lean meat (a
  mixture of pork and veal or
  beef)

1 large onion, finely chopped	3 tablespoons butter or
2 eggs, beaten	margarine
3 flat anchovy fillets, drained	3 tablespoons flour
and minced	Juice of 1 large lemon
Pepper to taste	3 tablespoons drained capers
4 cups beef bouillon	Salt

Soak the bread cubes in milk to cover. Squeeze dry and put in a large bowl. Add the ground meat and mix well. Then add the onion, eggs, minced anchovies, and pepper. Work with the hands to combine well. Shape into 2-inch balls. Bring the bouillon to a boil and drop the meatballs into it. Cook over medium heat, uncovered, until the meatballs rise to the top, about 15 minutes. Remove from the liquid with a slotted spoon and keep warm. Strain the liquid and reserve it. Melt the butter in a saucepan. Stir in the flour and blend well. Gradually add 3 cups of the strained liquid and cook slowly, stirring constantly, until thickened and smooth. Add the lemon juice and capers. Season with salt and pepper. Add the meatballs and heat through. Serves 8.

SWISS FONDUE BOURGUIGNONNE

Another delightful fondue which has become a favorite dish in America during recent years is this one of beef. It differs, however, from the famous cheese fondue in that the meat is cooked in oil and dipped in sauces afterward. There is great appeal to this type of cookery, as all the ingredients can be prepared beforehand and the beef is cooked by the guests at the table. Necessary for the cooking is a fondue pot or similar utensil, long-handled forks, dinner plates, and small bowls for the sauces. If the hostess wishes to serve a first course, she should plan a light one, such as a clear soup. Traditional accompaniments for the fondue are deep-fried, thinly sliced potatoes or baked potatoes and a green salad. The Swiss enjoy a dry red wine with the fondue. Although any good beef may be used, a tender cut such as sirloin is preferable. A few sauce recipes are included below but prepared sauces may be used, if desired.

These might include tartar or chili sauce or Russian dressing.

3 pounds boneless beef
tenderloin, sirloin or other
beef

Peanut or vegetable oil
Salt, pepper
Assorted sauces

Cut off any fat from the beef and discard it. Cut the meat into 1-inch cubes. Pile on a platter or wooden board. When it is time to cook the meat have the table set with an empty plate, long-handled fork, dinner fork (and other necessary implements if other foods are included) for each person. Enough oil to be 1½ to 2 inches deep is put into the fondue pot and heated. Each person spears a cube of meat with a long-handled fork and cooks it in the hot oil to the desired degree of doneness. The meat is then taken from the long-handled fork onto the plate and eaten with a dinner fork after dipping in one or more sauces. Continue the cooking until all the meat is used. Serves 4.

ASSORTED SAUCES

Garlic Sauce

Crush 4 cloves of garlic and mix with 1 cup of mayonnaise and 1 teaspoon curry powder.

Mustard Sauce

Combine 1 cup sour cream, 2 tablespoons prepared mustard, and 2 teaspoons prepared horseradish.

Tartar Sauce

Combine 1 cup mayonnaise, ¼ cup chopped sweet pickle, 3 tablespoons chopped green onion, 1 tablespoon minced fresh parsley, 1 teaspoon prepared mustard, salt, and pepper.

Russian Dressing

Combine 1 cup mayonnaise, ½ cup chili sauce, 3 tablespoons pickle relish, salt, and pepper.

SWEDISH BIFF À LA LINDSTROM

This version of a hamburger is an intriguing combination that is traditionally served in Sweden with a fried egg on top of each meat patty.

2 pounds ground beef
3 egg yolks
1 cup mashed cooked potatoes
Salt, pepper to taste
⅓ cup minced onions

1 cup finely chopped cooked
   beets
2 tablespoons drained capers
2 tablespoons heavy cream
Butter for frying

Put the beef, egg yolks, mashed potatoes, salt, and pepper in a large bowl and mix with a large spoon or the hands until all the ingredients are thoroughly combined. Mix together the onions, beets, capers, and cream and stir into the meat mixture. Mix until well combined. Shape into large flat patties and fry in butter on both sides until well cooked. Makes about 10 patties. Serve with a fried egg on top of each, if desired.

8

Vegetables and Salads

PERFECTLY PREPARED VEGETABLES, available in exceptional variety, and superb salads are Western European gastronomic delights. Each country is wealthy with an enviable number of these delectable and interesting dishes. Fortunately, cooks have long been experts in making the gifts of the garden into inviting creations that enhance the pleasure of dining.

A fascinating aspect of this cookery is the discovery of the wondrous ways that both familiar and unfamiliar vegetables can be prepared. Over the years a great deal of attention has been paid to their growth, method of cooking, seasoning, and presentation. In some instances even their proper culinary companionship has been divined. The French, as one example, have long understood that turnips and duckling, beans and lamb, and spinach and ham belong together.

Over the centuries the social status of vegetables has fluctuated remarkably. The early Romans were fortunate in having a good selection for their daily fare, including artichokes, asparagus, beans, beets, cabbage, carrots, celery, chickory, cucumbers, fennel, leeks, lettuce, radishes, and turnips. Many of their vegetable dishes were heavily flavored with sauces made

177

with a great number of ingredients. Lettuce, however, which
was sometimes sprinkled with wine, was a great delicacy and
was eaten as a salad. Mushrooms were so treasured that they
were reserved only for the upper classes. Cardoons, thistlelike
plants cultivated for their roots and stalks, were the costliest
of them all.

Vegetables did not fare too well on the tables of medieval
diners, who much preferred meat. By the fourteenth century,
however, European cooks were utilizing more of them, particularly in soups and stews. Well established on English menus
were "sallets," made generally with a number of the products
of field and garden. One recipe called for "the young Buds and
Knots of all manner of wholesome Herbs at their first springing." They were dressed with oil, vinegar, and sugar.

French menus gradually began to include more and more
vegetables and salads as separately featured dishes in their
many-coursed meals. An eleventh-century banquet had four
different salads, with sauces. One regal repast during the reign
of Louis XIV included cucumbers stuffed with marrowfat, beet-
roots blanched and sautéed in butter, purée of artichokes à la
ravigote, and celery in remoulade sauce. This, however, does not
seem like very many when one considers that there were 24
desserts.

By the eighteenth century, vegetables were very much in
vogue. Tender sweet peas were sought-after delicacies. Artichokes and asparagus were aristocratic foods. Alexander
Dumas's Dictionary of Cuisine, published in 1873, has some
interesting observations about the various favorites. Asparagus,
he noted, should be served hot on a folded napkin as it absorbed
the water; beets "should be washed in ordinary brandy"; cabbage with bacon was an "excellent plebeian dish"; turnips "have
their own aristocracy and their own privileges."

Dumas entertained at late evening suppers and became famous among his associates for his salads. He described the
preparation in his book:

> First I put the ingredients into the salad bowl, then overturn them
> onto a platter. Into the empty bowl I put one hard-boiled egg yolk
> for each two persons—six for a dozen guests. These I mash with
> oil to form a paste, to which I add chervil, crushed tuna, macerated
> anchovies, Maille mustard, a large spoonful of soya, chopped
> gherkins, and the chopped white of the eggs. I thin this mixture by

stirring in the finest vinegar obtainable. Finally I put the salad back into the bowl, and my servant tosses it. On the tossed salad I sprinkle a pinch of paprika, which is the Hungarian red pepper.

No matter how humble, each vegetable that could grow in Western Europe became a part of one or more of the cuisines. Thus, cooks are as well acquainted with the cookery of salsify, rutabaga, fennel, eggplant, celery root, kohlrabi, cardoons, sorrel, leeks, or endive, as they are with peas, carrots, beets, and beans. To understand the versatility and goodness of vegetable cookery, we can look to one of the oldest and best known "families," the onion. All of the members, chives, garlic, leeks, scallions (or green onions), shallots, and onion varieties—white, red, yellow—are highly esteemed throughout the Continent.

The most widely cultivated and used of all vegetables, onions have even had great power attributed to them. They were long ago employed medicinally and used for an untold number of illnesses. Some believed they could ward off evil. In medieval times, the Swiss wore them in necklaces as a charm against the plague.

Even today the Swiss accord the onion an unusual honor by setting aside one day each year—the fourth Monday of November—to celebrate the vegetable with a colorful Onion Market (*Zibele Marit*) in Berne. It is a festive occasion that includes buying and eating onions, dancing, and drinking wine. Visitors may sample a whole meal starring this vegetable: onion soup, sausages stuffed with onions, liver and onions, onion salad, fried onion rings, and a dessert of onion cake, a Berne specialty—truly a notable and befitting tribute to the onion!

Western European cooks have created a fascinating repertoire of onion dishes. They are, of course, important as seasonings and are treasured as flavorful additions to soups, stews, salads, and baked dishes. On the other hand, they may be stuffed, roasted, creamed, pickled, cooked with eggs, simmered in sauces, or added to breads and rolls.

Another vegetable of primary importance in central and northern European countries is the potato, a food that was introduced much later than the others. Spanish conquistadors brought the potato (as well as tomatoes, peppers, squashes, corn, and lima beans) to Europe, but it took some time for the white tuber to gain acceptance on the dining table. Potatoes were first planted in flower gardens as botanical curiosities, and eating them was frowned upon. Some persons actually blamed the vegetable for certain illnesses, and the upper classes considered them suitable only for cattle, the poor, and prisoners.

Fortunately, Antoine-Auguste Parmentier of France, who had subsisted on potatoes while a prisoner of the Prussians, worked tirelessly to change this attitude and ultimately succeeded in gaining acceptance of the potato as a valuable and economical food. The threat of famine was one of his weapons. Despite ridicule, he cultivated potatoes and served a dinner with 30 different potato dishes he had created. To further his ideas, he persuaded Louis XIV to accept a bouquet of their pretty blossoms in public acknowledgment of the value of the *pomme de terre* ("apple of the earth"). Marie-Antoinette loyally popularized them by wearing potato blossoms in her hair.

The French chefs elevated the stature of the potato by making it the feature of any number of delectable dishes. Some of them are named for Parmentier, who would have been pleased to know that the potato soon ranked first among France's vegetables. It is also most important in the cuisine of several other European countries.

Throughout Western Europe among the marvelous sights to see are the colorful displays of fresh vegetables, attractively arranged, in the open-air markets, sidewalk stalls, and groceries. Root and tuber, seed and pod, stem and flower, and leafy vegetables are delightful to behold. Although canned and frozen vegetables are available, cooks still prefer the fresh varieties and go to market daily to purchase the household supply. In most regions they are eaten in season, enjoyed while garden-fresh and tender.

Vegetables may be prepared and served as hors d'oeuvre, used in soups and stews, combined with eggs and cheese, cooked with meats and poultry, and used in some desserts. The recipes included here, however, are for dishes featuring vegetables that can be served as accompaniments to other foods or, in some cases, as entrées. Generally speaking, salads in Western Europe are enjoyed either as an appetizer or with the main course. Although salads feature vegetables as their most popular ingredients, some are made with fruit. Cooks will find this selection of recipes an extremely interesting and different one.

Belgian Endive

A great deal of confusion exists about the name of one of Western Europe's most highly prized vegetables, the endive of Belgium. For it is also called *witloof* (white leaf) and Brussels chicory (or *chicorée*), and is sometimes known by its botanical appellation, *Chicorium intybus*. Its growth is as curious as its name. The discovery was by accident. In 1845 a gardener in Brussels, experimenting to improve chicory roots, found that a group of them, left in a cellar for several days, began sprouting firm and white leaves. Further testing led to the development of the white-leaved heads. Over the years the pampered production of them in especially prepared underground "growing houses" became an important Belgian industry. Endive does not thrive as well anywhere else, and thus it is grown primarily in Belgium. Raw, the slightly bitter leaves are great favorites for salads, but they may be cooked also and served in a number of inviting creations. Given here are two favorite Continental endive preparations.

BRAISED ENDIVE

12 medium endive
Salt
4 tablespoons butter
2 tablespoons fresh lemon
  juice

Freshly ground pepper
3 tablespoons chopped fresh
  parsley

Trim and wash the endives. Drain well. Blanch in boiling salted water to cover for 10 minutes. Drain, pressing lightly, to remove all the water. Heat the butter and lemon juice in a skillet and add the endive. Cover and cook over low heat about 20 minutes, or until tender, the exact amount of time depending on the size. Season with salt and pepper and sprinkle with the parsley. Serves 4.

ENDIVE À LA MORNAY

This is an elegant dish for luncheon.

12 medium endive
2 tablespoons fresh lemon
 juice
Salt
12 thin slices cooked ham
3 tablespoons butter

3 tablespoons flour
1½ cups light cream
1 cup shredded Gruyère or
 Swiss cheese
Freshly ground pepper, grated
 nutmeg to taste

Trim and wash the endives. Drain well. Blanch with the lemon juice in boiling salted water to cover for 10 minutes. Drain well, pressing to release all the water. Roll each endive in a slice of ham. Set aside. Melt the butter in a saucepan. Mix in the flour and cook, stirring, 1 minute. Gradually add the cream and cook slowly, stirring, until smooth and thick. Add the cheese and season with salt, pepper, and nutmeg. Cook, stirring often, until the cheese melts. Spoon a little of the sauce into a buttered shallow baking dish and arrange the ham-wrapped endive over it. Pour the remaining sauce over the endive. Bake, uncovered, in a preheated hot oven (425°F.) for about 20 minutes, or until the cheese is melted and the sauce is bubbly. Serves 6 as an entrée or 12 as a first course.

IRISH COLCANNON

This humble dish of potatoes and cabbage, or sometimes kale, is traditional fare in Ireland and is also a Scottish favorite.

2 pounds potatoes, washed
Salt, pepper to taste
1 medium green cabbage,
 shredded

4 green onions, with tops,
 minced
¼ cup butter

Boil the potatoes in salted water until tender. Drain, peel, and mash. Season with salt and pepper. Keep warm. Meanwhile, cook the cabbage in boiling salted water until tender.

Drain. Sauté the green onions in the butter in a large saucepan until tender. Add the cabbage and sauté until heated. Mix with the warm potatoes. Serves 4.

A similar dish, called champ or thump, may be made by combining hot mashed potatoes with chopped green onions, including their tops, and a generous amount of butter.

ITALIAN FENNEL WITH PARMESAN

Fennel, an aromatic vegetable with an anise flavor, is highly regarded in Mediterranean locales. Called *finocchio* in Italian, the plant is valued for its seeds and leaves, used for seasonings; and for its bulb, which when cooked makes a good vegetable dish or, used raw, an interesting salad.

4 bulbs sweet fennel	Pepper to taste
Salt	½ cup freshly grated
½ cup melted butter	Parmesan cheese

Remove and discard the fernlike tops, tough outer stalks, and stems of the fennel bulbs. Wash and cut crosswise into thin slices. Cook in boiling salted water until tender, about 5 minutes. Drain. Spoon into a buttered shallow baking dish. Season with salt and pepper. Pour the melted butter over them. Sprinkle with the cheese. Put in a preheated hot oven (425°F.) for about 10 minutes, or until the top is golden. Serves 4.

SWISS RÖSTI

This national dish of Switzerland is eaten daily in the homes and appears on most restaurant menus. It is generally prepared with a special grater but any standard kind can be used. Grated Emmenthaler or Gruyère cheese may be added to the potatoes in place of the onion, if desired.

6 medium potatoes, washed	Salt to taste
1 small onion, minced (optional)	About ¼ cup butter

Boil the unpeeled potatoes in salted boiling water until just fork tender. Drain and cool. Remove the skins and grate the potatoes. Mix with the onion and salt. Melt 2 tablespoons of the butter in a skillet that is about 10 inches in diameter. Add the potato mixture and flatten with a spatula into a thin cake. Cook over a moderate fire until a golden crust forms on the bottom. Shake the pan occasionally so it does not stick. Loosen around the edges. Put a plate over the top and invert onto the plate. Add more butter and then return the potato cake to the pan. Cook until golden brown on the other side. Serves 4.

GERMAN POTATO PANCAKES

Kartoffelpuffer are internationally famous German creations made in a number of versions. They are often served with apple sauce and as accompaniments to such meats as roast pork or sausages.

4 medium (about 1⅓ pounds)   2 tablespoons flour
  potatoes   Salt, pepper to taste
1 small onion   Shortening for frying
1 large egg

Peel the potatoes and onion and grate into a large bowl. Drain off any liquid, pressing with a spoon to release all of it. Add the egg, flour, salt, pepper and mix well. Heat enough shortening in a frying pan to grease the surface. Drop spoonfuls of the potato mixture into the fat and fry a few minutes to brown. Turn over with a spatula and brown on the other side, adding more shortening if needed. Serves 4.

AUSTRIAN CREAMED SPINACH

This is an interesting manner of preparing a favorite Austrian vegetable, *Spinat*.

2 packages (10 ounces each)   Salt
  fresh spinach, washed and   2 tablespoons butter
  trimmed   1 small onion, minced

2 tablespoons flour
½ cup beef bouillon
1 tablespoon fresh lemon juice
2 teaspoons chopped fresh dill

Pepper to taste
½ cup sour cream at room
  temperature

Cook the spinach in a very small amount of salted water until tender. Drain and chop. Melt the butter in a large saucepan. Add the onion and sauté until tender. Stir in the flour and cook 1 minute. Gradually add the bouillon and cook, stirring, until thickened. Mix in the chopped cooked spinach, lemon juice, dill, salt, and pepper and stir together. Add the sour cream and leave on the stove over low heat long enough to heat through. Serves 4.

CHAMPIGNONS FARCIS PROVENÇALE

There are many fine French preparations for stuffing large mushrooms, which may be served as accompaniments to meats or as appetizers. This variation is favored in lovely Provence in southern France.

1 pound large fresh
  mushrooms
About ⅓ cup butter
¼ cup minced shallots or
  green onions
2 garlic cloves, crushed

5 tablespoons olive oil
2 medium tomatoes, peeled,
  seeded, and chopped
½ teaspoon dried basil
Salt, pepper to taste
⅓ cup chopped fresh parsley

Clean the mushrooms to remove any dirt by wiping with a damp paper towel or rinsing quickly in water. Pull off the stems. Cut off any tough ends and discard. Mince the stems and set aside. Brush the caps with melted butter and arrange, hollow sides up, in a buttered shallow baking dish.

Sauté the shallots and garlic in 2 tablespoons of butter and 2 tablespoons of olive oil until tender. Add the minced mushroom stems and sauté for 1 minute. Stir in the tomatoes, basil, salt, and pepper, and cook about 5 minutes. Remove from the heat and mix in the parsley. Spoon into the mushroom caps, filling them as full as possible. Sprinkle the tops with the remaining 3 tablespoons of olive oil. Bake in a preheated moderately hot oven (375°F.) for about 20 minutes, or until the caps are tender. Serves 4 to 6.

GERMAN HEAVEN AND EARTH

Himmel und Erde, a simple combination of potatoes and apples, is a specialty of the Rhineland and is eaten traditionally with slices of fried blood sausage.

2 pounds potatoes, washed and peeled	Pinch sugar
	Salt, pepper to taste
2 pounds apples, cored and peeled	¼ pound bacon, chopped and cooked

Cook the potatoes in water to cover until tender. Drain and mash. Cook the apples in water to cover until soft. Drain and purée. While still hot, combine the potatoes and apples. Season with sugar, salt, and pepper. Have the bacon already cooked and sprinkle it and a little of the fat over the potato-apple mixture. Serves 4 to 6.

DANISH RED CABBAGE

Rodkall, a Danish national vegetable dish, is eaten traditionally with roast pork, goose, or duck. It is a favorite holiday dish and is best if prepared the day before and reheated.

1 medium head red cabbage	2 to 3 teaspoons sugar
3 tablespoons butter	Salt to taste
⅓ cup water	¼ cup red currant juice or jelly
⅓ cup red-wine vinegar	

Wash and drain the cabbage. Cut out and discard the tough core and remove any wilted leaves. Shred the cabbage. Melt the butter in a large saucepan. Add the cabbage and sauté about 5 minutes. Pour in the water and vinegar. Add the sugar and salt. Cook over low heat, tightly covered, for 1 hour. Stir in the red currant juice or jelly and cook another 5 minutes. Serves 4 to 6.

VIENNESE CUCUMBER SALAD

Gurkensalat is Vienna's most popular salad and may be prepared in a number of inviting ways. Sometimes it is made with lemon juice instead of vinegar; without sugar; with garlic; or with a garnish of paprika. This is a common version.

3 medium cucumbers
Salt
¼ cup white-wine vinegar
¼ cup vegetable oil

1 teaspoon sugar
Freshly ground white pepper
Chopped chives or parsley

Peel the cucumbers and score with a fork. Cut into paper-thin slices. Put in a bowl and sprinkle with salt. Leave for 30 minutes. Drain well. Arrange in a bowl. Add the vinegar, oil, and sugar. Season with salt and pepper. Mix well. Serve garnished with chopped chives or parsley. Serves 4 to 6.

Sour cream may be added to the salad, if desired.

SWEDISH POTATO SALAD

This salad is ideal for a buffet or outdoor meal.

6 medium potatoes, about 2
  pounds, washed
Salt, pepper to taste
1 medium onion, chopped
1 cup chopped cooked beets
2 tablespoons drained capers

½ cup mayonnaise
½ cup sour cream
3 tablespoons chopped fresh
  parsley
Lettuce leaves (optional)

Cook the potatoes in boiling salted water until just tender. Cool. Peel and slice. Mix with the remaining ingredients, except the parsley and lettuce. Chill and serve cold on the lettuce leaves, if desired, and garnished with the parsley. Serves 4 to 6.

Add more mayonnaise if needed. The ingredients, however, should be thickly bound together.

PORTUGUESE GREEN BEANS

A flavorful vegetable dish to serve with any kind of meat but particularly lamb.

1 large onion, thinly sliced
1 garlic clove, crushed
3 tablespoons olive oil
2 large tomatoes, peeled and
  chopped

1 pound fresh green beans,
  trimmed and cut up
Salt, pepper to taste
⅓ cup chopped fresh coriander
  or parsley

Sauté the onion and garlic in the olive oil in a saucepan. Add the tomatoes and sauté for 5 minutes. Add the green beans, salt, and pepper and cook slowly, covered, for about 20 minutes, or until the beans are tender. Stir in the coriander and remove from the heat. Serves 4.

FRENCH CARROTS VICHY

This very popular Continental vegetable dish, found on the menus of many fine restaurants, is thought to have been named for the famous French town of Vichy, which is noted for its mineral springs, luxuriant parks, and gardens. Visitors who took the "cure" for their liver were given also carrots, said to be good for the ailment. But this dish is enjoyed for pleasurable rather than medicinal purposes.

18 small whole carrots, scraped
2 tablespoons sugar
⅓ cup butter
1 cup water

Salt, pepper to taste
3 tablespoons chopped fresh
  parsley

Put the carrots, sugar, butter, water, salt, and pepper in a saucepan and bring to a boil. Lower the heat and cook slowly, covered, until most of the liquid has evaporated and has boiled down to become thick and syrupy, about 30 minutes. Serve garnished with the parsley. Serves 4 to 6.

WHITE ASPARAGUS

The most luxurious of all the vegetables enjoyed in Western Europe is undoubtedly asparagus, and there are many great dishes made with the delectable stalks. Although the green variety is grown and savored in many locales, the most highly prized in such countries as Belgium, France, Germany, and Switzerland is the tender, thick pearl-white kind.

Asperges blanches were in great vogue in France by the time of Louis XIV, and those grown in Argenteuil near Paris are still very highly rated. The Germans began growing *Spargel* (white asparagus) seriously by the 1700s, and it has been a national culinary treasure ever since. In fact, each spring the country goes on a *Spargel* spree. The stalks, grown in dirt mounds without being exposed to light, are ready to harvest when the sun begins to crack the earth's surface. Timing is of utmost importance, as any exposure to the light will result in coloring the stalks and reduce their value. Harvesting is also difficult, as it must be done by hand with a special long-handled tool.

At the beginning of the season, in mid- or late April, housewives flock to the markets to get the earliest possible purchase of bunches of *Spargel*, which must be carefully peeled from just below the tip to the base with a special gadget before cooking. After being boiled the stalks are served whole and warm on platters with matching porcelain strainers, or they are left to cool and are served cold. The top grade, always served whole, is called *Stangenspargel*. Pieces of second and third grades, termed *Spargelgemüse*, are made into various dishes. The lowest grade is used for soups, and the peelings or leftover pieces are made into a broth, highly regarded as a tonic for its diuretic quality.

It is also a part of the spring *Spargel* mania to seek out favorite restaurants that specialize in an incredible number of dishes made with white asparagus. Many of them have menus specially printed for the short season. The Gastehaus Grundmuhle, a restaurant in Würzburg, features 23 warm specialties and 7 cold ones. The Hotel Rad in Tettnang, near Lake Constance, a 300-year-old half-timbered landmark, is famous for its 55 dishes. A particular mecca for *Spargel* lovers, however, is a delightful small town of Schwetzingen, near Heidelberg, which was once a summer playground for German royalty. The local restaurants serve a small number of the traditional *Spargel* favorites. At the Gasthof zum Ritter, the white stalks are eaten with a large *Pfannkuchen* (pancake), which actually consists of delicate pieces of golden deep-fried egg batter. In the Gasthof zum Erbprinzen, the asparagus is accompanied by thin slices of Westphalian ham served separately on small wooden boards. At the Adler Post, two particular treats are *Spargel* with a thin hollandaise sauce and a platter-sized *Speckpfannkuchen*, a pancake that includes chips of bacon in the batter, and a large pancake prepared with a batter mixed with champagne and mineral water.

During the spring it is certainly a worthwhile venture to seek out this specialty in the restaurants of any of the other above-mentioned countries in Europe. Canned white asparagus can be purchased in America and prepared in the same way as the green variety.

ONIONS MONÉGASQUE

This is one version of a vegetable dish from the lovely principality of Monaco, famed for its gaiety, gambling, and good living. This specialty is often served cold as a part of the hors d'oeuvre, but it may be enjoyed as an accompaniment to an entrée such as chicken or roast meat.

2 pounds small white onions
1 cup white vinegar
2 cups water
¼ cup vegetable oil
1 teaspoon sugar

Salt, white pepper
⅓ to ½ cup tomato paste
½ cup seedless raisins
⅓ cup chopped fresh parsley

Wash and peel the onions. Put in a large saucepan with the vinegar, water, oil, sugar, salt, and pepper. Bring to a boil. Lower the heat and cook slowly, covered, until the onions are just tender, about 15 minutes; the exact time will depend on their size. When tender, remove with a slotted spoon to a large bowl. Add the tomato paste and raisins to the remaining liquid and boil briskly to reduce to a thickened sauce. Stir in the parsley and pour over the onions. Let cool. Serves 6 to 8.

CHEESE SALAD À LA SUISSE

¾ pound Emmenthaler or Swiss cheese, cut into ½-inch cubes
1 medium onion, chopped
1 tablespoon grated horseradish

1 tablespoon white vinegar
2 tablespoons vegetable oil
2 teaspoons prepared mustard
2 tablespoons mayonnaise
Salt, pepper to taste
Lettuce leaves

Garnishes:
tomato slices, gherkin slices

Combine the cheese and onion in a bowl. Mix together the horseradish, vinegar, oil, mustard, mayonnaise, salt, and pepper. Combine with the cheese mixture. Serve on lettuce leaves garnished with the tomato and gherkin slices.

SALADE LIÉGEOISE

This is a specialty of Liège, one of Belgium's gayest cities and very French-oriented, noted for fine fare. A superb restaurant in Liège that features elegant creations is a hillside gastronomic temple called Clou Doré.

1 pound fresh green beans
4 large potatoes
1 small piece bacon

¼ cup vinegar
1 large onion, minced
Salt, pepper to taste

Remove the stems from the beans and break the beans into 1-inch pieces. Put in a saucepan with a little salted water. Bring to a boil. Lower the heat and cook until tender, about 20 minutes. Drain. Meanwhile, peel and cube the potatoes. Cook in water to cover until just tender. Drain. Dice the bacon and cook in a skillet. Add the vinegar and then the beans and potatoes. Mix well. Stir in the onion and season with salt and pepper. Serve hot. Serves 4.

NORWEGIAN LETTUCE SALAD

1 small head lettuce
½ cup sour cream
1 teaspoon sugar
2 teaspoons vinegar

¼ teaspoon prepared mustard
Salt, pepper to taste
1 hard-cooked egg, shelled and
   cut into wedges

Wash the lettuce. Drain and dry well. Tear into bite-size pieces and put in a large salad bowl. Combine the sour cream, sugar, vinegar, mustard, salt, and pepper and mix with the lettuce, tossing lightly. Serve garnished with the egg wedges. Serves 4.

RIVIERA STUFFED ARTICHOKES

Once deemed by Pliny "monstrous productions of the earth," artichokes are now aristocratic vegetables prepared in fascinating creations. The Romans even use them to make artichoke ice cream. This is a favorite Mediterranean dish that often appears on menus of inviting restaurants along the Riviera.

2 cups coarse dry bread
   crumbs
2 tablespoons minced
   anchovies
½ cup chopped fresh parsley
½ cup grated Parmesan
   cheese

3 garlic cloves, minced
Freshly ground pepper to taste
4 large artichokes
1 large lemon, sliced
¼ cup olive oil
Melted butter (optional)

Combine the first six ingredients and mix well. Wash the artichokes thoroughly in cold water and drain. With a sharp knife, cut off about ⅓ inch from the top. Cut off the stem ends so that the artichokes will stand upright. With kitchen scissors, snip off the sharp leaf tips of each artichoke. Tear off and discard any loose or spotted leaves. With a teaspoon or knife, scoop out the choke. Spread out the leaves gently with the hands. Spoon the stuffing into the center and between the leaves of each artichoke. Pour hot water, enough to be 1 inch deep, into a large kettle and bring to a boil. Arrange the artichokes, one next to another, in it. Add the sliced lemon and sprinkle the artichokes with the oil. Turn down the heat and cook slowly, covered, about 45 minutes, or until the artichokes are tender. Carefully remove with a slotted spoon and drain. Serve with melted butter, if desired. Serves 4.

Sauerkraut

A very popular dish in northeastern France, Norway, Switzerland, Austria, and Germany is fermented green cabbage or sauerkraut. This very old creation, dating back some 2,000 years, is believed to have originated in the Orient, where it was eaten by laborers building China's Great Wall. Invading Tartars some 700 years ago are credited with introducing sauerkraut to central Europe, where it has long been popular. Sauerkraut is so important in the German cuisine that it appears in a wide number of variations. It may be simmered in white wine, beer, bouillon, or champagne; cooked with apples, pineapple, caraway seed, or juniper berries; and appear as an accompaniment to or topped with such meats as pork, sausages, or game. Some cooks thicken sauerkraut with grated raw potatoes or flour. Others do not thicken it at all. Visitors to Germany are ever amazed at the interesting ways sauerkraut appears on their plates. The sauerkraut of Norway is somewhat different in that it is not fermented in salt but is made by cooking cabbage with tart flavorings and caraway seeds. Following are three good sauerkraut recipes. Two others are Alsatian Choucroute Garnie (p. 160) and Berner Platte (p. 164).

GERMAN SAUERKRAUT WITH APPLES

1 medium onion, chopped
3 tablespoons lard or bacon fat
1 pound sauerkraut, drained
½ cup beef bouillon
2 tart apples, cored, peeled,
  and chopped

1 teaspoon sugar
½ teaspoon caraway seeds
1 small potato, peeled and
  grated
Salt, pepper to taste

Sauté the onion in the lard or fat in a large saucepan until tender. Add the sauerkraut and sauté for 5 minutes. Put in the remaining ingredients and cook slowly, covered, for 45 minutes. Serves 4.

GERMAN SAUERKRAUT WITH PINEAPPLE

During the past few years the Germans have become great devotees of pineapple, which they have added to many of their traditional dishes including sauerkraut. This is served often with game birds or ham.

1 pound sauerkraut, drained
3 tablespoons butter
¾ cup sweetened pineapple
  juice

1 cup drained crushed
  pineapple

Sauté the sauerkraut in the butter in a large saucepan for 5 minutes. Add the pineapple juice and cook slowly, tightly covered, for 1 hour. Add the pineapple and leave on the stove over low heat long enough to heat through. Serves 4.

NORWEGIAN SAUERKRAUT

3 tablespoons butter or pork
  drippings
1 pound green cabbage,
  shredded (about 5 cups)
1 tablespoon caraway seeds

About 2 tablespoons cider
  vinegar
2 teaspoons sugar
½ cup beef bouillon or water
Salt, pepper to taste

Melt the butter in a large saucepan. Add the remaining ingredients and bring to a boil. Lower the heat and cook slowly, covered, for about 1 hour, or until the cabbage is cooked. Add more vinegar after the dish is cooked if a tarter flavor is desired. Serves 4.

ITALIAN SAUTÉED BROCCOLI

A very popular vegetable in Rome is the tender and delectable broccoli. This dish appears often on Italian menus as *broccoli alla romana.*

1 bunch broccoli	1 or 2 garlic cloves, minced or
¼ cup olive oil	crushed
	Salt, freshly ground pepper

Wash the broccoli and cut off and discard the tough part of the stem and large outer leaves. Put in a large saucepan with 1 inch of salted boiling water. Cook slowly, covered, for about 12 minutes, or until just tender. Remove from the heat and drain well. Divide into florets. Heat the oil in a large skillet. Add the garlic and broccoli and fry until covered with the oil and garlic. Season with salt and pepper and serve. Serves 4.

DANISH CARAMELIZED POTATOES

The most characteristic way of preparing potatoes in Denmark is to sugar-brown them. *Brunede Kartofler* are served with traditional fare such as pork and game.

2 pounds small potatoes,	¼ cup sugar
washed	½ cup butter

Cook the potatoes in water to cover until tender. Drain and peel. Put the sugar in a skillet and heat until golden brown. Do not burn. Add the butter. When melted, add the potatoes and cook them, shaking the pan occasionally, until they are covered on all sides with the golden mixture. Serves 4.

GERMAN PURÉED CELERY ROOT

Celery root or celeriac, a gnarled and knobby brown root with a celerylike flavor, is widely used in Germany as well as other northern European countries. The French enjoy it with remoulade sauce for an hors d'oeuvre. In Germany it is served as a salad, with a cream or another sauce, or as this simple preparation.

2 celery roots
8 tablespoons butter
1 cup beef bouillon or water

4 teaspoons sugar
Salt, pepper to taste

Wash, peel, and dice the celery roots. Melt 6 tablespoons of the butter in a large saucepan and add the diced celery root. Sauté 1 minute. Add the bouillon, sugar, salt, and pepper and bring to a boil. Lower the heat and cook slowly, covered, for about 15 minutes, or until tender. Mash well or put through a sieve. Add the remaining 2 tablespoons of butter and season again with salt and pepper if necessary. Serves 6 to 8.

SPANISH PISTO LA MANCHA-STYLE

In Spain a flavorful vegetable stew is called *pisto* and can include such varieties as onions, eggplant, tomatoes, green peppers, string beans, squash, or pumpkin. The variation that originated in the famous central plain of La Mancha is one of the best and includes pumpkin. In this recipe zucchini is used as a substitute.

⅓ cup diced cooked ham
About ⅓ cup olive oil
1 large onion, chopped
2 medium garlic cloves,
  minced

2 zucchini, sliced
1 small eggplant, unpeeled and
  cubed
4 medium tomatoes, peeled
  and chopped

2 medium green peppers,
  cleaned and chopped
Salt, pepper to taste

4 eggs
¼ cup chopped fresh parsley

Fry the ham with 2 tablespoons of oil in a large skillet. Add the onion and garlic and sauté until tender. Push aside and add more oil, the zucchini, and the eggplant. Sauté, adding more oil as needed, until the vegetables are tender. Stir in the tomatoes, green peppers, salt, and pepper. Cook slowly, covered, for 20 minutes. Beat the eggs lightly and stir into the vegetable mixture. Add the parsley. Cook another few minutes on low heat, stirring occasionally, until the mixture is set. Serves 6.

LEEKS À LA NIÇOISE

Although the French commonly use leeks, *poireaux*, for flavoring soups and stews, they have also devised some excellent dishes starring the vegetable. Many are baked creations with cream or cheese sauces. This one utilizes the typical foods of Nice, the beautiful Mediterranean resort city with its famed Promenade des Anglais along the seafront.

12 fresh leeks
⅓ cup olive oil
1 or 2 garlic cloves, minced
3 medium tomatoes, peeled,
  seeded, and chopped
1 tablespoon fresh lemon juice

½ cup pitted black olives
Salt, pepper to taste
3 tablespoons chopped fresh
  parsley
Wedges of hard-cooked egg
  (optional)

Cut the roots and top green leaves from the leeks. Remove any wilted leaves. Wash the leeks thoroughly to remove all the dirt. Drain well. Leave whole or cut into halves lengthwise. Heat the oil in a skillet and add the leeks. Cook covered, over medium heat for about 10 minutes, until just tender. Add the remaining ingredients, except the parsley and eggs. Cook, uncovered, for 5 minutes. Remove from the heat and sprinkle with parsley. Serve garnished with the eggs. Serve hot or cold. Serves 6.

SALAD VALENCIANA

The region of Valencia on Spain's eastern Mediterranean coast is noted for many glories, including flavorful oranges. Such is the beauty of their white flowers that open in the evening that the area has been called the Coast of Orange Blossoms. This is a typical salad featuring oranges.

2 large oranges, peeled and sliced
1 large white onion, peeled and sliced
3 or 4 tablespoons olive oil
1 or 2 tablespoons wine vinegar
Salt, pepper to taste
Salad greens
Pitted black olives

Combine the orange and onion slices, oil, vinegar, salt, and pepper in a bowl and leave for 1 hour. Stir the ingredients now and then. Serve over or mix with salad greens. Garnish with the olives. Serves 4.

EGGPLANT ALLA PARMIGIANA FROM ITALY

This flavorful eggplant casserole is one of the best of the many dishes made with this favorite Mediterranean vegetable. The handsome purple treasure, grown in round and elongated shapes, achieves added appeal when married with olive oil, tomatoes, and pungent herbs, as in this dish. This can be served as a luncheon dish or accompaniment to roast meat, particularly lamb.

2 eggplants, about 1 pound each
Salt
Olive oil
1 medium onion, minced
1 can (4 ounces) tomato paste
3 cans water
1 teaspoon dried basil
½ teaspoon dried oregano
Pepper to taste
Flour
2 or 3 eggs, beaten
¾ pound mozzarella cheese, sliced
½ cup grated Parmesan cheese

Wash the eggplants; remove the stems; cut crosswise into slices about ¼ inch thick. Put in a colander and sprinkle with salt. Leave to drain for 30 minutes. Meanwhile, heat 2 tablespoons of oil in a skillet and add the onion. Sauté until tender. Add the tomato paste, water, basil, and oregano. Season with salt and pepper. Cook over a low fire, uncovered, about 20 minutes. Stir occasionally while cooking.

Drain the eggplant slices and wipe dry with paper toweling. Dredge each slice with flour and dip in beaten egg. Fry on both sides in hot oil until golden. Drain on paper toweling.

Line a shallow baking dish with a little of the tomato sauce. Arrange a layer of the eggplant slices over it. Cover with a layer of mozzarella slices, one of sauce, and a sprinkling of Parmesan cheese. Repeat the layers until all the ingredients are used. Top with a generous sprinkling of Parmesan. Bake in a preheated moderate oven (350°F.) about 30 minutes, or until tender. Serves 6.

MIXED SALAD FROM LIECHTENSTEIN

The tiny principality of Liechtenstein, a storybook paradise tucked in between Switzerland, Italy, Austria, and Germany, is truly a pleasure to visit. Its scenery is breathtaking, and the way of life is a page from yesteryear. One most pleasurable experience in Vaduz ("Sweet Valley"), the atmospheric capital, is to dine at the Hotel Real, a landmark on the main square. The indoor restaurant and outdoor café are noted for their charm and particularly fine cuisine. There is nothing pretentious about the décor, but one appreciates the warmth of the Old World surroundings and the geniality of the clientele. Tourists mingle with local residents, including scions of Europe's royal houses. A luncheon there remains one of my most memorable European meals. The menu included: consommé with tiny liver noodles, pork fillets with a morel sauce, buttered thin green noodles, carrots Vichy, mixed vegetable salad, and a delicate pink raspberry sherbet with a champagne sauce. It was topped with a single wild mountain strawberry and accompanied by *petits-fours*.

1 cup drained corn niblets
1 can (1 pound) kidney beans, drained
1 cup chopped cucumber
1 medium onion, finely chopped

2 medium tomatoes, peeled and chopped
3 tablespoons vegetable oil
2 tablespoons red wine vinegar
Salt, pepper to taste

Combine all the ingredients in a large bowl and mix well. Chill. Serves 6 to 8.

HOP SPROUTS

Hop sprouts, called in French *jets de houblon* and in German *Hopfensprossen,* are the edible flowers of a perennial herb important to the brewing of ale and beer. The young shoots are cut in spring from the hop vines, tall climbing plants, and are considered great delicacies in Belgium, France, and Germany. Although not actually vegetables, they are boiled and served with butter and cream, with sauces, or cold as a salad. Many cooks point out that the hops may be prepared in the same way as asparagus. Available for only a few weeks in spring, they are generally found in the markets beginning in early March and perhaps through April. I first purchased the shoots at the colorful Victualian Markt in Munich where they were on display among vegetables, fruits, nuts, and other foods from all over Europe and the Middle East. One of the best places to sample hop sprouts is the restaurant of the Hotel Rad in Tettnang, Germany, where a special menu includes 30 dishes featuring hop sprouts, prepared in much the same way as asparagus.

FRENCH POMMES SOUFFLÉS

One of the delights of the French cuisine is this potato creation. Although termed soufflés, they are actually slices of potatoes, fried twice in hot fat until puffed up. The technique requires some practice to perfect, but it is well worth attempting. These are beautifully prepared and are served in France's great restaurants.

Cut firm, pared potatoes into thin oval slices ⅛ inch thick and of equal size. Discard any small end slices. Put in ice water for 30 minutes. Drain and wipe dry. Drop into hot fat (350°F. on a frying thermometer) and cook until the potatoes begin to rise to the top and puff a little. Turn once while cooking. Drain in the frying basket and remove to absorbent paper for 5 minutes. Plunge a few at a time into a second pan of hot fat which is 450°F. on a frying thermometer. As soon as the potatoes puff up again and become golden take out of the fat and drain. Serve at once lightly sprinkled with salt.

NORTHERN EUROPEAN CREAMED KOHLRABI

Kohlrabi, a very popular vegetable in northern Europe, particularly Germany, is a member of the cabbage family. The name in German means "cabbage turnip." It is an excellent accompaniment to roast pork. When the leaves are tender they are customarily cooked and served with the root vegetable, as in this recipe.

2 small kohlrabi	Salt, pepper, nutmeg to taste
7 tablespoons butter	¼ cup flour
¼ cup light cream	⅓ cup chopped fresh parsley

Cut off the kohlrabi leaves and cook them in salted water to cover in a saucepan for about 15 minutes, or until tender. Drain and chop. Add 3 tablespoons of the butter and the cream. Season with salt, pepper, and nutmeg. Keep warm. Meanwhile, trim the kohlrabi roots; peel and slice. Cook the slices in 2 cups of boiling salted water in a saucepan for about 25 minutes, or until tender. Drain, reserving the liquid. Melt the remaining butter in a saucepan and stir in the flour to blend well. Season with salt, pepper, and nutmeg. Add the reserved vegetable liquid and cook slowly, stirring, until a thick and smooth sauce. Add the cooked kohlrabi slices and parsley and leave on the stove over low heat long enough to heat through. Serve surrounded by the cooked leaves. Serves 4.

ROMAN PEAS WITH PROSCIUTTO

Piselli al prosciutto is a very popular dish in the great restaurants of Rome where it is made with very sweet and tender peas and the superb prosciutto ham.

2 pounds fresh peas, shelled	Salt
1 small onion, minced	Freshly ground pepper to taste
1/3 cup butter	1 cup chopped prosciutto or
Pinch sugar	other smoked ham

Cook the peas in a little salted water in a saucepan until just tender, about 8 minutes. Drain. Sauté the onion in the butter in a saucepan until tender. Add the peas, sugar, salt, pepper, and ham and sauté about 2 minutes. Serves 4.

DUTCH BRAISED BEETS

In Holland many of the vegetable dishes such as these beets, *bieten,* have a piquant flavor derived from vinegar.

1 can (1 pound) or 2 cups	2 teaspoons sugar
sliced beets, drained	1 tablespoon red-wine vinegar
1 small onion, minced	Salt, pepper to taste
3 whole cloves	Cornstarch (optional)

Combine the beets, onion, cloves, sugar, vinegar, salt, and pepper in a saucepan and simmer, covered, for 10 minutes. Remove and discard the cloves. Thicken with a little cornstarch mixed with cold water if a thicker consistency is desired. Serves 4.

9

Sauces

"ONE CAN LEARN to cook, and one can be taught to roast, but a good sauce-maker is a genius born, not made," declared Brillat-Savarin, the eminent French gastronome. In the realm of cookery the art of preparing sauces is truly of utmost importance. Their ingredients must be expertly blended to produce creations that will harmonize with and enhance the flavors of the various foods. Often they will also make them visually more attractive. The triumph of many a culinary presentation has been attributed to the selection of the sauce.

Our word for sauce evolved from *sauco*, a derivation of the Latin word *saltus*, meaning salted. The early sauces of the Imperial Romans were curious combinations of incredible numbers of diverse ingredients which appear to have had the purpose of disguising the flavors of the particular foods. In the cookbook *Apicius* we find that a sauce was used by the Romans in just about every dish and was devised to "change the original taste radically." The author boasted that after the cook prepared the fare "not one at table will know what he is eating."

Among the Roman sauces were those with pungent sweet-and-sour flavors, a legacy that still persists in many of the

Western European cuisines. One of the great English favorites, catsup or ketchup, would become the national sauce of America. The Romans also used anchovies in their sauces, another characteristic that has persisted in other lands through the ages.

During the Renaissance, Italian cooks reversed the culinary practices of their forefathers, and a large repertoire of refined sauces began to evolve. It was the French chefs, however, who perfected the art of sauce-making and gave the world the great classic creations. In the *Larousse Gastronomique* we can read recipes for some 200 sauces, all of these deriving from a few fundamental ones called by the French *sauces mères*, ("mother sauces") or sometimes *grandes sauces*. The first of these is brown sauce or *sauce espagnole,* one of the best and most complicated, as it is made with a rich stock. An offshoot of it is *demi-glace.* Two white sauces are *velouté,* made also with a rich stock, and *béchamel,* a simpler preparation of butter, flour, and milk. The primary emulsified sauces are hollandaise, made with egg yolks, melted butter, and lemon juice; and mayonnaise, an uncooked combination of egg yolks, oil, and seasonings. *Vinaigrette* is prepared with oil, vinegar, and seasonings.

These mother sauces and the many others based on them are important to the cuisines of Western Europe. In addition, each of the countries also has its own characteristic kinds. Over the years housewives and chefs devised a fascinating repertoire of national sauces that were not necessarily complex creations but nevertheless were good and interesting. Many of the Spanish dishes have a typical base sauce called *sofrito,* made generally with garlic, onions, ham, tomatoes, peppers, and perhaps other ingredients, which are fried lightly in olive oil. Others, such as *chilindrón* or *romescu,* include similar ingredients, perhaps adding herbs and nuts. Sherry is added to a few sauces.

An important addition to the Italian sauce repertoire occurred in the sixteenth century with the introduction of the tomato from the New World. Many of the southern sauces, now exported around the world and very popular with pasta dishes, are made with this favorite red vegetable. This is not to say, however, that the Italian cuisine does not include a fascinating number of other innovative sauces. *Pesto,* for example, a sauce specialty of Genoa, is a thick flavorful combination of fresh basil, garlic, pine nuts, olive oil, and cheese. The Sicilians have a sauce called *alla Sarde,* which is a mixture of fresh sardines, onions, raisins, black olives, and herbs.

In addition to the great classic sauces, the French have regional favorites that range from the Mediterranean staple of garlic and oil to a rich cream-and-butter combination of Normandy. Central Europeans favor piquant or tart flavorings in many of their sauces. Thus they will include such favorite foods as cucumbers, capers, vinegar, horseradish, mustard, tart fruits and berries, and sour cream. Dill and parsley are popular herbs.

Some of the same flavorings can be found in the Scandinavian sauces, for each of their cuisines has one or more sauces seasoned with dill, mustard, or horseradish, and with berries, particularly lingonberries or cloudberries. Egg and shrimp sauces are commonly served with the many seafood dishes.

Some of the more interesting sauces of Western Europe can be found in Great Britain. The Normans introduced sauces, as well as their word *sausse,* to the island, and since then some very cherished characteristic examples have become important to the everyday cookery. The five basic sauces prepared in the home are apple, mint, onion, bread, and horseradish. Additional favorites are variations of white sauce, including such flavorings as hard-cooked eggs, capers, anchovies, mushrooms, and mustard. Possibly the best known English sauce is the bottled Worcestershire, which is used frequently in the cookery.

Included here is a collection of some of the classic sauces and national favorites that can be made easily in the home kitchen.

SWISS SAUCE VERTE

This is an excellent green sauce to serve with cold fish. In Switzerland it accompanies the superb salmon.

½ cup chopped fresh spinach
½ cup chopped fresh
  watercress
⅓ cup chopped fresh herbs
  (parsley, tarragon, or
  chervil)

2 egg yolks or 1 whole egg
½ teaspoon dry mustard
Salt, pepper to taste
2 tablespoons fresh lemon
  juice or white wine vinegar
1 cup olive or salad oil

Combine the spinach, watercress, and herbs with a little water in a saucepan. Cook slowly until tender, about 2 or 3 minutes. Drain well, pressing firmly to remove all the liquid. Put through a sieve or mince finely. Cool. Combine the egg yolks or egg, mustard, salt, and pepper in a bowl. Beat with a whisk or fork until well combined. Stir in 1 tablespoon of the lemon juice or vinegar. Add ¼ cup of the oil drop by drop, beating while adding. Add more oil, a little more quickly, still beating while adding. Then add the remaining tablespoon of lemon juice and oil alternately, beating constantly until thick. Mix in the· chopped vegetables and herbs. Serve cold. Makes about 1¼ cups.

ENGLISH CUMBERLAND SAUCE

This traditional English sauce is served with roast game, boiled ham, or other pork.

½ cup red currant jelly
½ cup port wine
1½ teaspoons grated orange
  peel
1½ teaspoons grated lemon
  peel

2 teaspoons fresh lemon juice
2 teaspoons fresh orange juice
½ teaspoon dry mustard
Pinch each of cayenne and
  ground ginger
Salt, pepper to taste

Heat the jelly in a small saucepan. Mix in the remaining ingredients. Remove from the heat and cool. Serve at room temperature. Makes about 1¼ cups.

DANISH MUSTARD SAUCE

This is one version of *Sennepssovs,* mustard sauce, which is served in Denmark with boiled cod or other fish.

2 tablespoons butter
2 tablespoons flour
2 cups fish stock or milk

2 or 3 teaspoons powdered
  mustard
Pinch sugar
Salt, pepper to taste

Melt the butter in a saucepan. Stir in the flour to form a *roux*. Gradually add the stock or milk and cook slowly, stirting, until a thick and smooth sauce. Add the mustard, sugar, salt and pepper and cook 1 minute to blend the flavors. Makes about 2 cups.

MINT SAUCE FROM ENGLAND

Serve with roast lamb or mutton.

1 cup chopped fresh mint
 leaves
1 or 2 tablespoons sugar

½ cup malt or white vinegar
½ cup water

Put the mint, sugar, and vinegar in a small saucepan. Mix well. Add the water and bring to a boil. Remove from the heat and cool. Makes about 1½ cups.

SWEDISH GRAVLAXSAS

This sauce, *gravlaxsas*, is served traditionally in Sweden with *gravlax*, Dill Salmon (page 5).

2 tablespoons mild mustard
1 teaspoon powdered mustard
1 tablespoon sugar
1½ tablespoons wine vinegar

3 tablespoons salad oil
Salt, white pepper to taste
3 tablespoons chopped fresh
 dill

Combine the mustards, sugar, and vinegar in a bowl and mix well together to form a paste. Gradually add the oil, beating with a spoon or whisk while adding. Beat until the sauce has the consistency of mayonnaise. Season with salt and pepper and add the dill. Makes about ½ cup.

AUSTRIAN CAPER SAUCE

Serve with veal or poultry.

1/4 cup butter
3 tablespoons flour
1 1/2 cups beef bouillon

1/3 cup light cream
2 tablespoons drained capers
Salt, pepper to taste

Melt the butter in a saucepan. Stir in the flour. Gradually add the bouillon and cook, stirring, over medium heat until thickened. Add the cream, capers, salt, and pepper and cook for 1 minute. Makes about 1 3/4 cups.

CENTRAL EUROPEAN HORSERADISH SAUCE

This is one of the many horseradish sauces that are great favorites in Austria and Germany. Serve with cold cooked meat or fish.

1/2 cup heavy cream
3 tablespoons freshly grated or
   prepared horseradish,
   drained

1 teaspoon sugar
1/2 teaspoon vinegar
Pinch salt

Whip the cream until thick. Stir in the remaining ingredients. Mix well. Serve cold. Makes about 1 cup.

PESTO ALLA GENOVESE

This traditional sauce from Genoa is served over pasta, with fish, or added to soups, particularly minestrone.

3 or 4 garlic cloves, crushed
1/2 cup minced sweet basil
2 tablespoons chopped fresh
   parsley
1/2 cup grated Sardo or
   Parmesan cheese

2 tablespoons finely chopped
   pine nuts
Salt, pepper to taste
About 1/2 cup olive oil

Pound the garlic, basil, parsley, cheese, and nuts with a pestle in a mortar or with a spoon in a bowl. Season with salt and pepper. Gradually add the oil, mixing as added, the exact amount depending on the desired thickness. Makes about 1 cup.

FRENCH SAUCE BOURGUIGNONNE

A sauce prepared "in the style of Burgundy," one of France's great gastronomic and wine-producing regions, may be served with beef or game.

½ pound fresh mushrooms
2 tablespoons butter or
  margarine
1 teaspoon lemon juice
¼ cup minced cooked ham
⅓ cup finely chopped onion
⅓ cup minced carrot
1 garlic clove, crushed

1 tablespoon olive or salad oil
¼ teaspoon dried thyme
1 small bay leaf
1 cup dry red or white wine
Salt, pepper to taste
2 tablespoons chopped fresh
  parsley

Clean the mushrooms and cut into halves from the caps through the stems. Sauté in the butter and lemon juice for 4 minutes. Remove from the heat and set aside. Combine the ham, onion, carrot, garlic, and oil in a skillet. Sauté the vegetables for 5 minutes. Add the thyme, bay leaf, wine, salt, and pepper. Bring to a boil. Lower the heat and cook, uncovered, for 15 minutes. Add the sautéed mushrooms and leave on the stove over low heat long enough to heat through. Mix in the parsley. Makes about 3 cups.

FINNISH EGG SAUCE

Serve with cooked fish, especially salmon, or eggs.

2 tablespoons butter
2 tablespoons flour
2 cups hot milk
Salt, pepper to taste

4 hard-cooked eggs, shelled
  and chopped
2 teaspoons fresh lemon juice
1 tablespoon chopped fresh dill

Melt the butter in a saucepan. Stir in the flour. Gradually add the milk and cook slowly, stirring, until thickened and smooth. Season with salt and pepper. Add the eggs, lemon juice, and dill and leave on the stove long enough to heat through. Makes about 3 cups.

RAGÚ ALLA BOLOGNESE

This is a variation of a rich sauce enjoyed in the northern Italian city of Bologna, famous for its fine cuisine. Serve with white or green noodles, or any other cooked pasta.

1 medium onion, chopped
1 medium carrot, scraped and
  diced
2 medium celery stalks,
  cleaned and minced
2 tablespoons butter
4 thin slices bacon, chopped
¼ cup chopped cooked ham
2 tablespoons olive oil
½ pound minced uncooked
  lean beef

1 pound combined ground
  pork, veal, and beef
1 cup dry white wine
¼ cup tomato paste
About 1 cup beef bouillon
Salt, pepper, freshly grated
  nutmeg to taste
3 uncooked chicken livers,
  chopped
1 cup chopped fresh
  mushrooms
¾ cup heavy cream (optional)

Put the onion, carrot, celery, butter, bacon, and ham in a large skillet. Cook, stirring occasionally, for 5 minutes. Remove to a saucepan. Heat the oil in the same skillet. Add the minced beef, ground pork, veal, and beef and cook, mincing with a fork, until the redness disappears. Add the wine, tomato paste, bouillon, salt, pepper, and nutmeg and mix well. Return the sautéed onion-bacon mixture to the pan and mix well. Bring to a boil. Lower the heat and cook over a slow fire, uncovered, for 45 minutes. Add a little more bouillon if needed. The final sauce should be thick. Stir in the chicken livers and mushrooms 10 minutes before the sauce is finished. Stir in the cream a few minutes before serving time and leave on the stove long enough to heat through. Makes about 5 cups.

CHEESE SAUCE FROM HOLLAND

Serve with hard-cooked eggs, pasta, or vegetables.

3 tablespoons butter
3 tablespoons all-purpose flour
1½ cups hot milk
1 cup grated Gouda or Edam
cheese

1 teaspoon prepared mustard
¼ teaspoon paprika
Salt, pepper to taste

Melt the butter in a saucepan. Stir in the flour to form a *roux*. Gradually add the milk, stirring, and cook slowly until thickened and smooth. Add the cheese, mustard, paprika, salt, and pepper and cook slowly until the cheese melts. Makes about 2 cups.

FRANKFURT GREEN SAUCE

Grüne Sosse is a great specialty of the German city of Frankfurt where it is served in restaurants with hard-cooked eggs, meat, or fish. It is difficult to duplicate authentically unless one has access to an herb garden, as it is made traditionally with perhaps as many as seven or eight herbs.

½ cup olive oil
3 tablespoons white wine
vinegar
¼ teaspoon sugar
Salt, pepper to taste

1 cup mixed chopped fresh
green herbs (chives, parsley,
dill, watercress, tarragon,
chervil, borage)

Combine the oil, vinegar, sugar, salt, and pepper in a bowl. Stir in the herbs. Serve cold. Makes about 1¼ cups.

SHRIMP SAUCE FROM NORWAY

Rekesaus, a flavorful shrimp creation, is served traditionally in Norway with boiled fish or fish pudding, Fiskepudding (p. 120).

1 pound uncooked shrimps	1 tablespoon sour cream
6 tablespoons butter	Salt, pepper to taste
3 tablespoons flour	2 tablespoons chopped fresh
1½ cups fish stock	dill
1½ cups milk	

Cook the shrimps in boiling salted water until they become pink. Drain and cool. Remove the shells and devein. Cut into pieces. Melt 3 tablespoons of butter in a large saucepan. Stir in the flour and mix well. Gradually add the fish stock and milk, stirring constantly. Then add the remaining butter and the sour cream, stirring constantly. Season with salt and pepper. Cook slowly until thick and smooth. Add the shrimps and cook 1 minute. Mix in the dill and remove from the heat. Serve hot. Makes about 3 cups.

If desired, the sauce may be made with 3 cups of milk instead of the mixture of fish stock and milk.

SAUCE CHASSEUR

This French sauce, which means "sauce hunter's style" is an excellent one to serve with veal or chicken.

2 tablespoons butter	1 cup *espagnole* or brown
1 tablespoon salad oil	sauce
2 tablespoons chopped shallots	Salt, pepper to taste
or green onions	1 teaspoon chopped fresh
½ pound fresh mushrooms,	parsley
cleaned and sliced	½ teaspoon chopped fresh
2 tablespoons tomato paste	tarragon
½ cup dry white wine	

Melt the butter in a skillet or saucepan. Add the oil and shallots and sauté until they are tender. Add the sliced mushrooms and sauté for 4 minutes. Stir in the tomato paste. Add the wine, *espagnole* or brown sauce, salt, and pepper. Cook slowly, stirring occasionally, for 10 minutes. Stir in the parsley and tarragon and remove from the heat. Makes a little more than 2 cups.

BÉCHAMEL SAUCE

This basic French white sauce, made by blending butter, flour, and milk in various degrees of thickness, was named for Louis de Béchamel, Lord Steward of Louis XIV. It is not certain whether or not he created the sauce, but we do know that at that time it was an intricate creation made with a well-flavored stock and rich with cream. Béchamel may be further enriched with the addition of other ingredients, such as cheese, herbs, chopped hard-cooked eggs, tomato paste, mustard, curry powder, and/or seafood, but it is then called by another name. That which has cheese added to it, for example, becomes Mornay sauce. This is one of the most widely used of all sauces.

2 tablespoons butter	Freshly grated nutmeg
2 tablespoons all-purpose flour	Salt, pepper
1 cup hot milk	1 egg yolk (optional)

Melt the butter in a saucepan. Stir in the flour to form a *roux* and cook about 1 minute. Gradually add the milk, stirring as you do so, and cook until smooth and thickened, about 5 minutes. Season with nutmeg, salt, and pepper and remove from the heat. If the egg yolk is used, mix it with some of the hot sauce in a small bowl. Return to the sauce and leave over low heat just about 1 minute. This makes a medium-thick sauce. Makes about 1 cup.

SCANDINAVIAN DILL SAUCE

The Scandinavians have several fine sauces flavored with dill. In Sweden there is a special one made with lamb stock that is served with lamb; the Finns have a dill-mayonnaise-type sauce; and in all the countries there is a good salad dressing made with oil, vinegar, and dill. This is an appealing sauce that can be served with meat, fish, vegetables, or eggs.

1 tablespoon butter or margarine	2 teaspoons sugar
2 tablespoons flour	1 tablespoon fresh lemon juice or vinegar
1½ cups stock or milk	2 tablespoons chopped fresh dill
Salt, pepper to taste	

Melt the butter in a saucepan. Stir in the flour to form a *roux*. Gradually add the stock or milk and cook slowly, stirring, until a thick and smooth sauce. Season with salt and pepper. Mix in the sugar and lemon juice. Cook slowly for 3 or 4 minutes. Mix in the dill and remove from the heat. Makes about 1½ cups.

SPANISH ROMESCU

This is a very spicy sauce that is served with shellfish, grilled meat, or game in the northeastern Spanish region of Catalonia.

3 or 4 garlic cloves, crushed	1 small dried hot chili pepper or 1 teaspoon cayenne
1 medium tomato, peeled, seeded, and chopped	Salt to taste
½ cup blanched almond slivers, toasted	1 cup olive oil
	¼ cup wine vinegar

To toast the almonds, put in a preheated moderate oven (350° F.) about 10 minutes, until golden. Combine the garlic, tomato, almonds, chili pepper, and salt and grind or mix together to form a paste. Very slowly add some of the oil, mixing as you add it. Gradually add the vinegar and remaining oil and continue to mix to form a thick sauce. Makes about 1½ cups.

DUXELLES

A sautéed preparation of seasoned chopped mushrooms, called *duxelles* in French, takes its name from a seventeenth-century gourmet, the Marquis d'Uxelles, who is credited with inventing the mixture. This sauce, or filling, can be used to stuff mushroom caps, fish, or vegetables, or when mixed with bread crumbs, as a stuffing for poultry. It may also be mixed with eggs, added to sauces, or used as a spread for canapés or sandwiches.

1 pound fresh mushrooms	3 tablespoons minced onions
¼ cup butter	1 garlic clove, crushed
2 tablespoons olive or salad oil	Salt, pepper to taste
3 tablespoons minced shallots or green onions	1 tablespoon chopped fresh parsley

Clean the mushrooms and chop finely. Put in cheesecloth and press to remove any moisture. Heat the butter and oil over a high flame. Add the shallots, onions, and garlic and sauté for 1 minute, stirring frequently. Lower the heat and add the minced mushrooms. Sauté until all the moisture has evaporated and the mixture is quite thick. This will take some time. Season with salt and pepper. Stir in the parsley. Makes about 2 cups.

VINAIGRETTE SAUCE

One of the most widely used and best sauces, *vinaigrette*, is the primary dressing for salads in Western Europe. The name derives from the French word for vinegar, *vinaigre*, and the sauce is simply made with 3 or 4 parts oil to 1 part vinegar, seasoned with salt and pepper. Sometimes minced fresh herbs are also added to it, and one variation includes chopped capers, onions, and herbs. One version that has become popular in America is called French dressing, which is *vinaigrette* made with additional seasonings such as mustard and garlic.

AÏOLI

Garlic sauce, called *aïoli* in French, is a potent type of mayonnaise that is a beloved food in both southern France and the neighboring region of Catalonia in Spain. It is

added to the Provençal soup, *bourride,* and is served as a
dip for such foods as boiled fish, hard-cooked eggs, seafood,
and a large assortment of raw and cooked vegetables. The
sauce is traditionally made with several more cloves of garlic than are used in this recipe.

6 garlic cloves   1 tablespoon fresh lemon juice
2 egg yolks   Salt, pepper to taste
1 to 1½ cups olive oil

Crush the garlic in a mortar or bowl with a pestle or spoon.
Add the egg yolks and beat well with a wooden spoon. When
thoroughly combined, begin adding the oil, drop by drop, beating
as you add it. When the mixture is fairly thick add the remaining oil in a steady stream, then the lemon juice, salt, and pepper.
Leave at room temperature. Some cooks add also 1 tablespoon
lukewarm water. The consistency should be that of a fairly
thick mayonnaise. Makes about 1½ cups.

ITALIAN MARINARA SAUCE

Serve with cooked pasta—spaghetti, macaroni, or noodles—or meats.

3 tablespoons olive oil   ½ teaspoon dried basil
1 large onion, chopped   Pepper to taste
1 or 2 garlic cloves, crushed   ⅓ cup chopped fresh parsley
4 cups chopped and peeled   4 to 6 flat anchovy fillets,
  fresh tomatoes   minced
½ teaspoon dried oregano

Heat the oil in a saucepan. Add the onion and garlic and
sauté until tender. Add the tomatoes, oregano, basil, and pepper. Cook, uncovered, over a brisk fire for 10 minutes. Add the
parsley and anchovies, the number according to taste, and cook
another 2 minutes. Makes about 3 cups.

FRENCH REMOULADE

Serve with cold fish, meats, or poultry.

2 hard-cooked eggs, shelled
  and chopped
2 tablespoons Dijon or other
  sharp mustard
Salt, pepper to taste
⅓ cup minced green onions
1 cup olive oil

1 tablespoon drained capers
2 tablespoons minced gherkins
2 tablespoons fresh lemon
  juice or vinegar
⅓ cup finely chopped parsley
1 tablespoon minced fresh
  chervil

Combine all the ingredients and mix well. Serve cold. Makes
about 2 cups.

GERMAN ANCHOVY SAUCE

Serve with fish.

2 tablespoons butter or
  margarine
1 small onion, minced
1 tablespoon flour
1 cup beef bouillon

1 tablespoon lemon juice
1 can (2 ounces) anchovy
  fillets, drained and minced
Pepper to taste
1 egg yolk

Melt the butter in a saucepan. Add the onion and sauté until
tender. Stir in the flour. Gradually add the bouillon and cook
for 1 minute. Add the lemon juice, anchovies, and pepper and
simmer, stirring frequently, for 10 minutes, or until thickened.
Pour a little of the hot sauce to mix with the egg yolk. Stir well
and return to the sauce. Remove from the heat. Makes about
1¼ cups.

HOLLANDAISE

This very popular sauce, which is used extensively in
Western Europe, is believed to have originated in Holland.

It is widely used throughout Western Europe with fish, eggs, and vegetables.

½ cup (¼ pound) butter, at room temperature
3 egg yolks

1 or 2 tablespoons fresh lemon juice
Salt, white pepper, and cayenne pepper

Cut the butter into slices. Put the egg yolks in a bowl set in a pan of hot water. Stir with a whisk until foamy. Add the lemon juice, the amount according to taste, and season with a little salt, pepper, and cayenne. Stir vigorously until well mixed. Add ⅓ of the butter and beat vigorously until the butter melts and the sauce is thick. Keep adding more butter and beating until all of it is used. Serve lukewarm. Makes about ¾ cup.

If the sauce begins to separate add a little hot water, drop by drop, and continue to beat vigorously.

VARIATIONS OF HOLLANDAISE:

Béarnaise: Put 2 teaspoons minced shallots or green onions, 2 tablespoons tarragon vinegar, 2 teaspoons minced fresh tarragon (or 1 teaspoon dried tarragon), and a little pepper in a saucepan and bring to a boil. Cook over fairly high heat to reduce to about 1 teaspoon. Add to the water in the above recipe and omit the lemon juice. Serve with meat.

Choron: Add 1 tablespoon tomato paste to the Béarnaise recipe. Serve with fish or meat.

Maltaise: Make the hollandaise with ¼ cup orange juice instead of the water and add 1 teaspoon grated orange peel. Serve with vegetables.

Mousseline: Add ½ cup heavy cream, whipped, to 1½ cups of Hollandaise and serve with eggs, fish, or vegetables.

ENGLISH BREAD SAUCE

This classic English sauce is served with roast chicken, pheasant, or partridge.

1 cup milk
1 small onion stuck with 2
  whole cloves
Pinch ground mace or nutmeg

½ cup white bread crumbs
2 tablespoons butter
Salt, pepper to taste
1 tablespoon cream

Put the milk, onion, and mace in the top of a double boiler over boiling water. Heat until the milk becomes scalded. Add the bread crumbs, 1 tablespoon of butter, the salt, and pepper. Beat vigorously to mix the ingredients. Cook for 20 minutes, beating from time to time. Add the remaining tablespoon of butter and the cream. Remove the onion and cloves. Serve at once. Makes about 1 cup.

MAYONNAISE

This great French sauce is of ancient origin and has become a favorite around the world. Using this recipe as a basis, many variations of mayonnaise can be made. Included below it are a few of them.

2 egg yolks
½ teaspoon powdered mustard
Salt, pepper, cayenne to taste

2 cups olive oil
2 tablespoons fresh lemon
  juice

Put the egg yolks in a bowl after removing any white threads. Add the mustard, salt, pepper, and cayenne and beat with a whisk or rotary beater until well blended. Add ¼ cup of the oil a drop at a time, beating while you add it. Add the remaining oil a little more quickly and continue beating until the mixture is well blended. Stir in the lemon juice and beat again. If the mixture should curdle add another egg yolk and 1 tablespoon of water and beat vigorously. Makes about 2 cups.

VARIATIONS OF MAYONNAISE:

Sauce Niçoise: To 1¼ cups of mayonnaise add ½ cup minced green pepper, 2 tablespoons tomato paste, 1 minced garlic clove, and 1 teaspoon minced fresh tarragon.

Sauce aux fines herbes: Add 2 or 3 tablespoons minced fresh green herbs to 1 cup of mayonnaise.

Sauce tartare: To 1 cup mayonnaise add 2 tablespoons minced green onions, 3 tablespoons minced gherkins, 1 tablespoon minced capers, and 2 tablespoons chopped parsley.

Russian dressing: Add ½ cup chili sauce, ¼ cup pickle relish, 2 tablespoons chopped stuffed olives, and 1 tablespoon minced chives to 1 cup mayonnaise.

10

Desserts

WHEN DINING IN WESTERN EUROPE it is always difficult to choose among the inviting and delectable pastries, puddings, cookies, cakes, ices and ice creams, and cheese and fruit specialties for dessert, the last course of luncheon or dinner. Fortunately, however, it is customary to partake of these toothsome sweets, handsomely displayed in bakeries, pastry shops, and confectioners' stores, throughout the day and evening as in-betweens or snacks. Thus, one is not limited to enjoying them only at the end of a meal.

Our word dessert derives from the French verb *desservir*, meaning "to clear the table." At one time in Europe it was customary to offer an elaborate presentation of sweets after everything had been removed from the dining table. Now the selection is confined to one or a few dishes, but each will be a superb creation carefully prepared with only the very best of materials. Western Europeans take great pride in making and serving their illustrious national specialties.

Probably the first European desserts were puddings made by combining grains, fruits, and nuts, sweetened with wine and honey. The Romans enjoyed a simple form of pastry, as well as

221

a type of cheesecake, honey-flavored custard, cake fried in oil and sprinkled with honey, and confections of nut-stuffed dates. The Gallo-Romans did not lack for variety, as their banquets ended with "hot or cold tarts, honey cakes, soft cheese, grilled escargots, medlars, chestnuts, figs, Gaul peaches and fresh and dried grapes."

During the Renaissance European cooks were developing more refinements in the art of making pastries, cakes, and, particularly, fruit desserts. The extensive orchards yielded an increasing variety of delectable fruit, which was fashioned into compotes, tarts, pies, cakes, dumplings, fried batters, and confections that are still enjoyed today. Widely enjoyed also are candied fruits. The peels of such favorites as oranges and lemons are utilized extensively in the cookery.

In Elizabethan England, when ships returning from the East and New World explorations brought increasing supplies of such luxuries as spices, nuts, raisins, dates, figs, fruits, oil, and the most important sugar, the cooks toiled to make amazing desserts of incredible variety. Their portions, however, are a little overwhelming for the present-day homemaker. "Take five or six pounds of currants, five pounds of flour, sixteen eggs, a pound and a half of butter, half pound of sugar, a pint of cream, spices, and a pint of ale-yeast," read one recipe for a cake.

The Elizabethans entertained with lavish tables of desserts arranged artistically to create scenes and with each creation garnished as ornately as possible. For them the cooks prepared marchpane castles and dragons. Jellies appeared into the form of "flowers, herbs, trees . . . beasts, fish, fowl and fruit." Baskets were heaped with rare and colorful fruits. Fountains gushed forth with favorite beverages. Ices, biscuits, candles, cheeses, custards, meringues, compotes, and pies were all handsomely adorned.

This elaborate presentation of desserts was common throughout the Continent. Perhaps it reached its zenith during the nineteenth century with the artistic creations of the great French chef, Marie-Antoine Carême, who astonished and pleased diners with sculptures of *Pièces Montées*, extraordinary decorative pieces made with an incredible array of ingredients designed to glorify pastries. His book, *Le Pâtissier Royal*, which dealt primarily with pastries, remains today a respected work, and Carême is credited with founding the classic French cuisine. No other pastry maker has surpassed his accomplishments.

Over the years there was some confusion in France, as well
as in other European countries, about what to serve for dessert
and what to call that particular course of the meal. A simple
French banquet menu of 1571, for example, consisted of two
preliminary courses called first and second plates and a final one
named *issue*. Presumably this was taken from an old meaning
of the word which was "at the end of." The term was evidently
still in use in 1652, as an account in *Larousse Gastronomique*
by a food authority stipulated that the dinner eighth course, or
issue, "should consist of all sorts of preserves, in syrup and
dried, marzipans, bunches of fennel, sprinkled with sugar in all
colours, studded with tooth-picks, musk pastilles or Verdun
(sugared) almonds in small pieces of sugar paste flavored with
musk and amber." This, however, the author pointed out, should
follow a seventh course, to "consist only of fruit, with creams
and a few biscuits. Almonds and green walnuts should be
served on dish-stands."

Later on it became the custom to serve a course of sweets and
also some vegetable dishes as *entremets* ("between dishes").
The French still called desserts *entremets* but have dropped the
inclusion of the vegetable creations.

Throughout the Continent the choice of a typical dessert
might vary considerably. In southern European countries light
desserts such as fruit, cheese, or custards are preferred. Sweets
are eaten, however, with morning coffee or afternoon tea, or
at other times. The French dinner menu properly includes a
course of cheese to be served after the entrée and before the dessert. The English do just the opposite. The Germans and Austrians are particularly fond of sweet dumplings, pancakes, cakes,
and such pastries as *Strudel* and *Torte*. Puddings, waffles, and
pancakes are great Scandinavian favorites.

Of all the great Continental desserts particular mention
should be made of the ices and ice creams that appear as glorious creations in all the cuisines. Since the days of the Romans,
iced fruit-flavored waters were sought-after and luxurious fare.
To keep them cool, the Romans devised a system of preserving
ice during the hot summer months. From the Arabs, the Italians
learned the secrets of preparing *sharbats* (sherbets) and *sorbets*
(sorbets), and introduced them to other Europeans. Cooks of
Catherine de' Medici featured them at banquets of the French
court. So impressed was the English King Charles I with the
creations of two Italians who served him ices that the monarch

enjoined them never to reveal the secret formula for making them.

It was a Sicilian who opened a café in Paris about 1670 and discovered that his business flourished when he began offering refreshing iced beverages. But it was not until the 1700s that vendors began selling ice creams as we know them today. Once the consistency of these treasures had been strengthened with the addition of eggs and cream, the repertoire of frozen desserts knew no bounds. Across the Continent cooks enhanced the basic ice or ice cream mixture with fruit juices, fruit purée, candied fruit peel, liqueurs, nuts, chocolate, and other flavorings to make such great dishes as *coupes, bombes, parfaits, melbas, mousses,* sherbets, and *granite,* which became celebrated finales for elegant dinners.

To describe the Western European repertoire of cakes is an impossibility. Each of the countries has its own variations of light custards, hot and cold soufflés, rich nut cakes, fragrant yeast loaves, intricate layered pastries, puff-paste creations, sweet omelets, appealing pancakes, gelatine treasures, and marvelous meringues. Whether served at the end of a meal or with a beverage during the day or evening, it is always a joy to savor an éclair, hot fritter, fruit tart, cream puff, *brioche, baba,* slice of fruit cake, *Strudel, savarin, tote,* or pie anywhere on the Continent.

The American cook may enjoy this representative collection in his or her own home.

CITRUS GRANITA FROM ITALY

In Italy there are two kinds of ice cream. *Gelati* resembles our firm milk or cream type and *granita* is a type of sherbet that has fine ice crystals. This is particularly refreshing.

2 cups water
1 cup sugar
6 tablespoons fresh lemon juice
6 tablespoons fresh orange juice
1 teaspoon grated lemon peel

Combine the water and sugar in a saucepan and bring to a

boil. Cook over fairly high heat for 5 minutes. Remove from the heat and cool. Add the lemon and orange juice and grated peel. Pour into a refrigerator tray and freeze about 2 hours, until firm and granular. Serves 4.

SPANISH ALMOND SIGHS

Suspiros de almendras ("almond sighs") were probably so named because the cookies are so light.

6 egg whites
1 cup sugar

1 cup chopped blanched
almonds

Beat the egg whites until stiff. Fold in the sugar and almonds until well mixed. Drop by large spoonfuls onto a floured cookie sheet. Bake in a preheated moderate oven (350°F.) for 12 to 15 minutes. Makes about 2 dozen.

BAKED APRICOTS OF PROVENCE

In France's lovely southern region of Provence the fresh fruit is particularly sweet and appealing. One of the great treasures is the flavorful golden apricot, which is made into compotes, tarts, ice cream, or this appealing dessert.

12 ripe fresh apricots
Lemon juice
¾ cup sugar

1 cup water
1 teaspoon vanilla extract
Whipped cream

Wash and peel the apricots. Cut into halves along their natural lines. Remove the pits. Sprinkle with a little lemon juice. Combine the sugar, water, and vanilla in a small saucepan. Bring to a boil and simmer 5 minutes. Arrange the apricots in a shallow baking dish. Pour the syrup over them. Bake in a preheated moderate oven (350°F.) for 45 to 60 minutes, until fork tender. Cool and then chill. Serve with whipped cream. Serves 4.

WINE CREAM FROM GERMANY

Weincreme can be a cold dessert or may be served warm as a sauce over plain cake.

2 cups dry white wine   1 teaspoon grated lemon rind
½ cup sugar   1 teaspoon grated orange rind
4 eggs

Combine all of the ingredients in the top of a double boiler. Cook, beating with a whisk or fork, until frothy and thickened. Pour into serving dishes and chill. Serve with whipped cream, if desired. Serves 4.

NORWEGIAN CHRISTMAS CAKE

This traditional fruit loaf called *Julekake* is one of Norway's most treasured desserts. Each household will have an ample supply of the cakes for the festive winter holidays.

¾ cup milk, scalded   4½ cups unsifted all-purpose
¾ cup sugar   flour
½ cup butter   1 teaspoon ground cardamom
¾ teaspoon salt   ½ cup seedless raisins
2 packages active dry yeast   ¾ cup diced citron
½ cup lukewarm water

Combine the scalded milk, sugar, butter, and salt in a large bowl and cool to lukewarm. Dissolve the yeast in the lukewarm water and after a few minutes (about 4), stir into the milk mixture. Sift the flour and cardamom together and add a little at a time. Mix well after each addition. Turn out on a floured board and knead firmly until smooth and elastic. Turn into a greased bowl; turn over. Let rise, covered, in a warm place for about 1½ hours, or until doubled in bulk. Punch down. Turn out onto a floured board. Push the raisins and citron into the dough and knead until well combined. Form the dough into two balls. Place several inches apart on a greased cookie sheet.

Let rise again, covered, in a warm place until doubled in bulk. Bake in a preheated moderately hot oven (375°F.) for about 30 minutes, or until done. Cool. Makes 2 loaves.

The loaves may be frosted with a white confectioners' sugar icing and decorated with chopped citron or candied cherries.

IRISH COFFEE

Throughout a great part of Western Europe a very popular after-dinner drink, sometimes called a dessert, is the inviting Irish coffee. I have many recipes for this great favorite, but the most appealing is one that I found in an Irish cookbook, *250 Irish Recipes,* which I bought in Dublin.* It reads:

Ingredients:
   Cream: rich as an Irish brogue.
   Coffee: strong as a friendly hand
   Sugar: sweet as the tongue of a rogue.
   Whiskey: smooth as the wit of the land.

Method:
   Heat a stemmed whiskey goblet. Pour in one shot of Irish whiskey—the only whiskey with the smooth taste and full body to make this beverage satisfactorily. Add two coffee-spoonfuls of sugar. Fill goblet with strong coffee to within one inch of the brim. Stir to dissolve sugar. Top off to the brim with whipped cream, slightly aerated, so that it floats on coffee. N.B.—Do not stir after adding cream—as the true flavour is obtained by drinking the hot coffee and Irish whiskey through the coolness of the cream.

VIENNESE PALATSCHINKEN

This is one of the many pancake desserts that have become beloved fare in Vienna.

* *250 Irish Recipes* (Dublin: Mont Salno Press, 1959).

2 eggs, separated
½ cup milk
½ cup water
1 tablespoon sugar
¼ teaspoon salt

2 tablespoons brandy or rum
1 cup all-purpose flour
Butter for frying
Fruit jelly
Confectioners' sugar

Combine the egg yolks with the milk, water, sugar, salt, and brandy in a bowl. Stir in the flour and mix well. Beat the egg whites until stiff and fold into the mixture. Melt a little butter in a 7- or 8-inch skillet and add 3 tablespoons of the batter. Tilt the pan to spread evenly. Cook over medium heat until the underside is golden. Turn over with a spatula and cook on the other side. Slip onto a warm plate and keep warm in a preheated 250°F. oven. Continue to cook the other pancakes. Spread each with a thin layer of jelly and fold into quarters. Serve at once sprinkled with confectioners' sugar. Serves 6.

BELGIAN BEER WAFFLES

Gaufres bruxelloises are light and crisp creations that can be served for dessert or as snacks.

2 cups sifted all-purpose flour
4 eggs, separated
1 teaspoon sugar
5 tablespoons melted butter
Salt to taste

½ teaspoon vanilla
½ cup light beer
⅔ cup milk
Confectioners' sugar
Whipped cream

Combine the flour, egg yolks, sugar, butter, salt, vanilla, beer, and milk in a bowl and beat until smooth. Whip the egg whites until stiff and fold into the dough mixture. Spread a little of the batter on a waffle iron and cook. Serve with confectioners' sugar and whipped cream. Serves 4 to 6.

FRENCH CHESTNUT SOUFFLÉ

Marron, the French word for a superb cultivated chestnut, is a highly prized food. Either sweetened or unsweetened, the chestnuts are used creatively in the French cuisine. This traditional dessert can be made with imported canned chestnut purée.

2 tablespoons butter	2 squares (2 ounces each)
2 tablespoons flour	unsweetened chocolate,
1 cup milk	melted
1 cup chestnut purée,	4 eggs, separated
unsweetened	1 teaspoon vanilla extract
½ cup sugar	Granulated sugar

Melt the butter in a saucepan. Stir in the flour. Mix together the milk, chestnut purée, and sugar with a rotary beater. When well blended, mix into the butter and flour. Cook over low heat, stirring constantly, until thickened. Stir the melted chocolate into the chestnut mixture. Beat the egg yolks in a large bowl and gradually add the chestnut mixture to them. Mix well and cool. Beat the egg whites until stiff. Fold them and the vanilla into the cooled mixture. Turn into a well-buttered 1½-quart soufflé dish or mold that has been sprinkled with granulated sugar. Put the dish into a pan of hot water and cook in a preheated moderately hot oven (375°F.) for about 45 minutes, or until done. Serve at once. Serves 6 to 8.

AUSTRIAN LINZER TORTE

This attractive lattice-top cake is one of the most popular of all the great Austrian pastries. It is handsomely displayed in most of the *Konditorei* ("pastry shops"), but is also prepared in the home.

¾ cup softened butter	1½ cups all-purpose flour
¾ cup sugar	½ teaspoon ground cinnamon
2 egg yolks	⅛ teaspoon ground cloves
1½ cups finely ground	1 cup raspberry or strawberry
hazelnuts or almonds	preserves
2 teaspoons grated lemon rind	

Cream the butter in a large bowl and add the sugar, beating until light and fluffy. Add the egg yolks and mix until well blended. Stir in the nuts and lemon rind. Sift the flour, cinnamon, and cloves and stir a little at a time into the creamed mixture. Mix well and chill for 1 hour. Spoon ¾ of the mixture into a 9-inch round cake pan with a removable bottom and spread evenly. Spoon the preserves over the top. Roll out the remaining ¼ of the dough and cut into 8 strips, each about ⅓ inch wide and of varying lengths. Arrange over the preserves to make a lattice. Bake in a preheated moderately hot oven (375°F.) for about 50 minutes, or until cooked. Cool and remove from the pan. Dust the top with confectioners' sugar, if desired. To serve, cut into wedges. Serves 6 to 8.

THE HAGUE BLUFF

In Holland this simple dessert is a great favorite of the children.

1 egg white
½ cup sugar

3 tablespoons red currant or
raspberry syrup

Beat the egg white until fluffy. Add the sugar and syrup, a little at a time, and continue beating until light and fluffy. Spoon into dessert dishes and serve with cookies. Serves 4.

GERMAN APPLE PANCAKES

Apfelpfannkuchen, apple-filled pancakes, are among the numerous great Western European desserts made with this popular fruit.

6 tablespoons butter or
  margarine
4 tart apples, peeled and
  thinly sliced
2 teaspoons grated lemon rind
½ to ¾ cup sugar

1 teaspoon ground cinnamon
1 cup sifted all-purpose flour
¼ teaspoon salt
1 cup milk
2 eggs, beaten
Confectioners' sugar

Melt 4 tablespoons of the butter in a skillet and add the apple slices. Cook slowly until tender. Add the lemon rind, sugar to taste, and the cinnamon. Mix well. Leave in the skillet over very low heat. Combine the flour, salt, milk, and eggs in a bowl and stir with a fork or whisk until smooth. Add the remaining 2 tablespoons of butter, melted, and mix again. Heat a 7- or 8-inch skillet, lightly greased, and add 3 tablespoons of the batter. Tilt the pan at once to spread the batter evenly. Cook over medium heat until the underside of the pancake is golden. Turn over with a spatula and cook on the other side. Turn out onto a warm plate and keep warm in a preheated 250°F. oven. Continue cooking the other pancakes. Spread ½ of each one with a thin layer of the warm apple mixture. Fold over and sprinkle with confectioners' sugar. Serve at once. Serves 8.

SCOTTISH DUNDEE CAKE

This rich and attractive fruitcake is famous throughout Britain and is a great favorite for tea and picnics.

1 cup butter
1 cup sugar
5 eggs
¾ cup seedless raisins
¾ cup currants
¾ cup chopped mixed candied
  fruit
½ cup blanched almonds,
  grated or whirled in a
  blender

2 tablespoons fresh orange
  juice
1 tablespoon minced orange
  rind
2½ cups all-purpose flour
1 teaspoon baking powder
½ teaspoon salt
⅓ cup blanched almonds, cut
  into halves

Cream the butter in a large bowl. Add the sugar and mix until well blended. Stir in the eggs one at a time, beating after each addition. Mix in the raisins, currants, candied fruit, almonds, orange juice, and orange rind. Stir well. Sift the flour, baking powder, and salt a little at a time into the bowl. Mix the ingredients until well combined. Turn into a greased 8- or 9-inch tubular pan. Decorate the top with the almond halves. Bake in a preheated slow (300°F.) oven about 1¼ hours, or until the cake is baked. Cool and remove from the pan. Cut into slices to serve. Serves about 12.

PORTUGUESE EGG PUDDING

This typical Portuguese *pudim* is one of their many great desserts made with sugar and eggs. It is a type of custard but richer than most.

2½ cups sugar
½ cup orange juice
8 large eggs

2 tablespoons grated orange rind

Combine the sugar and orange juice in a saucepan and cook over low heat until the mixture begins to thicken, about 15 minutes. Take from the stove and cool a little. Beat the eggs together and stir into the sugar mixture. Add the grated rind. Mix very well. Turn into a mold or individual custard cups. Place in a pan of hot water and bake in a preheated slow (325°F.) oven for about 45 minutes, or until set. Cool. Serves 6 to 8.

AUSTRIAN EMPEROR'S OMELET

This very excellent and traditional dessert called *Kaiserschmarrn* is served in Austria with stewed plums as an accompaniment.

2 tablespoons raisins
Brandy or rum (optional)
2 eggs, separated
1 tablespoon sugar

½ cup all-purpose flour
Pinch salt
1 cup milk
Butter

Soak the raisins in brandy or rum until soft. (Or, if preferred, do not soak them at all.) Combine the egg yolks and sugar in a bowl and mix well until light and creamy. Sift the flour and salt into the egg mixture, adding alternately with the milk. Mix until smooth. Whip the egg whites until stiff and fold into the mixture. Turn into a well-buttered omelet pan or medium skillet. Sprinkle the raisins over the top. Leave over medium heat for 5 minutes, or until the bottom is golden and the surface is dry. Turn out onto a warm plate. Rebutter the pan, if necessary. Return the omelet to the pan and cook until golden on the other side and the mixture is set. Cut into shreds with two forks. Serve warm sprinkled with sugar. Serves 2.

POTS DE CRÈME AU CHOCOLAT

These elegant desserts, chocolate-flavored rich custards, are served in little covered pots called *petits pots*. If they are not available, other small containers can be used.

2 cups light cream
6 egg yolks
2 tablespoons sugar
Dash salt

6 ounces semisweet chocolate, grated
1 teaspoon vanilla
Whipped cream (optional)

Heat the cream to the boiling point, or when bubbles appear around the edge, in a saucepan. Meanwhile, combine the egg yolks, sugar, and salt but do not beat. Pour ⅓ of the hot cream mixture to mix with the egg mixture. Stir and return to the cream in the saucepan. Cook, stirring constantly, over medium heat until the mixture thickens and the spoon is coated. Stir in the chocolate. Remove from the heat and keep stirring until the chocolate melts. Add the vanilla. Pour into 8 small *pots de crème*, demitasse cups, or small bowls. Chill. Serve garnished with a dab of whipped cream, if desired. Serves 8.

DUTCH LEMON CREAM

An inviting light pudding to serve perhaps for a luncheon dessert.

4 eggs, separated
½ cup sugar
Juice of 3 large lemons

1 tablespoon unflavored gelatine
3 tablespoons water
3 tablespoons grated chocolate

Beat the egg yolks until creamy. Combine with the sugar and
lemon juice in the top of a double boiler. Cook, stirring constantly, over hot water until thick and creamy. Remove from
the stove. Soften the gelatine in the water and add at once to
the hot mixture. Stir to dissolve. Cool a little. Whip the egg
whites until stiff. Fold into the lemon mixture. Turn into a
mold and chill until set, 2 or 3 hours. Unmold onto a chilled
plate and garnish with the grated chocolate. Serves 6.

GERMAN FRUIT KUCHEN

In German *Kuchen* means cake and one of the most typical is a simple one topped with slices of fresh fruit and
decorated with whipped cream. It may be served as a dessert, for morning coffee, and for afternoon tea.

⅓ cup softened butter
⅓ cup sugar
½ teaspoon vanilla
2 eggs
1 teaspoon baking powder
1 cup sifted all-purpose flour

2 tablespoons milk
2 cups fresh fruit slices
  (peaches, apricots,
  strawberries)
Whipped cream

Cream the butter and sugar in a large bowl. Beat until light
and fluffy. Add the vanilla and eggs, one at a time, beating well
after each addition. Sift the baking powder with the flour into
the bowl, adding alternately with the milk. Mix well to combine the ingredients thoroughly. Turn into a 9-inch round cake
pan that is 1¼ inches deep, lined with wax paper, and spread
evenly. Bake in a preheated moderate oven (350°F.) for about
30 minutes, or until done. Cool for 5 minutes. Turn out onto a
rack and take off the paper. Cool. Arrange the fruit slices,
sweetened with sugar if desired, over the cake. Serve decorated
with whipped cream. Serves 6 to 8.

SPANISH FLAN

The national dessert of Spain is *flan*, known in other
Western European countries as caramel custard. There are
several variations, but the most common is this simple one.

15 tablespoons sugar	4 large eggs
2 teaspoons water	½ teaspoon orange or vanilla
2 cups milk	extract

Put 12 tablespoons (¾ cup) of the sugar in a heavy skillet. Add the water and heat over a medium flame. When the sugar begins to melt, stir it and shake the pan a little. Leave over the heat until the mixture becomes a deep golden syrup. Pour at once into 6 custard cups or a baking dish. Scald the milk. Mix together in a bowl the eggs, the remaining 3 tablespoons of sugar, and the extract. Pour in the hot milk and beat to blend well. Pour over the caramelized mixture. Place the dishes in a pan of hot water and bake in a preheated moderately hot oven (375°F.) for about 1 hour, until a knife inserted into it comes out clean. Remove from the oven; remove from the hot water; cool. Invert and serve. Serves 6.

OMELETTE SURPRISE

A delectable and popular French dessert made with ice cream on a layer of cake and covered with meringue before baking is known by various names in Western Europe. It is called *omelette surprise, omelette norvégienne* or à la *norvégienne,* and sometimes *glace au four.* In America it is called baked Alaska. The French version, however, is generally a richer and more elaborate creation than the American dessert. It may be in oval, round, or square form, made with any kind of ice cream, and the meringue covering may be simply garnished with sugar or with more elaborate decorations such as crystallized violets. Sometimes the cake layer is sprinkled with a liqueur and spread with puréed fruit. There are several stories concerning the invention of this lovely dessert. *Larousse Gastronomique* states that it "was launched into popularity about 1895, at the Hôtel de Paris in Monte Carlo, by Jean Giroix, who was then in charge of the kitchens there." The book also points out that the creation was possibly the invention of a master cook of a Chinese Mission visiting Paris in the 1800s. Another possible creator, they relate, was an American-born physicist who worked in England. There is no doubt about the appeal of the ice cream treasure, a glorious presentation whether served in a French restaurant or at a home table. This is one version.

1 quart brick ice cream
1 layer sponge cake cut 1 inch
  thick
1 cup sweetened raspberry or
  apricot purée (optional)

Kirsch, Framboise, or
  Mirabelle (optional)
4 egg whites
¾ to 1 cup granulated sugar
Dash salt
Confectioners' sugar

Before starting the preparation of the dessert decide if it is to be in an oval, square, or round form. Also be sure that the ice cream is frozen as hard as possible and molded in the same form as the cake. The cake should be cut to extend 1 inch beyond the ice cream which will be placed over it. To prepare, place a piece of brown paper on a cookie sheet. Arrange the cake on it, spread with the purée, and sprinkle with the liqueur. Then put the ice cream on top. Spread all the surfaces with a meringue made by beating together the egg whites, granulated sugar, and salt until stiff. Sprinkle the top with confectioners' sugar and put in a preheated hot oven (475°F.) for about 5 minutes or until delicately browned. Slip onto a chilled platter and serve at once. Cut into slices. Serves 6.

SWEDISH PANCAKES

Plättar, small pancakes, are made in Sweden in a special pan with five or seven sections. They are often served traditionally at family suppers for dessert on Thursday evening following hearty pea soup. In Sweden typical accompaniments are lingonberry, cloudberry, or blueberry preserves.

2 large eggs
1 tablespoon sugar
Salt to taste
2 cups milk

1 cup all-purpose flour
Butter
Berry preserves

Beat the eggs in a bowl. Add the sugar and salt and mix again. Pour in the milk and mix to combine the ingredients thoroughly. Gradually add the flour, beating as you do so, and mix until you have a thin batter. Grease a 7- or 8-inch skillet with butter. Pour 1 tablespoon of batter for each pancake. Cook until bubbles form on the top. Turn over and cook until done on the other side. Keep warm in a preheated low oven or serve at once. Cook the others. Serve with berry preserves. Serves 6 to 8.

BRITISH TIPSY CAKE

Very elaborate and rich English desserts, made with sponge cake, ladyfingers, fruit purée, liqueurs, custard, whipped cream, nuts, and candied fruits, are called trifles. The name is curious as certainly the rich and complex creation is anything but a trifle. Another and perhaps more appropriate name is tipsy cake. According to some ancient recipes for this favorite dessert, the quantity of spirits used in its preparation could very well make the diner tipsy. This is a simplified version.

6 egg yolks, slightly beaten
1/3 cup sugar
3 cups milk, scalded
1 teaspoon vanilla
2 layers sponge cake

Apricot, strawberry or
  raspberry jam
1/2 to 3/4 cup dry sherry
1 cup heavy cream, whipped
1/3 cup blanched almond slivers
Candied cherries

Combine the egg yolks, sugar, and milk in a heavy saucepan. Beat with a wire whisk or rotary beater to mix well. Heat over a medium flame, stirring often, until the mixture coats a spoon and is thickened. Remove from the heat and stir in the vanilla. Cool. Place one layer of sponge cake in a glass bowl. Spread evenly with a thin layer of jam. Sprinkle with half the sherry. Top with the other layer of sponge cake. Spread with jam and sprinkle with sherry. Leave long enough for the sherry to soak through the cake. Pour the cooled custard over the cake. Decorate with the whipped cream, almonds, and cherries. Serves 8.

ITALIAN PANETTONE

This light yeast bread or cake, studded with raisins and candied fruit, is a specialty of Milan and is said to have been created by a baker named Toni. It is a breakfast specialty throughout Italy and a particular favorite at Christmas.

1 cake compressed yeast	5 to 5½ cups sifted all-purpose
½ cup lukewarm water	flour
¾ cup butter, softened	½ cup milk, scalded
¾ cup sugar	1 cup seedless raisins
5 eggs	¾ cup chopped candied citron
½ teaspoon salt	1 teaspoon grated lemon rind

Crumble the yeast into the lukewarm water in a small bowl. Leave a few minutes and then stir to dissolve. In a large bowl cream the butter. Add the sugar and cream until light and well mixed. Add 4 of the eggs one at a time, beating after each addition. Stir in the salt and 1 cup of flour. Add the milk and mix well. Add the remaining flour, enough to make a stiff dough. Stir in the raisins, citron, and lemon rind. Mix well and form into a large ball. Place in a greased bowl and turn over. Let rise, covered, in a warm place until doubled in bulk. Punch down and beat well. Form into two round loaves. Place the loaves on a greased cookie sheet, leaving several inches between them. Let rise, covered, in a warm place until doubled. Combine the remaining egg with 1 tablespoon of water. Brush the tops with the egg mixture. Bake in a preheated moderate oven (350°F.) for about 45 minutes, or until baked and golden on top. Remove and cool. Serve warm or cooled. Serves about 24.

RAISED DOUGHNUTS FROM BERLIN

These delectable filled doughnuts, called *Pfannkuchen*, are a specialty in Berlin at New Year's and are sold in the pastry shops and at stalls along the streets.

1 cake compressed yeast
1 cup lukewarm milk
¼ cup butter, melted
½ cup sugar
3 eggs, beaten
1 teaspoon grated lemon rind
1 teaspoon salt

1 teaspoon almond extract
  (optional)
About 5 cups sifted all-purpose
  flour
Apricot or plum jam
Fat for deep frying
Confectioners' sugar

Crumble the yeast into ¼ cup of the lukewarm milk. After a few minutes, stir to dissolve. Combine the butter, sugar, eggs, lemon rind, salt, almond extract, and yeast in a large bowl. Mix well. Add 1 cup of flour and the remaining milk. Mix well. Gradually add the remaining flour, enough to make a soft dough. Mix well again. Place in a warm place and let rise, covered, until doubled in bulk. Turn out on a floured board and knead well. Roll out to a thickness of ¼ inch and cut into rounds about 2½ inches each. Place a spoonful of apricot or plum jam in the center of ½ of the rounds. Top with the other rounds and moisten the edges with water. Press firmly together. Let rise until doubled. Drop several at a time into a kettle of hot deep fat (375°F. on a frying thermometer) and cook until golden brown on both sides. Remove with a slotted spoon and drain. Serve sprinkled with confectioners' sugar. Makes about 30 doughnuts.

ITALIAN ZABAIONE

This very popular dessert, a wine-flavored custard, is sometimes also called *zabaglione*. It is made in several variations and is sometimes used as a sauce. The French have an adaptation of it, which they call *saboyan*.

4 egg yolks
4 tablespoons sugar

¾ cup Marsala wine

Put the egg yolks and sugar in the top of a double boiler over simmering water. Beat with a wire whisk or rotary beater until foamy. Gradually add the Marsala. Continue beating until the mixture thickens. Spoon at once into stemmed glasses and serve. Serves 4.

DANISH APPLE CAKE

Although this dessert is called a cake, it is actually a pudding made with layers of applesauce and buttered bread cubes.

4 cups dried bread cubes,
 crusts removed
1/4 cup sugar
About 1/2 cup butter

1 teaspoon vanilla
4 cups thick applesauce
Whipped cream
Red currant or raspberry jelly

Brown the bread cubes in the sugar and butter over low heat in a skillet, stirring until they are golden and crisp. Add additional butter if needed. Cool slightly. Place a layer of the cubes in a glass bowl or serving dish. Combine the vanilla and applesauce and spread a layer of it over the bread cubes. Repeat until all the ingredients are used. Have a layer of crumbs over the top. Chill. Decorate the top with whipped cream and dots of jelly. Serves 6 to 8.

ENGLISH FRUIT FOOL

This is a beloved traditional English dessert that was made originally with green gooseberries. Today it is also prepared with other fruit such as raspberries. The name supposedly came about because a fool was a simple mixture. No matter, it is a delectable dessert.

1 quart fresh gooseberries or
 raspberries
1 cup sugar

1 cup water
2 cups heavy cream, whipped

Wash and clean the fruit. Put in a saucepan with the sugar and water and cook slowly until tender. Put through a sieve to purée. Cool. Fold in the whipped cream and turn into dessert glasses. Chill. Serves 4 to 6.

For raspberries you may wish to use less sugar, if desired.

SCOTCH NUT SHORTBREAD

This is one variation of the shortbread that Scottish cooks have made famous around the world.

1 cup softened butter or margarine
½ cup sugar
¼ teaspoon salt
2½ cups sifted all-purpose flour

¼ teaspoon almond extract (optional)
½ cup finely chopped shelled almonds or walnuts

Cream the butter or margarine and add the sugar. Mix well. Stir in the remaining ingredients and mix again. Form into a ball. Chill in the refrigerator. Roll out on a floured board to ⅛-inch thickness. Cut into lengths 1 inch by 2 inches. Prick the tops with a fork. Place on an ungreased cookie sheet. Bake in a preheated slow oven (325°F.) for about 20 minutes, or until cooked. Makes about 4½ dozen. Store in a canister until ready to serve.

Or roll out to a thickness of ¼ inch, if desired.

ALSATIAN RASPBERRY PARFAIT

The French have given to other nations a marvelous ice cream dessert called *parfait*, taken from their word for perfect. Very often it is a type of single, flavored *mousse* frozen in a mold. But it may also be a delicate ice served in a tall, narrow, short-stemmed glass. One of the most refreshing parfaits I ever tasted was after a superb dinner in the hotel-restaurant Aux Armes de France, an Alsatian gastronomic temple in the picturesque wine town of Ammerschwihr. It was a simple combination of lemon sherbet covered with champagne and a little *kirsch*. Not only was the dessert delectable but it fulfilled the function of a pleasant digestive after a very rich meal. No wonder the French developed the very noble and practical custom of serving delicate ices to clear the palate between courses at lengthy banquets.

Index

245